T0153139

HEALING the JEWISH-CHRISTIAN RIFT

Growing Beyond Our Wounded History

**Ron Miller and
Laura Bernstein**

Foreword by Dr. Beatrice Bruteau

Walking Together, Finding the Way

SKYLIGHT PATHS®
PUBLISHING

Woodstock, Vermont

Healing the Jewish-Christian Rift:
Growing Beyond Our Wounded History

2006 First Printing
© 2006 by Ron Miller and Laura Bernstein

All rights reserved. No part of this book may be reproduced or reprinted in any form or by any means, electronic or mechanical, including photocopying, recording, or by any information storage and retrieval system, without permission in writing from the publisher.

For information regarding permission to reprint material from this book, please write or fax your request to SkyLight Paths Publishing, Permissions Department, at the address / fax number listed below, or e-mail your request to permissions@skylightpaths.com.

Library of Congress Cataloging-in-Publication Data
Miller, Ron, 1938–
Healing the Jewish-Christian rift : growing beyond our wounded history / Ron Miller and Laura Bernstein.
    p. cm.
Includes bibliographical references.
ISBN 1-59473-139-X (pbk.)
1. Bible. N.T. Matthew—Commentaries. 2. Jesus Christ—Teachings. 3. Jesus Christ—Jewishness. 4. Christianity and other religions—Judaism. 5. Judaism—Relations—Christianity. 6. Jews in the New Testament. I. Bernstein, Laura, 1947– II. Title.

BS2575.53.M55 2005
261.2'6—dc22
                                                              2005022070

10 9 8 7 6 5 4 3 2 1
Manufactured in the United States of America
Cover Design: Tim Holtz

SkyLight Paths Publishing is creating a place where people of different spiritual traditions come together for challenge and inspiration, a place where we can help each other understand the mystery that lies at the heart of our existence.

SkyLight Paths sees both believers and seekers as a community that increasingly transcends traditional boundaries of religion and denomination—people wanting to learn from each other, *walking together, finding the way.*

SkyLight Paths, "Walking Together, Finding the Way," and colophon are trademarks of LongHill Partners, Inc., registered in the U.S. Patent and Trademark Office.

Walking Together, Finding the Way
Published by SkyLight Paths Publishing
A Division of LongHill Partners, Inc.
Sunset Farm Offices, Route 4, P.O. Box 237
Woodstock, VT 05091
Tel: (802) 457-4000   Fax: (802) 457-4004
www.skylightpaths.com

We dedicate this book with gratitude to some of our friends and colleagues in the field of Jewish-Christian dialogue:

Herbert Bronstein

Beatrice Bruteau

James Carroll

Yechiel Eckstein

Douglas Goldhamer

Sidney Hood

Shana Lowitz

John Pawlikowski

Rosemary Ruether

Rami Shapiro

SkyLight Paths Books by Ron Miller

The Gospel of Thomas: A Guidebook for Spiritual Practice

Healing the Jewish-Christian Rift: Growing Beyond Our Wounded History

The Hidden Gospel of Matthew: Annotated and Explained

Contents

Foreword

Dr. Beatrice Bruteau

Some years ago a group of us here in Winston-Salem were reading and discussing Rabbi Michael Lerner's *Jewish Renewal*. Several times in that book he says something to this effect: Jews need to mourn for all the wounds we sustained from the various peoples we have tried to live among, being persecuted by Christian nations and finally subjected to the extermination efforts of the Nazi regime. It is right and proper for us so to mourn. Let us do it thoroughly. And then let us move forward from it. The world still remains to be healed, and we are still called to heal it. And God is still the power that can transform the world from the way it is to the way it ought to be.

Our discussion group was much moved by this appeal and exclaimed, "We're the ones who should be mourning! We represent the people and the institutions that caused or prepared the way for this terrible suffering." So we organized a year-long program to acquaint Christians with the history of Jewish persecution and distress. We started study groups in churches, we presented public lectures, and at the end of the year we offered a formal liturgy of repentance as a part of the Selichot (penitential prayer preparation) observance in the local synagogue.

The rift between Judaism and Christianity is still a sore matter. It cries out for healing on a broad level. And this means that we still need knowledge—information and explanation, interpretation and exhortation—to help bridge the divide. The sources of these wounds need to be held up for public inspection. What is wrong and hurtful needs to be emphatically rejected and replaced with fresh insight, respect and appreciation, outreach in friendship, trust-building, and side-by-side feelings.

This book is a contribution to that large effort. Anti-Jewish feeling in Christian countries grew out of the New Testament itself, and this is why it is important for us all to understand how this literature was created and how it can best be reinterpreted and dealt with.

The authors of this book bring to their task vigorous action on the two most important dimensions: Ron Miller, as a Christian scholar, shows where the negativity comes from and how the location, history, and political forces of the time contributed to the dire influence these texts have had on subsequent generations. Laura Bernstein, as a devout Jew trained in a Jewish seminary, illumines the essentially and characteristically Jewish root and core of the historical Jesus's ministry, and presses us to appreciate him properly in his own context and in terms of his own efforts at healing the world.

This challenge and this call highlight the loss we have sustained through this dreadful rift. The Christians idolized Jesus and therefore the Jews abandoned him. That's the pity of it, both ways. Jesus's own point of view was lost, and he has been effectively alienated from his own people, his own religion, his own aspiration and work. Both religions have been distracted from paying attention to him in his original reality.

I support our authors' efforts because I believe that, behind the miracle stories, the local polemics, and the theological claims of the gospels, we can discern a vision of the value of every person that grounds a social program of revolutionary proportions. Demonstrated on a small scale and startling in its own day, never thoroughly copied, not even by the communities that compiled the literature that gives us our only knowledge of the Jesus movement, this social program still remains to be tried.

If all persons (regardless of age, sex, race, nationality, wealth, political or religious position or affiliation, or any other description) are unconditionally valuable in their *personhood, which comes from God,* then all are socially equal and are to be accorded the equal and high respect due such "children of God," which means no social ranking or deference behaviors. It follows from this that all people are to be cared for equally, as though they are your neighbor (Lev. 19:18); even your enemies deserve your love, just as God sends sun and rain impartially on all (Matt. 5:44–48).

It can well be argued that the shift in attitude and social practice such a view requires is intrinsically and vitally consistent with the tradition of the Torah, the Prophets, and the Talmud, and in fact has been put forward in some way by numerous practitioners of the Jewish tradition. Could we not together examine and consider such possibilities as a way not only to heal our painful rift but also to continue our shared commitment to work at healing the world? I hope so.

This book is not a lone voice in this area of human need. There is a commendable amount of work directed toward this end. This particular conversation between a Jew and a Christian is especially helpful as the Christian relieves us of the false and hurtful passages in the New Testament, and the Jew understands Jeshu from the inside, sharing his outlook and feelings, recognizing her kinship with him in developing the depths and beauties of this ever-renewing religion.

All Will Be Well

> "All will be well, and all will be well, and every kind of thing will
> be well."
>
> —*Julian of Norwich*

Is it kosher to work on a poem on shabbos?
This one calls to me like ripe grain begging to be picked,
like honey offering to be sucked from the rock
of my wilderness journey, training hard
for the spiritual Olympics.

The scene: A table laden with books, Bibles,
a silver *yad,* a Buddhist bell.
My twelve-year-old Torah study partner Daniel—
face, an anemone; mind, the Grand Canyon;
heart, the Milky Way …
And me, technically his teacher,
old enough to be his grandma,
wise enough to know how much he has to teach me.

As usual we've veered off course, this time from Genesis
to an analysis of the New Testament. He's bothered
by the line from Matthew: "His blood be on us
and on our children." (I'm bothered by it, too.)
"Couldn't it be a lament," he wonders,

"rather than a self-inflicted curse?"
I lament that it could not. I explain
the historical context, the anti-Jewish subtext,
the hideous harm the words have wrought.
He is glad I am working on a book with another partner
to redress this wrong, to heal this rift.
He is "captivated" (his word) by the project,
eager to see us fix all that is wrong
and make it right.

Then he's concerned that I am less confident than he
about the ease with which this righting of wrongs
can be accomplished. Touching hearts and changing
minds set for centuries on a mistaken course requires
stamina, steadfastness, a burning bush, a pillar of cloud.
Suddenly he is sad at my perceived pessimism
about the world, the slow evolution of consciousness,
and I, an ardent optimist, am at a loss to convince him
otherwise. I rest a moment beside his beseeching
bottomless eyes, and take the plunge.

I am not a pessimist, I insist.
Just uncertain of exact outcome
and willing to marinate in mystery,
to do the work unattached to the fruit.
We earthlings are still toddlers, I tell him,
arguing over mine and yours, grabbing
and biting, throwing tantrums, needing
daily hugs and hourly loving reminders
of who we are, of the greater things that we will do,
of the vastness we have to grow into.
"Will we grow up?"
I hope so, but I'm a poet, not a prophet, dearest.

Still, in spite of everything—
from ancient hatreds to modern holocausts,
from Jesus turned into the weapon
used to crucify his own people,
to airplanes turned into the missiles
used to incinerate our own people—
I know
the way a rose knows how to flower and fade,
the way a cloud knows how to dance and dissolve,
the way a galaxy knows how to burst into being and die,
the way Daniel knows how to evoke tenderness and trust,
that ultimately, indisputably, irrevocably, unfathomably,
all will be well.

—Laura Bernstein

Introduction

This book is a collaboration many years in the making. We have been teacher and student, spiritual mentor and aspirant, loving friends and respected colleagues. All these aspects of our relationship have contributed to the writing of this dialogue. We share a passion for interfaith understanding and religious pluralism, and a yearning to see Christians and Jews—indeed, all faith traditions—in a place of harmony. It is our belief that religious differences are part of a tapestry that is intended to have threads of many colors; each thread contributes to the integrity and beauty of the whole. As a Christian and a Jew, we celebrate our diversity, knowing we have much to learn from one another. At the same time, we embrace our commonality, knowing that we come from the same Source and at our core we are much more alike than different. As humanists and religious pluralists, we share a deep desire to heal the wounds that have separated our two traditions.

Judaism and Christianity have had a volatile relationship in their two-thousand-year history. Like contentious siblings, there has been anger and rivalry, bitterness and recrimination. Like Cain and Abel, there has been insensitivity and infamy, bloodshed and murder. But it was not always that way. The roots of this hostility go back to the writing of the Christian Testament during a time of tremendous

1

upheaval and brutality, as the Roman Empire's unrelenting grip wreaked violence and fear throughout its occupied territories, including first-century Palestine. The destruction of the Second Temple by Rome in the year 70 CE, with the enormity of suffering and privation that accompanied it, marked a pivotal shift in Jewish and Christian identities. Tension between these two communities intensified during this period of turmoil and identity crisis, as did a growing antagonism.

The gospels were written in the years following this catastrophe, decades after the death of the Jewish carpenter from Nazareth who is their guiding star, and light-years away from the life-world he inhabited. This awareness begins to shed light on the question: how did a Jewish teacher, healer, sage, and mystic become the vehicle for so much hatred and harm directed against his own people? The premise that the growing anti-Jewishness found in the gospels (which later would turn into the most virulent anti-Semitism) stems from this later period of antagonism, and not from the heart and mind of Jesus, is central to this book.

Context is vital to understanding the truths in our sacred texts. We have chosen to examine specific verses from the Gospel of Matthew, which gradually reveal those dramatically different contexts hidden in the strata of the text. Matthew was written in the mid-80s; Jesus taught in the late 20s. Differentiating between the authentic voice of Jesus and the voice of Matthew's community becomes an essential process of discernment in reading this text and, by extension, the other gospels as well (which each has its own communal context). This work was begun in *The Hidden Gospel of Matthew: Annotated and Explained* (by Ron Miller, SkyLight Paths), which contains a new translation of the entire gospel. We use this translation and refer, at times, to its commentary. While it is not essential to read it in conjunction with this volume, it is a helpful companion piece to our current work.

Why did we choose the Gospel of Matthew as the foundation of this book? Initially, we thought to include the entire Christian Testament; when that became daunting, we considered all four gospels. Finally, we realized that Matthew's gospel contained the heart of what we were striving to elucidate, and that readers could extrapolate from what is learned about this gospel to the rest of the Christian scriptures. Some background: Matthew is the first book of the Christian Testament and the first gospel, although not the earliest chronologically; the Gospel of Mark was written about the year 70, and Matthew was finalized about the year 85. The text has multiple sources, including Mark's gospel, and various editors, so the name "Matthew" is actually a corporate persona for all who contributed to the final version of the gospel. But Matthew's gospel is especially well suited to this project for two major reasons: it is paradoxically the most Jewish and the most anti-Jewish book in the Christian Testament, and it contains the largest body of teaching material attributed to the historical Jesus. These two interacting realities provided us with exactly the material we needed to examine the conflicting layers that coexist within the text—the earlier material from the 20s is more Jewish and more like Jesus; the later material from the 80s is more anti-Jewish and decidedly not like Jesus.

Thus, a second premise of the book is that what doesn't ring true for a Jew when reading the gospel is not likely to have come from Jeshu. Note that we are using his Hebrew name throughout the book (pronounced yay-shoo, short for Jehoshua, which translates to Joshua; Jeshu would be Josh, more or less), because that name speaks to his Aramaic language and Jewish context in first-century Palestine. No one who knew him would have used the Greek name Jesus. Looking for what is discordant from a Jewish standpoint helps to discriminate the early, authentic gospel layers from the later community's bias: words, phrases, or ideas that are subtly or overtly anti-Jewish are out of sync with the Judaism that Jeshu so richly embodied. We hope this will encourage a Christian audience to notice what familiarity, immersion, and deep affection make difficult to see—that scattered among the spiritual jewels of the gospel is an increasingly fierce polemic that has had devastating consequences for Jews (including Jeshu). Those consequences include every anti-Semitic remark, incident, brutality, and outrage of the last two millennia, culminating in the Holocaust of the last century. They are extremely painful to contemplate.

Becoming aware of this polemic and how it degenerates into a pervasive anti-Jewish stance that turns into demonization of Jews in the gospel is a crucial step toward mitigating the enormity of harm that has been done, and in some quarters continues to be done, both to Jews and to Jeshu. For when it is understood that this extreme antagonism is not of Jeshu (himself most emphatically a Jew), but a product of the historical and religious turbulence that occurred decades after his death, an opening can occur. Far from lessening the power of these sacred scriptures, such scrutiny adds to their impact. It allows the universal truths of Jeshu's teachings to emerge in their fullness, unsullied by the atrocities that have been committed in his name. It allows the connection between those atrocities and their antecedents in the gospels to be acknowledged and broken—by examining the bias, putting it into historical context, and teaching new generations of Christians how to understand this material better. We hope this can open the door to repentance, to dialogue, and to a much-needed healing of the two-thousand-year rift between Christians and Jews.

We also hope this study will encourage Jeshu's Jewish brethren to take a fresh look at the actual teachings of this God-intoxicated Galilean hasid (a passionate lover of God and humankind) when uncontaminated by the animosity that surrounds them. For another devastating consequence of the anti-Jewish polemic in the Christian Testament has been the loss of this spiritual genius from the canon of Jewish wisdom. That this Jewish sage and mystic has been excluded from the vast body of Jewish thought (albeit for understandable historical reasons) adds another dimension to the tragedy.

Jeshu has something vital to say to Jews, as well as to all humankind, because of the universality of his teachings. And in accord with our pluralistic bent, we frequently refer to other spiritual traditions in this commentary. But the particularity of his being Jewish is evident throughout this first Christian Testament gospel, where much of his teaching is an extended midrash (commentary) on Leviticus 19:18, which commands us to love our neighbor as ourselves. It is ironic and terrible that this zaddik (holy leader) who taught so eloquently about love and nonviolence became the unwitting standard-bearer of so much hatred and violence for those who distorted his message and abused his name. That such hatred and violence was directed so regularly against his own people is another hideous irony. We hope this writing will contribute to the effort to clear Jeshu's name of undeserved infamy, and will encourage Jews to embrace him as a Jewish brother and teacher. Welcoming Rabbi Jeshu back into the fold and drawing sustenance from his remarkable Jewish wisdom is another indispensable aspect of healing the rift between Jews and Christians.

The timing of this book is purposeful. It was in 1965, forty years ago, that the Second Vatican Council released its document on non-Christian religions *(Nostra Aetate),* a text that included several paragraphs on the church's relationship to Jews and Judaism. Though not as courageous and forthright a statement as many had hoped for, it was nonetheless a watershed in Jewish-Christian relations. We honor that document through our joint participation in the preparation of the book you are reading.

Dialogue has been integral to our friendship and collaboration these many years, so we find it fitting that this project takes the form of a dialogue. We hope that you, the reader, will feel yourself a part of this conversation as you interact with what we have written. The questions at the end of each chapter are designed to facilitate that interaction, both between you and us and between you and others in your community. We look forward to your comments and, of course, to your corrections to any statements where you feel that we are in error.

A word about our format: We are following the text of Matthew in the SkyLight Paths edition that was translated by Ron, using selected passages that speak to our concerns. Each chapter begins with one or more extracts from the text of Matthew, followed by Laura's commentary (LB), followed by Ron's response (RM). Questions for reflection close each chapter.

Thank-yous are in order to SkyLight Paths for encouraging us to write this book and to Maura Shaw and Emily Wichland for their editorial assistance. We appreciate the hard work of Lora East, a student at Lake Forest College, in bringing the manuscript to its final form. Finally, we are grateful to our family members—Joel, Jason, Adam, Jim, and Carrie—and friends too many to name who have supported us, to countless scholars who have preceded us, and to all our readers who will take this work forward into their lives and into our larger global community.

1

What Is a Messiah?

The genesis of Jeshu the Messiah, the child of David and of Abraham. (Matt. 1:1)

LB

Names are powerful and evocative. I appreciate Ron's use of the Hebrew name "Jeshu" in his translation (and later the use of "Miriam" for Mary). This puts Jeshu more squarely and appropriately in his Jewish context. The Hellenized name "Jesus" was certainly never applied to the historical Jehoshua ben Josef (Joshua son of Joseph), who, like his fellow Jews, spoke Aramaic (a Semitic language similar to Hebrew), and not the Greek of the gospels.

To a Jew, the word *messiah* (*mashiach* in Hebrew) has a number of implications. It means (literally) "God's anointed one." In biblical times, first priests and then kings were anointed with sacred oil as part of their induction into high office—the oil was a symbol of their appointment. So *messiah* signifies "the anointed king" in a general sense, and the Messiah is also a descendent of King David in a specific sense; in this regard, the term's meaning has evolved considerably.

Jewish tradition holds that this monarch of David's lineage will accomplish a number of specific tasks. He will gather all Jews from the four corners of the world and bring them to a sovereign land of Israel, as well as restore them to full observance of Torah (which means devotedly following the *mitzvot,* or commandments, in the Torah: loving God and one another). Moreover, as the prophet Isaiah promises, this Messiah will bring peace, justice, and harmony to the whole world, heralding a messianic age when the wolf will dwell with the lamb and war will be obsolete (Isa. 11:16, 2:4). Clearly, Jeshu did not accomplish those tasks: Roman oppression continued, wars and brutality continued, and Israel's lack of sovereignty continued. By the Jewish standard, the messianic age remains a future reign rather than a current reality. With our world so full of violence and injustice—war, greed, and corruption; prejudice, callousness, and environmental plunder; a gaping disparity between the rich and the poor—how could the *Mashiach* have come?

More recently, in some Jewish circles (particularly the Jewish Renewal movement), *mashiach* has come to be regarded as the collective human effort to bring about *tikkun olam*—the healing and transformation of the world—through compassion and social justice. Rather than waiting for an individual Messiah to come, we can each strive to attain messianic consciousness, perfecting the world through thoughts, words, and deeds that reflect our deepest values and most God-saturated awareness. When enough of us have answered this call, the messianic age will open. This understanding accords well with the hasidic insight (Hasidism, which began in the eighteenth century, being the most recent flowering of Jewish mysticism) that every thought, word, and deed on an individual level impacts the world on a collective level. What we think, utter, and do is felt in the universe.

While "Jeshu the Messiah" is discordant to Jewish ears, "the child of David and of Abraham" puts Jeshu in good Jewish company. It makes him a descendent of both the first patriarch and the shepherd-soldier-king whose bloodline would produce the Messiah. *Messiah* can also be used figuratively to refer to individuals favored by God (as in Ps. 105:15 when God exhorts, "Do not touch My anointed ones [literally, My messiahs]; do not harm My prophets"). Isaiah puts the Persian King Cyrus in this privileged category of God's anointed for having allowed the Judean exiles to return from Babylonia to Jerusalem and rebuild the Temple (see Isa. 45:1). In this sense, Jeshu could be understood as *a* messiah, if not *the* Messiah.

In his provocative article "Who Do You Say That I Am?" in *Jesus Through Jewish Eyes,* Rabbi Byron Sherwin proposes that Jeshu be considered a "Messiah son of Joseph," which classic Jewish literature regards as a preliminary messiah who suffers and dies and paves the way for the final redemption to take place via the Messiah son of David. As Sherwin remarks, "This would give Jesus a place within Jewish theological discourse and would end the centuries-long tradition of his virtual excommunication from the faith community of which he was a part."[1] However, even if most Jews could embrace a messianic role for Jesus, it is unlikely that most Christians would find this "preliminary" status satisfying.

Can we reconcile the tension between the Christian view that the Messiah has come in the person of Jeshu, and the Jewish view of the Messiah as a future reality or as an ideal to be striven toward? Perhaps the past and future can come together in the present. Or do we simply agree to disagree on this point? In his introduction to *The Hidden Gospel of Matthew,* Ron regards the declaration of Jeshu as the Messiah by the disciple Shimon (known to most Christians as Simon Peter) as "a clear climactic moment," forming "the watershed of the gospel" and "the gospel's center."

Certainly the longing for a Messiah to come and right the wrongs of Roman cruelty had to be fierce (and Jeshu was one of a number of first-century candidates for such messiahship). It is not surprising that Shimon would have wished it to be so and believed it was so (just as the great talmudic sage Rabbi Akiva granted the freedom fighter Bar Kokhba this title a century later out of the same longing for justice and peace). However, Ron then notes that acknowledging Jeshu as the Messiah marks the transition from his role as teacher, helper, and healer to "the deeper issues of suffering and death."[2] This is based on a developing tradition of Jeshu as a suffering Messiah.

Is it essential to see Jeshu as God's anointed before moving into these deeper waters of suffering, of dying to self in order to be born to eternal life? For me, his status as the Messiah is not the real issue here, but rather his example of how to live and die as a fully God-conscious individual in a world that has yet to attain messianic consciousness. It is not necessary for the man of sorrows who leads us into the deepest realms of awareness and shows us how to transform suffering and death into joy and renewed life to be the Messiah.

A bit further on in the commentary, Ron remarks that "Jeshu fulfills the deepest longings attached to the title of Messiah and thus is the true child of David as well." Given his failure to bring about a harmonious, sovereign state of Israel, let alone a world of peaceful coexistence, how could Jeshu be said to have fulfilled those deepest longings? This is in no way to diminish the profound effect that he has had on the world (as Ron affirms, "Most deeply … Jeshu is God's child");[3] it is simply to point out that this effect was not and is not what is attributed to the Messiah. Jeshu could be viewed as the Prince of Inner Peace, but such internal transformation has yet to be widespread enough to produce a peaceful world order. Although Jeshu gives us an extraordinary road map, we are a long way from collectively experiencing the kingdom of heaven here on earth.

RM

It always amazes me how carelessly we Christians use those titles: Christ, Son of God, Lord. For most of us, "Christ" is simply Jeshu's last name and "Jesus" is how his mother called him in for dinner. Laura's remarks definitely help clarify this matter. We Christians need to remind ourselves of the original meaning of the word *messiah* and not get swept away by its later theological baggage. After all, the Qur'an refers to Jeshu as messiah, and yet Muslims, like Jews, in no way connect this term to any claim to divinity.

Laura's question about the significance of Shimon's confession of Jeshu as the Messiah is a good one. In the theology of the synoptic gospels (Matthew, Mark, and Luke) Jeshu is a suffering messiah and that's why Shimon's affirmation of him as the Messiah is followed by Jeshu's remarks about his coming arrest and death. This theology is based on the conflation of two traditions in the voice that Jeshu hears when he is immersed in the Jordan by John the Baptist: "This is my child, the child I love, the child in whom I take great delight" (Matt. 3:17).

The divine sonship ("my child") goes back to Psalm 2, in which the king of Israel's intimate relationship to God is described as one of father and son: "Let me tell of the decree: the Lord said to me, 'You are My son, I have fathered you this day'" (Ps. 2:7). The words about "great delight" are from a verse in Isaiah dealing with the "suffering servant": "This is My servant, whom I uphold, My chosen one, in whom I delight. I have put My spirit upon him, He shall teach the true way to the nations" (Isa. 42:1). The servant is an unnamed prophet who was with the Jewish exiles in Babylon after the destruction of the First Temple in 586 BCE. He was captured, tortured, and killed by his Babylonian captors.

In Jewish theology, these three strands of tradition (sonship, messiah, and suffering servant) are not ordinarily connected, much less identified. But in the theology of the synoptic gospels, these separate currents are conflated, resulting in the idea of a suffering messiah. This is why it makes sense that Matthew's focus on Jeshu's imminent arrest and death follows Shimon's confession that Jeshu is the Messiah. Laura makes a valid point when she argues that, from a Jewish perspective, there seems to be no relationship to Jeshu's status as the Messiah and the manner of his death.

The deeper Jewish issue, of course, which Laura articulates very well, is why Christians regard Jeshu as the Messiah when the world has clearly not been changed by his ministry. My mentor in Judaism at Northwestern University, Dr. Manfred Vogel, remarked one day in class that for Jews, messianism is not a matter of faith but of vision. If you look out your window and the world is unchanged, then the Messiah has not come.

Rosemary Ruether, a contemporary Catholic theologian, argues that Jeshu is "proleptically" the Messiah. He is an anticipation of the messianic reality, much like the Sabbath in Judaism is a foretaste of messianic times. In other words, his consciousness reveals to us what the consciousness of all humankind will someday be. It's a bit like tasting the soup before you serve it to your dinner guests. Jeshu gives us a taste of the messianic age, but the dinner has not yet been served. In that sense, Judaism and Christianity are not that far apart. They each have a foretaste of messianic times (the Sabbath and Jeshu, respectively), but neither community is celebrating yet the full messianic banquet.

REFLECTIONS

1. How is the concept of messiah used by Jews and by Christians I know?

2. Does it make sense that from their diverse perspectives Jews can be correct in saying that the Messiah has not come and Christians can be correct in saying that he has?

3. How can Jews' and Christians' different understandings of Jeshu's messianic identity be a useful topic for Jewish-Christian dialogue?

2

A Miraculous Birth?

[18]This was how the birth of Jeshu the Messiah took place. When his mother Miriam had been engaged to Josef, but before they were living together, she became pregnant by a holy spirit. [19]Her husband Josef, being a God-centered person and not wanting to disgrace her, resolved to break off the engagement with as little publicity as possible. [20]But while he was contemplating this, an angel of the Lord appeared to him in a dream and said, "Josef, son of David, don't be afraid to take Miriam as your wife, for the child she carries is from a holy spirit." (Matt. 1:18–20)

LB

Both angels and miraculous births are familiar occurrences in the Hebrew scriptures. Three angels come to tell Abraham that he and Sarah are going to conceive a child (at the respective ages of one hundred and ninety!). While Sarah laughs at the very idea, God answers,

"Is there anything too hard for the Lord?" (Gen. 18:14). Isaac (whose name derives from the word laughter) is born nine months later. It is not too much of a leap to assume that impregnation by a holy spirit would not be "too hard" for the Lord to accomplish. *Ruach haKodesh* is the Hebrew term for "holy spirit." While less commonly found in mainstream Judaism, it is a well-recognized concept in Jewish mystical theology. *Ruach* translates as "spirit," "breath," or "wind;" it is a soul dimension connected to spiritual depth and our sense of meaning in life. However, it is not essential that one understand this impregnation as a literal event to appreciate it as a midrash about a deeply spiritual encounter.

Midrash, it should be noted, is a form of commentary that fills in the gaps between the words and lines of scripture. The word comes from a Hebrew root that means "to search out." It attempts to clarify and explain or interpret the text, often using stories and sometimes requiring imaginative, intuitive leaps of consciousness to do so. This, of course, does not make midrash untrue. On the contrary, such creative wrestling with the text can uncover deeper truths that mere factual accounts cannot access. Midrash is a vast branch of rabbinic literature, which was largely oral in Jeshu's time, but was later compiled into many collections of books over many hundreds of years. It remains an essential part of Torah study today.

Is the absence of a human father for Jeshu pure midrash, or does it suggest, as Ron says, "some problematic but historical realities" regarding the unusual circumstances of Jeshu's birth?[1] Obviously, these questions do not lend themselves to definitive answers. Nor is it necessary to resolve the controversies that they arouse. Whether this story involved a miraculous birth or an illegitimate one (or both), we are left with the spiritual reality of God's child coming into the world to change it. That this Jewish baby will profoundly impact the world is uncontestable.

> [22]Now all of this had come about to fulfill what God spoke through his prophet: [23]"Look, a young woman will become pregnant and bear a son, who will be called Immanuel." This name means "God is with us." [24]So when Josef woke up, he did what the angel told him and took Miriam as his wife. [25]And yet, they didn't have any sexual relations up to the time she gave birth to the child to whom Josef gave the name Jeshu. (Matt. 1:22–25)

LB

In most Christian Bibles, verse 23 contains a misleading English translation of the verse from Isaiah 7:14, because it substitutes the word *virgin* for *young woman*. This is not surprising because, as Ron points out, the Greek *parthenos* used in Matthew does usually translate as "virgin." The Hebrew word in Isaiah's text, however, is *almah*, which means "young woman, maiden, damsel, marriageable girl"—not necessarily "virgin." (The Hebrew word that is specific for virgin is *betulah*.) The correction in Ron's translation is appreciated. Matthew's use of a mistranslation of the Hebrew clearly furthers the gospel writer's intention of presenting a virgin-birth story, which appears to be a later midrash (Ron notes that earlier writers such as Mark and Paul do not refer to it).[2] This view of a virgin Jewish mother is a departure from Jewish tradition, which considers healthy sexuality to be an asset and a blessing.

Translation aside, it is a stretch to connect this citation from Isaiah to the birth of Jeshu. This was written seven hundred years prior (in the year 734 BCE), and the son to be named Immanuel ("God is with us") was to be a sign assuring King Ahaz of Judah (the southern kingdom) of the coming destruction of both the northern kingdom (also called Ephraim, as well as Israel) and Syria by Assyria (because both Ephraim and Syria were threats to Judah at the time). Immanuel can be understood as a metaphorical name for the kingdom of Judah, which Isaiah prophesies will have divine protection. Indeed, Judah does withstand the onslaught of the powerful Assyrian army, which is miraculously stopped outside the walls of Jerusalem in 701 BCE during the reign of Hezekiah (the son and successor of Ahaz). All 185,000 Assyrian soldiers were said to have perished in one night (Isa. 36:1–37:38).

However, spiritual meaning transcends historical or factual data if it enlarges our understanding of profounder realities. This expansion is the role of midrash. Indeed, an enlightened teacher, sage, healer, prophet, or mystic *is* an example of *Immanu-El*—a representative of "God with us." And so are we all called to be—we are each charged with the task of realizing God's with-ness, of knowing the indweller who is our deepest reality. Union with God is the essence of Jewish mysticism (and of all mysticism). Jeshu is one example of how to embody that deepest reality—to be God's beloved, ready to serve and love one another in the here and now.

RM

Laura's introduction of the term midrash is crucial here. Most Christians are unfamiliar with this concept. This leads them to read the Bible as though it were all one literary genre. That would be like reading the morning newspaper as though it were all front-page reporting, without recognizing that an op-ed piece is a different genre. In reality, a newspaper contains several genres of writing—from front-page reporting to op-ed pieces, cartoons, obituaries, and book reviews. Being socialized as Americans, we know how to change gears as we move from one genre to another. We would be surprised if an opinion were printed as a front-page headline, but we take it for granted that opinions will be found on the editorial page.

The sophistication we bring to reading a newspaper is often lacking to readers of scripture. Because they read everything as front-page reporting, they fall into genre confusion. The virgin-birth story, for example, becomes a gynecological report, something pertaining to the nature of Miriam's unbroken hymen and the insemination of her ovum by a divinely created sperm. This is no longer theology but fairy tale. It is precisely this phenomenon of Christian genre confusion and the resultant literal approach to midrashic materials that leads so many Jews to regard Christianity with a kind of benign incredulity (somewhat the way we regard the remaining members of the Flat Earth Society). Can Christians really believe this as literal truth? But when the text is properly understood as midrash on a verse of scripture (Isa. 7:14), albeit a mistranslated verse of scripture, then some rapprochement between the two communities is possible, and that can lead to the very sensitive and sensible commentary that Laura suggests.

Mistaking midrash for gynecological reporting has had other disastrous consequences for Christianity. These have led to further misunderstanding between Jews and Christians. The image of Miriam as a virgin mother has profoundly hindered the development of a healthy sense of sexuality in Christian thought and practice. Miriam as both virgin and mother models an ideal of womanhood that no other woman can achieve. Women are doomed to be second class, settling for half of the model by being virgins or by being mothers, but forever banned from being both. When this inimitable sexuality of Miriam is coupled with the apparent asexuality of Jeshu, it is small wonder that sexuality is such a weak point in Christian theology and that there have been so many obstacles to developing a sound marriage of sexuality and spirituality in Christian practice. This contrasts sharply with Judaism, which has a much healthier and even celebratory awareness of sexuality.

I can still recall my surprise when my rabbi/professor in graduate school pointed out that sexual intercourse between loving partners was part of the celebration of the Sabbath. I was still a Jesuit priest at that time and I immediately had the fantasy of announcing to a Christian community from the pulpit some Sunday morning that from now on part of their preparation for coming to church on Sunday should be the enjoyment of wonderful lovemaking with their partner. A far more typical reaction among Christians would be for one partner to say to the other, "Not this morning, honey. It's Sunday and we're going to church later on."

The misunderstanding of the virgin-birth midrash as literal fact has had dreadful consequences in Christian life and practice. I remember talking about this whole issue one Sunday morning to an adult education group at a nearby church. I pointed out that Miriam's virginity was not physiological fact but was a metaphor for Jeshu's birth as willed by God, not by the mere decision of his human parents to conceive a child. In other words, Jeshu's birth came about not only through human agency but also as part of God's plan. It is in that metaphorical sense that the conception of Jeshu was virginal. After hearing this explanation, a woman came up to me afterward and accused me of "insulting the Virgin Mary." Did I really think that Mary engaged "in all that sweating and grunting of sex"? My first reaction was to wonder what kind of sex life that woman experienced, but my response was simply to point out that God was the author of all that sweating and grunting, because our sexuality is part of our created reality. The woman was not impressed with my answer and stormed away.

This negative attitude toward sex throws a real obstacle in the path of Jewish-Christian dialogue. The text of Deuteronomy assures us that when Moses died at the ripe age of 120 years, "his sight was unimpaired and his vigor had not abated" (Deut. 34:7). Some rabbinic commentators find here an allusion to the fact that without the later benefits of Viagra, he was still sexually potent at the age of 120. What a different perspective from the protests that followed the posting of a banner at a conference at a Catholic college that stated: "Jesus Had a Penis." Many Christians prefer to think of Jeshu as a Ken doll without genitalia, and Miriam as asexual as her son. Some medieval artists liked to picture Miriam as having her legs tied together when she gave birth, suggesting that Jeshu didn't enter the world the normal way but passed through her body just as he later passed through walls in his risen state.

As a Jesuit, I had studied the rules of St. Ignatius of Loyola given to the first members of the Society of Jesus. I admired the subtlety of his thought when he dealt with the vows of poverty and obedience. But the third vow, the promise of chastity, was dismissed with three words: *Sint sicut angeli*—"Let them be like the angels." But human beings are not angels, even when they don religious habits or take religious vows. And striving for an essentially inhuman goal often results in subhuman behavior, as the recent sex scandals in the Catholic Church make so abundantly clear. What is denied and repressed does not go away; it simply learns to live underground in secrecy and shame. The healthiness of Jewish spirituality on this point would be extremely salutary for Christians and would provide an excellent topic for greater Jewish-Christian discussion.

REFLECTIONS

1. How can I identify the different genres of writing found in scripture?

2. How can I understand the kind of meaning found in midrash, the spiritual sense of the story, rather than the literal sense of it?

3. How might I develop a forum of Jewish-Christian dialogue that includes the topics of midrash, sexuality, and spirituality?

3

A Homicidal Jewish King

¹In the days of King Herod, Jesus was born in Bethlehem of Judea. Seers from the east came to Jerusalem, ²asking, "Where is the one born to be king of the Jews? We've seen his rising star and are here to honor him." (Matt. 2:1–2)

LB

This is the stuff of myth and midrash, echoing the story of Moses, whose life was also threatened by the decree of a wicked ruler (Pharaoh in Egypt), but who escaped death and went on to help liberate his people. This new "king of the Jews" (although Moses was never declared a king) is similarly going to provide leadership in an oppressive time under a cruel regime. By using the word "myth," I am not being dismissive or suggesting that this story is untrue; I am distinguishing between literal, factual truth and sacred, symbolic truth that speaks not to the historical facts, but to a deeper reality. Such symbolic narratives illuminate our understanding of who we are and where we are going. As contemporary theologian Marcus Borg says, "Though not literally true, they can be really true; though not factually true, they can be actually true."[1]

For Matthew to create a midrash on Jeshu's early life (about which nothing is actually known) is perfectly in keeping with his Jewish sensibility and the cultural reality of midrash as a popular literary genre of his time. What is ironic is the misunderstanding of midrash in the Gentile world, such that the very term *gospel* (as in, "I swear it's the gospel truth") has become synonymous with factual or literal truth. As the dictionary defines it, gospel truth is "something absolutely true; something as true as the gospel." Yet this is precisely not the kind of truth that midrash conveys.

I am intrigued by the seers' reference to having observed "his rising star." It reminds me of the midrash that Moses's home was so filled with light at the time of his birth that Miriam (his sister) recognized his importance and resolved to save him. Of course, light as a metaphor for God's providence and guidance is a time-honored reference on the spiritual journey. As the psalmist declares, "Your word is a lamp to my feet, a light for my path" (Ps. 119:105).

When King Herod heard this, he was upset, as was all of Jerusalem. (Matt. 2:3)

LB

That Herod would be upset by a potential rival is not shocking, since he, a convert to Judaism without a shred of genuine religiosity, was, as Joseph Telushkin says, "perhaps the most vile human being ever to serve as a Jewish king,"[2] a man whose ruthlessness extended to murdering his own sons. But why would "all Jerusalem" quake with him, when he was universally despised by the Jews he ruled (when a popular uprising erupted against his regime, he had forty-two of its leaders burned to death)? On the contrary, Jerusalem would have welcomed any competition or threat to Herod.

> ⁴Calling together all the chief priests and Torah scholars, Herod asked them where the Messiah was to be born. ⁵"In Bethlehem of Judea," they told him. "For this is what the prophet wrote: ⁶'And you, Bethlehem, in the land of Judah, are far from the least among Judah's leading cities, for from you will come a leader who will shepherd my people Israel.'" (Matt. 2:4–6)

LB

This verse (with a somewhat altered translation) from Micah 5:1 foretells of the messianic king who will restore the Israelites to their land and bring peace to the world. The Hebrew uses "Beth-lehem Ephrathah" to refer to the family of David (who were Ephrathites of Bethlehem in Judah; the town itself is also known as Ephrath; Bethlehem translates as "house of bread"). The prophet declares that out of this family will come the Messiah, as in the better-known prophecy of Isaiah 11, which refers to a "shoot … out of the stump of Jesse"— David's father. King David was originally a shepherd and, as the youngest and smallest of stature of the eight sons of Jesse, a surprising choice for the role of monarch and the messianic lineage. Again, the gospel writer seeks midrashically to connect Jeshu with this lineage.

> ⁷At this point Herod secretly brought in the seers and asked them when this star first appeared. ⁸Then he sent them to Bethlehem with the request "Go and search carefully for the child and let me know when you have found him, so that I too

might come and honor him." 9When the seers heard what the king had to say, they set out, and the same star they had seen before led them to the place where the child was.

10They were incredibly happy when they saw the star again, 11and on entering the house and seeing the child with Miriam, his mother, they prostrated themselves and honored him. They opened their treasures and offered him gifts of gold, incense, and myrrh. (Matt. 2:7–12)

LB

Certain parallels with the Moses saga in the book of Exodus call out here. The baby Jeshu is in danger from Herod, just as the baby Moses was threatened by Pharaoh's cruel decree to murder all Hebrew newborn males. Herod uses deception, pretending that he will honor the child, just as Pharaoh pretended he would let the Israelites go but repeatedly went back on his word. The seers are led by a star, just as the Israelites are led through the wilderness by a pillar of cloud and a pillar of fire.

12Afterward, since they had been warned in a dream not to go back to Herod, they took a different road home to their own country. 13As soon as they had gone, an angel of the Lord appeared to Josef in a dream and said, "Get up! Take the child and his mother, and flee to Egypt. Stay there until I give you further word. Herod wants to kill the child and will be looking for him." 14Josef got up, took the child and his mother while it was still night, and left for Egypt. 15He stayed there until Herod's death. (Matt. 2:12–15)

LB

This episode of taking refuge in Egypt and then returning to the land of Israel mirrors the coming and going of the Jews in the Torah. As

Ron points out, this is more midrash, linking Jeshu to the trajectory of his Jewish ancestors, but with a disturbing, anti-Jewish twist.[3] In this parody of the Exodus story, the cruel Pharaoh is replaced by the villainous and Jewish King Herod, and instead of fleeing Egypt, the family finds safety there.

The gospel writer makes no effort to put Herod in context. This lackey of Rome and convert to Judaism cared nothing about Jewish values and behaved hideously throughout his reign, murdering anyone (including his own family members) who stood in his way. In no way did he represent the Jewish people on whom his kingship was foisted. Yet this midrash makes it appear that legitimate Jewish leadership (and "all Jerusalem," according to Matt. 2:3) opposed Jeshu from his birth. Such an interpretation comes from Matthew's life-world of the 80s (when opposition and rivalry between Matthew's Jeshu community and the rabbinic Jewish community was intensifying), not from the time of Jeshu. It is the beginning of an anti-Jewish thread that will be woven throughout the Gospel of Matthew.

RM

Laura's comments are right on target. This is one of many stories in Matthew's gospel that define the emerging Jeshu movement against its sibling rival, the rabbinic Jewish community. It all goes back to the year 70 CE when the Roman destruction of the Second Temple effectively ended biblical Judaism, a form of religion utilizing animal sacrifice and the accompanying sacrificial cult. The question of the day in 70 CE was: how can Judaism survive with neither cultic center (the Temple) nor cultic sacrifice? Judaism needed a viable interpretation of this tragedy, one that would open up a path to the future. The study of interpretation is called hermeneutics, and so another way of saying this is that Judaism needed a hermeneutics of survival. Two such hermeneutical paths opened up: a path laid out by the Pharisees (who are now called the rabbis) and a path described by the Jeshu movement (soon to be known as Christianity).

The rabbinic way saw the daily prayers as replacing the Temple sacrifices and the table in every Jewish home replacing the Temple's altar. Whereas there had been only one Temple as Judaism's center, the synagogue with the Torah as its center could be multiplied the world over. Judaism could thus be defined as a living relationship with God independent of any tie to a particular cultic site. The Jeshu movement represented a rival hermeneutics. The whole meaning of sacrifice had always been a total gift of the human heart and soul to God. Jeshu so fully embodied this stance of surrender to God that his life and death constituted the quintessential sacrifice, making any further sacrifice both unnecessary and impossible.

It was thus by two diverse routes that rabbinic Judaism and messianic Judaism found a way both to understand and to move beyond the Temple's destruction. They were competitors for the larger Jewish community's loyalty. As the second century began, the results of this competition were clear. The rabbinic community won the allegiance of most Jews of that time and thus defined Judaism up to our own day. Christianity ended up with very few adherents of Jewish ethnicity. But, to the surprise of many Christians, the non-Jewish world was showing increasing interest in coming forward to join their ranks.

Matthew's community, probably located in Syrian Antioch, is almost certainly a mixed community of Jews and Gentiles. Their rivals, the rabbinic Jews, are increasingly understood simply as "the Jews" or "the Pharisees." Both Pharisees and Jews in general now become the whipping boys in Matthew's story, and it is in this context that the Herod story needs to be understood. The story is once again midrash, not history. For readers who know the Moses story that it parodies, the narrative reflects a macabre humor, for it reverses the story of the Jewish people who fled from a homicidal Egyptian king by portraying the archetypal Jewish family (the "holy family" of Jeshu, Miriam, and Josef) fleeing not from, but to Egypt to escape a homicidal king, who in this case is not Egyptian but Jewish.

These kinds of stories have come to define damaging Christian attitudes toward Jews and Judaism: That, just like the Jewish king and the inhabitants of Jerusalem, the Jews missed their chance. That Jews had the opportunity to acknowledge their long-awaited Messiah and they ignored it. That the perspicacious Gentiles proved wiser (thus the "wise men") and saw the star that the Jews failed to notice. That Judaism since the time of Jeshu is now an irrelevancy, a failed option, a lost opportunity. That more than being merely wrong, Jews have actively opposed the community proven to be right, the Christians. That Jews are thus depicted as the enemies of the light and the allies of Satan, symbolized by Herod's massacre of the "holy innocents," the children murdered in his attempt to eliminate one who might prove to be the Messiah.

REFLECTIONS
1. As I go through the Herod midrash verse by verse, can I identify the step-by-step vilification of the Jews?
2. How have I encountered this Christian attitude that sees Jews as the people who missed their chance?
3. How can this story be used in a context of contemporary Jewish-Christian dialogue?

4

A Maverick Mentor

¹Some time later, Jochanan the Immerser went into the Judean desert, telling the people, ²"Turn your lives around; the reign of God is approaching." (Matt. 3:1–2)

LB

Jochanan the Immerser—emphasizing his Jewish identity and distinguishing the Jewish immersion practice from the Christian sacrament of baptism—had an apocalyptic view of God's reign (more commonly called the kingdom of heaven); he saw it as an end-time phenomenon. From a Jewish standpoint, that meant a messianic age when, after a period of suffering and strife, a divinely ordained ruler would come to bring peace and harmony to Israel and the world. With all the suffering that stemmed from the Roman occupation and its attendant brutality, messianic longings were intense in first-century Palestine. It is not shocking that a fervent Jewish preacher like Jochanan would be predicting the coming kingdom of God, presided over by the messianic king.

> 5Many people went out to see him—people from Jerusalem, from the whole province of Judea, and from the area around the Jordan River. 6They publicly admitted their sins and were immersed by him in the river. (Matt. 3:5–6)

LB

Jochanan's immersion of the people in the Jordan stems from the traditional Jewish purification rite involving the *mikvah,* or "ritual bath." This ritual entails immersion in preferably "living water" (a river or a spring, although a lake, an ocean, or even a swimming pool in modern times may substitute; most *mikvaot*—plural of *mikvah*—are now located in buildings). This immersion (which includes prayer and is used largely by orthodox Jews) happens monthly for married women upon completing their menstrual cycle (to make sexual relations with their husbands permissible). It is also used for conversion of non-Jews to Judaism, and among hasidic males (or the mystically inclined of either gender) as a preparation for the Sabbath or before Jewish holidays. It is an ancient purification ritual, prevalent during Jeshu's time, too, although not for confessing sins.

Jochanan is using immersion as a substitute for sin offerings at the Temple in Jerusalem. The system for making these offerings was seen as unfair to the poor, who encountered a double financial burden. First, they had to pay the money changers, who charged to convert Roman coins into shekels. Then they had to buy their animal to be sacrificed. This made sin offering an expensive proposition. Jochanan is offering them a free substitute, in part as a protest against

Temple policy (which was also discriminatory in that the poor could not afford the larger, more prestigious animals to sacrifice, such as bulls; they had to settle for doves, making them feel inferior to the wealthier sinners). This policy is what Marcus Borg calls "God brokering." Jochanan's free-for-all immersion in the Jordan was a creative and revolutionary Jewish alternative.

> But when Jochanan saw many of the Pharisees and Sadducees coming to be immersed, he said to them, "You brood of vipers! Who warned you to flee from the anger of God that's coming?" (Matt. 3:7)
>
> *LB*

Here we encounter the beginning of a highly negative "spin" on the Pharisees and Sadducees as a whole. While the Sadducees represented a wealthier class of Temple aristocracy (the priestly class) who were justly resented by most Jews for collaborating with Rome, not all were of this ilk, and certainly the Pharisees were in another class altogether. They were theological innovators, largely respected by the Jewish people and at odds with the biblical literalism of the Sadducees. The Pharisees were the group with which Jeshu would have felt most at home, indeed the group with whom he dialogued, discussed, argued, and dined. It is noteworthy that Mark's earlier gospel omits any reference to Pharisees or Sadducees and states instead: " … and everyone flocked to him from the countryside of Jerusalem and the city of Jerusalem" (Mark 1:5).

> ¹³Sometime later, Jeshu came from the Galilee and stood before Jochanan at the Jordan to be immersed by him. ¹⁴Jochanan tried to stop him, saying, "I ought to be immersed by you, and yet you come to me!" ¹⁵But Jeshu answered him, "Let things alone for

now; this way we'll be doing all that God requires." So Jochanan went along with this, ¹⁶and as soon as Jeshu had been immersed, he came up out of the water. Then heaven opened up for Jeshu, and he saw a spirit of God coming down like a dove and resting on him. ¹⁷And a voice from heaven said: "This is my child, the child I love, the child in whom I take great delight." (Matt. 3:13–17)

LB

That Jeshu insists on being immersed by Jochanan suggests that he sees himself as an ordinary human being desiring *teshuvah*, or "repentance." This comes through in spite of the awkward embellishment of Mark's story by Matthew in the form of Jochanan's hesitation and Jeshu's weak response: "This way we'll be doing all that God requires." The story meets the "embarrassment criterion" for authenticity that Ron cites in *The Hidden Gospel of Matthew*: if a story is embarrassing to the community it's being written for, chances are good that it really happened (or at least comes from an earlier tradition).[1] Jeshu thus firmly plants himself in the world of humanity, which includes the need for purification of *his* sins.

What were those sins? Where did he fail? What did his vulnerability look like? Did it resemble impatience? Tribalism? Judgment? Was it resentment in relation to family members who thought he was a fanatic or a lunatic? Or anger against the Pharisees with whom he argued? Did he sometimes retaliate? Any of these possibilities could lead to a need for purification. Just as the high priest of the Temple needed to be washed before being anointed for service (see Exod. 29:4–7), Jeshu would require a ritual cleansing to prepare him for divine service. At issue is what it means to be fully human. Is there anyone fully human who is fully free from sin?

The image in the last two verses of the heavens opening (which could be understood as Jeshu's consciousness deepening) and the *Ruach haKodesh* descending like a dove upon him is beautiful and touching. So also is the voice from heaven (a *bat kol* in Hebrew) declaring what each of us longs to hear: you are my beloved child, in whom I delight. Franz Rosenzweig (an esteemed twentieth-century Jewish philosopher) writes about each of us needing to discover ourselves as "beloved souls" in relation to God. This discovery is part of the great transformation of our spiritual journey.

RM

Laura's commentary raises a number of important points. It is fascinating to read this narrative aware of the fact that Matthew is writing this with a copy of Mark at hand. The ways in which Matthew expands the brief Marcan narrative are telling. First of all, as Laura notes, Matthew adds the Pharisees. This is just the first of many times he will add an antipharisaic or anti-Jewish highlight to a story he has received from the tradition. Pharisaic Judaism, emerging rabbinic Judaism, is the enemy in Matthew's life-world, and this becomes a repeated theme in the later strata of this gospel. This is of critical importance to understanding the way in which this gospel can simultaneously be Jewish and anti-Jewish.

We also sense the growing embarrassment in Matthew that is barely visible in Mark. In Mark, Jeshu is simply one of the crowd immersed by Jochanan. And the heavenly voice in Mark's story addresses Jeshu, not the crowd. In Mark, the theophany belongs to Jeshu; in Matthew, the revelation about Jeshu belongs to the bystanders—including, of course, the Pharisees, who not only refuse its truth but become its enemy, thereby showing their alliance to the power that stands in the way of truth, the power of Satan.

The embarrassment of Jeshu submitting to a ritual of repentance begins with Mark's assertion that Jochanan had a premonition that although he baptized in water, one would come after him who would rank higher than he and would immerse people in God's Spirit (Mark 1:7–8). This comment, of course, makes no sense. If Jochanan were really only immersing people in water, then he would be performing nothing more than the service provided by a bath attendant. Obviously Jochanan's immersion ritual is Spirit-filled. This early Christian attempt to downplay Jochanan's real significance as a spiritual teacher and leader ends up making the story ludicrous.

But the slight inconsistency in Mark's narrative reaches new heights in Matthew's story. Jeshu is not even there to participate in the ritual. He is, after all, the sinless Son of God. He is simply play-acting in order to do something that "God requires" (Matt. 3:15). Why would God be requiring an empty and meaningless act? Apparently to create a scene in which a lot of bystanders from various places could hear God announce the true nature of this man from Galilee. This is why Matthew changes the heavenly voice from speaking in the second person directly to Jeshu into the third person addressing the crowds. Thus, it is that Matthew robs Jeshu of what was perhaps his greatest experience of God. Matthew's Jeshu cannot be allowed to learn anything new about his relationship to God. So it is the crowd that becomes the benefactor of this blessing.

Matthew's unwillingness to allow Jeshu to be fully human empties the whole story of its power. Yes, Jeshu was human, and as Laura states so well in her remarks, he was undoubtedly thinking of some of his own limitations that day when he submitted to Jochanan's ritual of repentance. And the voice was indeed intended for him and for no one else. We, of course, have no idea what words, if any, Jeshu heard that day, but the event was certainly a turning point in his life, analogous to the Buddha's enlightenment under the bo tree, Moses's wonder at the God who was manifested in the burning bush, Muhammad's awe at the voice he heard at the entrance to a cave on a hillside outside of Mecca. We know nothing about the circumstances of Jeshu's physical birth, but we stand here at the very time and place of his spiritual birth.

As in the similar experiences of other giants of the Spirit, the revelation implies a calling, the beginning of a ministry. Moses will lead the people out of bondage as the Buddha will lead people out of ignorance and as Muhammad will lead people to a community of justice and peace. Jeshu, too, emerges from the waters of the Jordan with a mission and a message: he will proclaim God's reign to one and all. It will no longer be the vengeful coming of Jochanan's angry God, but the enveloping presence of a God of forgiveness and peace, a peace that is powerfully symbolized in the manner in which the Spirit's presence is revealed to Jeshu, descending on him with the gentleness of a dove.

REFLECTIONS

1. When I remove Matthew's agenda from the text, what do I learn about Jeshu?
2. How would I compare Jewish and Christian holy people who have had a powerful experience of the Divine?
3. How can this story be a focus for a discussion of spiritual growth in all of us? How are Jews and Christians today called to become Spirit-people, people with a message for the world?

5

The Message and the Messenger

Hearing of Jochanan's arrest, Jeshu withdrew into the Galilee. (Matt. 4:12)

LB

Then, as now in many places in the world, there is danger in speaking out against the status quo. As I write this commentary, today's newspaper has a headline regarding Afghan women who were attacked (some injured, some killed) by an explosion in their minibus as they championed the right to vote in upcoming elections. Jochanan has angered the powers that be—in this case, Herod Antipas—by criticizing Herod's mistreatment of his first wife and condemning his immorality in marrying his brother's wife. Jeshu wisely withdraws to a safer district (still ruled by Herod Antipas, but closer to the region ruled by his brother Philip, to which Jeshu could escape, if necessary).

He has been immersed by Jochanan in the waters of the Jordan, he has been declared God's beloved, and he has resisted temptation in the desert. Now he is ready to begin his public ministry.

> From that time on, Jeshu began to proclaim the message, "Turn your lives around; the reign of God is approaching." (Matt. 4:17)

LB

The word for "repent" in Hebrew (here translated as "turn your lives around") means to return or come back to a God-centered awareness. Neil Douglas-Klotz, who writes about the Aramaic Jeshu, probes deeper: "In a Hebrew-Aramaic sense, to repent means to unite with something by affinity because it feels like going home."[1] To be centered in God is our native state, so to undergo *teshuvah* (the process of repentance in Hebrew, from a root that means "to turn") is to come home to God. Jeshu is advocating just such a homecoming, not in some faraway afterlife, but in the immediacy of the present moment. The talmudic sage Rabbi Eliezer taught: "Repent one day before your death" (*Pirkei Avot* 2:15). Since none of us knows with certainty when that day is, the time to repent is always now. Jeshu's proclamation would be at home with such talmudic teachings.

What is this "reign of God" (usually translated as "kingdom of heaven") that Jeshu is proclaiming? Douglas-Klotz points out that a more accurate translation from the Aramaic would be "queendom of heaven," since the word for kingdom is gendered feminine in both Aramaic and Hebrew (*malkuta* and *mamlacha,* respectively).[2] I am reminded that the word *malkhut*—another Hebrew rendering of "kingdom" and also feminine—is one of the ten *Sefirot* (or Divine emanations) in Jewish mysticism. *Malkhut* is that aspect of the Divine that permeates our earthly existence, present in the here and now, and sometimes referred to as *Shekhinah*, or "She Who dwells with Us." The nearness of God that Jeshu refers to seems clearly related to the Divine Presence that is *Shekhinah*.

So while Jeshu echoes the words of Jochanan (Matt. 3:2), here they convey a very different understanding of the nearness of God's reign, as the upcoming Sermon on the Mount will reveal. Jeshu is not an apocalyptic preacher as Jochanan is; that is, he is not primarily focused on end-time phenomena. Rather, he is sapiential—he is a teacher of the wisdom inherent in living deeply in the present moment. The kingdom of heaven he proclaims is not a place but a state of being, a consciousness where seeing God means experiencing the Divine in the everyday, commonplace realities of living. It is finding the sacred hidden in the profane and opening to the abundance of blessings here and now. This is utterly Jewish in its ethos.

> 18While he was walking by the Lake of Galilee, Jeshu saw two brothers, Shimon, called "Rock," and his brother Andri. Being fishermen, they were throwing their net into the lake. 19Jeshu said to them, "Follow me, and I'll teach you to fish for people." (Matt. 4:18–19)

LB

The metaphor of fishing for people suggests pulling them out of their submerged consciousness of unawareness into a new reality. The power of Jeshu's message to attract those ready to hear it is evident in the way these fishermen drop everything and follow him. This God-intoxicated Jewish hasid (or holy man) must have been charismatic and convincing to achieve such an effect. God-centeredness attracts a following. Once caught in this new consciousness, his disciples can help awaken others. This is similar to Mahatma Gandhi's impact on people two thousand years later. And both leaders share a passion for what Gandhi called *satyagraha*—holding on to the truth. The truth of our authentic selves embodying love itself, the deep reality of our divine nature, is powerful bait. Thus, the new disciples leave their biological father to follow a greater authority and to encounter a deeper awareness.

> Jeshu traveled all around the Galilee, teaching in their synagogues, announcing the good news of God's reign, and healing every kind of sickness and infirmity found among the people there. (Matt. 4:23)

LB

The phrase "their synagogues" is inappropriate because it separates Jeshu from his fellow Jews. Better to leave off the possessive pronoun and say "teaching in synagogues" (or as Ron suggests, "his" synagogues).[3] This is a subtle detail, but adds to the misimpression that Jeshu was outside the Jewish fold. It also reinforces the anti-Jewish bias of the gospel.

Jeshu's ability to cure disease, relieve pain, and heal sickness is the physical counterpart to the deeper spiritual work he is accomplishing. Internists, psychiatrists, and clergy were not separate entities in Jeshu's life-world, as they are in our contemporary, fragmented world. Body, mind, and spirit are of a piece in ancient Hebrew understanding, and Jeshu embraces this holistic view. Not surprisingly, his reputation as a healer begins to spread throughout the region.

RM

I appreciate Laura's comments about the kingdom (or queendom) that Jeshu proclaims. It is without question the heart of his message, though it is also the source of some of the most dramatic differences in subsequent interpretation. I was attending a Bible study not too long ago with a group of college students and the session ended with the Lord's Prayer. I asked the students what they were praying for when they said, "Thy Kingdom come." They all responded that they were praying for the end of the world. I asked them why they wanted the world to end, and they had no answer. This was simply the way they had come to understand the prayer. I found that curious and a bit discouraging.

America today seems to be caught up in an end-time mania. This is reflected in the popularity of the novels by Tim LaHaye and Jerry Jenkins. This *Left Behind* series begins with the Rapture, when the true believers are taken to heaven, while the rest of humanity is plunged into the horror of seven years of tribulation to be followed by the establishment of a thousand-year reign (millennium) by Jeshu. Christians adhering to this theology are called premillennialists because they believe that Jeshu will return before the millennium. The nineteenth century saw a preponderance of postmillennialists, those who believed that Jeshu's coming will culminate a thousand years of peace brought about by Christians living the social gospel. And, of course, the vast majority of Christians are amillennialists, eschewing the whole idea of a literal millennium.

Premillennialism entails a dramatic political fallout, as wars and plagues, tsunamis and hurricanes constitute a kind of good news. They are, after all, the harbingers of the Rapture. It is only when the human situation hits rock bottom that Jeshu will step in to rescue his true church from the unbelievers who will remain behind. Premillennialists have no reason to try to cure AIDS, alleviate world hunger, or protect the environment. Bad news is good news in this

Orwellian theology. For it is only through disaster that Jeshu will be moved to rapture the church. This parallels the premillennialist view of personal salvation, which maintains that it is only the conviction of sin, of one's total helplessness to initiate a relationship with God, that can lead to salvation. It is only in realizing that we are completely alienated from God that we are motivated to turn to the atoning sacrifice of Jeshu for our salvation.

Premillenialists read the Bible as history written in advance. The scripture is a kind of *Farmer's Almanac* in which we can discern future events. From my perspective, everything falls apart from this false beginning. The message of Jeshu is not a news announcement about the future. It is something rooted in the mystical, sapiential, and prophetic traditions of his Judaism. It is mystical and sapiential because it is a way of knowing, of seeing, of being conscious. It is prophetic because it speaks to us in the present moment in which we exercise our conscience in addressing the complexity of our world. Finally, it calls forth a different kind of community, one of justice and peace. It is these three Cs (consciousness, conscience, and community) and their ramifications that display the mystery of God's reign in our lives.

Jeshu was indeed a God-intoxicated hasid. There were other hasidim in the Galilee at this time. Their lives, like that of Jeshu, were characterized by simple living, deep prayer, and healing. They also formed groups of disciples. Such a circle of students was called a *chavurah*. In Hebrew, a *chaver* is both a study partner and a friend. After all, what greater mark of friendship can there be than sharing with someone the study of Torah, God's teachings? In Jeshu's case, however, there is no indication that his *chavurah* spent the day studying Torah. What, then, characterized these disciples of Jeshu?

Like so many issues in Christian Testament scholarship, this question provokes widely disparate opinions. Like many Roman Catholics, I grew up with the idea that Jeshu started the Catholic Church. The apostles were the first bishops, and Shimon was the first pope. Others find nothing in Jeshu's ministry to support such a project or goal. And yet, it is clear that Jeshu formed a *chavurah*, and it follows that it must have had a purpose.

Perhaps the key to this problem lies in the verse about fishing for people. These companions were called apostles, a Greek word translating the Hebrew *shaliach*, one sent out on a mission or someone acting on the authority of a king or leader. Jeshu must have been sending these people out to do or say something. But what was the content of the message? A long answer to this question will come in our subsequent discussion of the abundant teachings attributed to Jeshu in this gospel. But a short answer is that the members of the *chavurah* were sent out to proclaim the kingdom of God, not only in words, but also in power and in healing. Once again, we're driven back to the all-important question of what Jeshu meant by the kingdom or reign of God.

One school of thought—and this includes but goes beyond the premillennialists—casts Jeshu as an apocalyptic preacher and consequently believes that the apostles were to proclaim a coming cosmic event, the in-break of God's kingdom. But as Laura and I have been claiming in this discussion, God's kingdom is not a future event (though it has implications for the future) but a present reality impacting consciousness, conscience, and community. It thus entails living with an intimate awareness of God's presence, dealing with the neighbor as a divinely imaged sister or brother, and striving for a community based on justice and peace.

REFLECTIONS

1. What are the consequences of seeing God's reign as a future event rather than as a present reality?

2. How can God's reign be understood as mystical, sapiential, and prophetic?

3. How can we discuss the petition "Thy Kingdom come" in the context of a dialogue between Jews and Christians?

6

A Program for
Jewish Renewal

¹Seeing what a crowd there was, Jeshu went up on the mount and sat down, and his disciples gathered around him. ²He then began to teach them, saying: ³"You're successful if you're spiritually receptive; you have room for God's reign." (Matt. 5:1–3)

LB

Jeshu's subversive wisdom rings out here, as he begins these extraordinary teachings. Using the traditional translation ("Blessed are the poor in spirit, for theirs is the kingdom of heaven") is a bit like wrestling with a Buddhist koan. Blessed are the poor? We wonder if we heard him correctly. Since when is it a blessing to be poor in anything? For the monetarily poor to be blessed might make some sense (although even that idea gives conventional wisdom a run for its money). There is the notion that material wealth is not the richness one truly desires and that big money often corrupts, but few pay much attention to it. "Poor in spirit" is more jarring yet. Typically, on a spiritual path one seeks abundance of spirit. So what is Jeshu talking about here?

Clearly, we have to chew on this verse to release the meaning. Ron's creative translation helps us with this task, but it's useful to unpack the familiar one. "Poor" suggests neediness and an awareness of need. In order for us to seek a deeper reality, we have to become dissatisfied with our more superficial satisfactions. The house in the suburbs, the cars in the garage, the Hawaii vacations may be the American dream, but they are not the answers to our longing for ultimate meaning. Even prizes, positions of power, honors, and accolades lose their ability finally to satisfy us.

When we experience our own *lack*—our impermanence and emptiness that longs to be filled with something lasting and unchanging; our mortality that craves to connect to what is immortal; our vulnerability that strives to know what is invulnerable, unassailable; our finiteness that seeks to confront the infinite—then we are capable of openness and receptivity. Awareness of our extreme dependence makes such receptivity possible. In our state of naked need we are humble. Such humility and longing lead to God-consciousness. The doors to the kingdom of heaven are flung open. And we are blessed.

"You're successful if you know how to mourn; God will comfort you." (Matt. 5:4)

LB

When we lose what we most deeply love, it puts us in touch with the profundity of our neediness, with the depth of our poverty. It reminds us that we are not self-sufficient, that our very lives and the lives of those we love are a gift to be cherished, a loan that can be withdrawn at any moment, a mystery in which we participate with joy and awe, with gratitude and wonder.

Loss and mourning awaken our need for God, which always awakens a divine response. Comfort comes in a multiplicity of forms, but it surely comes to those who open to it from out of the depths of anguish and despair. Very often, afflictive experiences are the ones that result in spiritual evolution. Mourning is universal—if we live long enough, we all will lose a loved one. It is part of our humanness. The comfort of God's nearness at such times of unrelenting pain (and sometimes the pain is all one feels, initially) results in growth, strength, new life, and healing.

Sometimes the loss we need to mourn is of a cherished part of the self that no longer serves and must be relinquished. Perhaps a dream or an ambition needs to be given up. Giving up the desire to possess people or control circumstances (and with it the illusion that we are in control) is another painful but necessary loss. Shedding old ego attachments and compulsions that once were a refuge of sorts requires a grieving period before a new orientation can take hold.

Then there are the "planetary" sorrows Ron speaks of,[1] the wounds of the world that cry out to be acknowledged and mourned. Environmental degradation, wars, hunger and homelessness, rage and violence plague our planet. Unenlightened leadership around these issues is another cause for mourning. When we open our hearts to the sorrows of others, allowing ourselves to feel their pain, God joins us in our efforts to be of service and comforts us. He "gives strength to our bones." In the words of Isaiah (58:9–10):

> Then, when you call, the Lord will answer;
> When you cry, He will say: Here I am.
> If you banish the yoke from your midst,

The menacing hand and evil speech,
And you offer your compassion to the hungry
And satisfy the famished creature—
Then shall your light shine in darkness,
And your gloom shall be like noonday.

"You're successful if you're gentle; you'll inherit God's earth."
(Matt. 5:5)

LB

Again we encounter unconventional wisdom, subversive wisdom, so different from the notion of a dog-eat-dog world or the belief that you have to be aggressive, unyielding, pushy, and uncompromising (even hardhearted) to succeed in our current world where the bottom line reigns supreme, where greed and corruption are rampant, where doing rather than being predominates.

What is usually translated from the Greek as "meek" has more the connotation of "gentle" than "timid" or "afraid" in Aramaic, Jeshu's native tongue. "Gentle" conveys a softening of the rigidities that bind us. When we soften what is hard (one thinks of Pharaoh's heart), we allow new insights and awareness to penetrate—compassion where there was anger, forgiveness where there was judgment, love where there was hatred. It is an opening to another point of view that permits diatribe to become dialogue, blame to soften into understanding. This softening enables us to receive, to inherit all the bounties that nature (the earth, of which we are a part) has available. Just as seeds cannot take root in hard, unyielding soil, so we, too, need earthworms to humbly turn over the soil of consciousness, to break up the clumps of anger, arrogance, and ignorance that prevent our growth. When we surrender our willfulness to God's will, we are nourished and sustained by the earth's productivity. We no longer exploit the earth and ravage its resources, destroying our very life-support system for personal, short-term gain. We are back in the garden, which is abundance and blessing indeed.

> "You're successful if you're starving to be God-centered; God will satisfy you fully." (Matt. 5:6)

LB

Again, the assumption is one of underlying emptiness, a famished space in ourselves that needs filling, that hungers and thirsts for something (the usual translation: "Blessed are those who hunger and thirst for righteousness, for they will be filled"). What does it mean to be "righteous" (here translated as "God-centered")? In Jewish tradition, righteousness is an attribute of God to be sought after by humanity—an attribute of justice, fairness, and perfect integrity. It signifies the truthfulness and uprightness that ideally permeate every aspect of life: what is right and just in business (equal weights and measures), in government (the laws of judges, rulers, and kings or, in our democracy, presidents and congressional leaders), and in personal relationships (mindful speech and ethical behavior). The Hebrew scriptures are saturated with this call for righteousness and justice, particularly in regard to the treatment of the poor, needy, marginalized, and oppressed. The Hebrew root for righteousness *(tzedek)* is the same as the word for charity *(tzedakah)*, indicating the close relationship between generosity and justice. To care for the widow, the orphan, and the impoverished is an act of righteousness.

> "You're successful if you're compassionate to others; God will be compassionate to you." (Matt. 5:7)

LB

Mercy or *compassion* usually translates *rachamim* in Hebrew, which comes from a root that means "womb." What is the relationship between a womb and compassion? We feel a deep, abiding connection to that which we birth—an intuitive, unconditional love, as well as a protective instinct. When our children suffer, we naturally feel compassion. We can extend this capacity for connection and empathy to those who are not our biological children. As the Buddha suggests: "Just as a mother protects her child, her only child from harm, so within yourself let grow a boundless love for all creatures."[2]

"You're successful if your purpose is always pure; you'll see God." (Matt. 5:8)

LB

When we are pure in purpose (the usual translation is "pure in heart") we have divested ourselves of all that is false, negative, or obstructive on our path. When we shed such ego attributes as greed, envy, or lust and transform hatred, ignorance, and fear, we deepen into our essential purity. This state of being is what Catholic theologian and mystic Thomas Merton calls our true self, aware of the unity of all life, unencumbered by the delusion of separateness.

As the Sufi mystic Rumi says, "Everyone sees the unseen in proportion to the clarity of his heart, and that depends on how much he has polished it. Whoever has polished it sees more—more unseen forms become manifest." Jeshu is advocating that we polish our hearts, removing the grime of anger and resentment and the grit of selfishness, so that our unsullied God-consciousness can shine through. Then we "see" God in the beauty and goodness of our own actions and intentions.

"You're successful if you work for peace; you'll be called God's children." (Matt. 5:9)

LB

The Aramaic root for peacemakers evokes planting images: laboring with commitment and regularity to till the soil, bringing forth an abundance of fruit, and celebrating the harvest. Planting peace must be done periodically, whenever the season calls for it.

Shalom, the Hebrew word for peace, comes from a root that means "wholeness" or "completeness," a kind of perfection that comes with fullness of being. We come full when all the disparate pieces of our lives have integrated harmoniously; then we are filled with an integral sense of well-being. This success is cause for celebration.

RM

Jeshu's renewal program takes concrete form in these seven signs of success, of blessedness, of a God-centered life. We stand here at the heart of Jeshu's message as he makes concrete and explicit the ways in which God-centeredness manifests in human experience. Anyone renewed in God's Spirit will be spiritually receptive, able to mourn, gentle, starving for God-centeredness, compassionate, pure of purpose, and an instrument of peace. We note the balance here of personal, interior qualities of consciousness and outer-directed activities of conscience. From this comes the harmony of a renewed community.

True religion entails a process of transformation. Not to be transformed is to be deformed by the forces shaping our lives: ego-driven family expectations, the idolatrous aims of organized religion, and the imperial goals of "the world." We find teachings of Jeshu in which each of these potential areas of deformation is addressed. We can't help but be struck by the similarity between the way these forces functioned in the life-world of Jeshu and the way they work in our own. If we live within the dictates of "the world," we will surely be depressed and distracted, addicted, destructive of our environment, suspicious of anything different, and buried up to our necks in the detritus of a materialistic society.

We are motivated to growth by our dissatisfaction with the current state of things, both in the external world and in our own hearts. This dissonance produces the irritant that so often proves to be the catalyst of growth. Hitting bottom can open us up, allowing our hearts to be receptive to growth and humble before the path by which we are transformed into our deepest and most divine selves. These stages of our growth are not from evil to good or from falsehood to truth. We ascend from good to good and from true to true. Yet each stage of the ascent is matched by a higher level of organization and complexity. And each step we take demands moving beyond an earlier rung on the ladder where we once found completeness.

The culmination of this transformative process is what Jeshu refers to as "God's reign" or "God's kingdom." This does not refer to some future cosmic event but rather to the present in-breaking of God's power and love in our lives. It does, however, have a future dimension insofar as we continue to move more deeply into this mystery and form communities of people whose lives are similarly being transformed.[3]

Fundamentalisms of all stripes and shapes are selective, simplistic, and static. They create a cartoon version of a complex, sacred tradition and provide us with the solace of not having to grow up. This is why the megachurches flourish in our land. This is why the Roman Catholic Church (at least in its hierarchical leadership) has all but abandoned the prophetic agenda of the Second Vatican Council, preferring the conservative piety of a church increasingly dysfunctional in its inability to address the modern world. Jeshu's program of renewal challenges the stale complacency of our day as well as his.

REFLECTIONS

1. How would adopting Jeshu's renewal program change my life?

2. How would adopting Jeshu's renewal program change the nature of the various communities in which I participate: family, religious, social, work-related, and political?

3. How might this program be a basis for Jewish-Christian conversations?

7

A Master of Metaphor

"You are the salt of the earth, but if salt were to lose its saltiness, what could restore its flavor? It would then be good for nothing except to be thrown out on the road." (Matt. 5:13)

LB

What does "salt of the earth" convey? It speaks to me of what gives our lives flavor, taste, and deliciousness. It refers to who we *are* authentically—God's seasoning. If we lose sight of our authentic flavor, our original goodness, our image-of-God identity, what good are we? Our false selves are good for garbage; we can throw them on the compost heap and transform them into food and flowers, or waste our lives in superficiality at best, malevolence at worst. Ron points to the historical reality of salt as a precious commodity that was diluted with sand by the poor so it would last longer. But dilute it too much and it becomes worthless; it is no longer worth its salt.

Salt has the quality of being a preservative, as well as a flavor enhancer. It is a sustaining substance. We need such continued sustenance on a spiritual path to keep from being corrupted or spoiled by the temptations of the socialized world, to keep from "going bad."

Our saltiness is also our uniqueness, each of us a particular, necessary manifestation of the Unity. To be bland is to be tasteless—to become "good for nothing" (Middle Eastern hyperbole, here—the culture's tendency to use exaggerated language to make a point). We no longer season the soup and might as well be tossed out. As the Sufi poet Rumi reminds us twelve centuries later, "The pot drips what is in it. The saffron spice of connecting, laughter. The onion smell of separation, crying." Rumi also compares the spiritual aspirant to a chickpea needing to be boiled by the cook (the teacher) to attain flavor, spice, and vitality—to become food for the Friend. We need to find and retain our genuine flavor, and instead of complaining, "You're torturing me," say to God, "I love your cooking."[1]

> "You are the light of the world. A city built on a hill can't be hidden." (Matt. 5:14)

LB

Jeshu is telling us more about our true nature. We are salty and shiny. We are light! And we are meant to shine like the sun, the moon, and the stars—for all to see. We are beings of light, God containers, and spark-centered wonders. This is a joyful reality.

> "We don't light lamps and then immediately extinguish them; we put them on lampstands so that they can provide light for everyone in the room." (Matt. 5:15)

We are encouraged to shine openly for others. We let our gifts, talents, and abilities be seen, not for self-glorification but for selfless service—to "provide light for everyone in the room." This can be done in countless ways: by cooking a meal, writing a poem, teaching a class, liberating a country. There is no end to the possibilities of giving light.

Spiritual practices are a way of bringing light into a household. In a home where only one person is meditating, for example, the rest of the family will benefit from that individual's enhanced security, patience, and selflessness. As we strive to become illumined (by removing the grit of self-will from our inner lamps), our radiance becomes a spiritual bonus to those around us.

> "In just this same way, your light should shine so brightly for others that they can both see your good works and praise your heavenly Parent." (Matt. 5:16)

Our good works inspire others to connect with their own basic goodness, called by many names: Buddha nature, *yetzer ha-tov* (Hebrew for the inclination to do what is good), Atman, Divine spark, Christ-consciousness. To "give glory" to God (an alternate translation for "praise") is to be like God in our thoughts, words, and deeds, which together comprise "good works." Compassion, justice, loving-kindness, fearlessness, firmness, generosity, wisdom, understanding, and forgiveness are both divine attributes and manifestations of good works, expressed in a thousand ways throughout each day. When we reflect God's light with a kind word, a firm but necessary "no," or a forgiving heart, we give glory.

A line from Proverbs (20:27) comes to mind: *Ner Adonai nish-mat adam* ("the candle of God is the soul of humankind"). God's light is our very soul, the legacy given to us as our birthright. Illumined teachers like Jeshu serve as an example that helps us access this light, which is our true nature and derives from the Divine Source. As a great flame may light an unlimited number of candles, so, too, are we extensions of God's radiance. But old wounds and ongoing ego issues cloud our awareness of this great spiritual truth. When we divest our-selves of these fetters, when we purify our hearts and minds of com-pensatory greed and anger, when we dispel the darkness of ignorance and fear, the resulting transformation is the kingdom of heaven. God's reign then reigns within us, and our lives are lamps for others.

RM

These images of salt and light are among the most powerful and enduring in Jeshu's teaching. At a subtle level, they represent both challenge and controversy. What is the piece of meat or fish needing to be seasoned? Where is the dark room needing the light of the lamp?

Jeshu saw the patriarchal family structure of his time, much of organized religion, and the socialized reality called "the world" as obstacles to his message and mission, his proclamation of God's reign. This world, after all, was essentially Caesar's world, the powerful empire wrapping itself around the Mediterranean Sea. The Romans arrogantly referred to that body of water as *mare nostrum,* "our sea." For all the land bordering that sea belonged to Caesar.

Despite its trained troops, the empire knew that it could not rule by military might alone. It therefore launched a campaign to win the minds and hearts of the people. This propaganda campaign was waged not only in literature but also in the very architecture of the empire—the roads and aqueducts, the amphitheaters and temples.

By every means at its disposal, the empire spread its fourfold message. First, the state is supreme. After all, the emperor was a god deserving of divine worship. Second, peace comes through conquest. The Roman motto boasted: *si vis pacem, para bellum,* "if you want peace, get ready for war." Third, possessions are the measure of a person's worth. You are what you own. Fourth, your attitude toward others should be one of dominance. In a patronage system where you bribed those above you and received bribes from those below you, the goal was to maximize the bribes you received and minimize the ones you paid.

What light does Jeshu's teaching bring to the empire's worldview? First, God is supreme, not the state. Second, peace comes from justice, not from conquest. Third, a person's value resides in the texture of her relationships, not in the things she owns. Fourth, one's attitude toward others should be one of compassion and service, not dominance. This contrary program, this salt for the meat and light for the room, does not originate with Jeshu. It's the basic message of the Torah and of Israel's prophets. It's what we find in virtually every page of the Qur'an. This program is taught today by the Dalai Lama, Sr. Joan Chittister, Rabbi Rami Shapiro, and Dr. Irfan Khan. It is the core of the spiritual challenge to every empire's ideology.

In one sense, this is a battle of metaphors. Where do we find life's flavor? In the panoply of empire or in a profound trust in God? How do we achieve peace? Through endless invasions and wars or through the achievement of equity and fairness? How do we understand self-worth? In the incessant accumulation of things or in the rich weave of relationships—our covenants with God, with intimate others, with larger communities, and with the earth itself? How should we approach our neighbors? By dominating and controlling them or by loving them and calling them into their own deepest reality? What is life's true salt, and what brings most light into the room—Caesar's reign or God's?

If these alternatives do indeed lie at the heart of all true spiritual teaching, why do we see so little of Jeshu and so much of Caesar in our contemporary world? This stems from what I refer to as the "Big Lie." This happens whenever the reign of God is confused with the empire of Caesar. Christianity bought into this lie when the emperor Constantine laid the foundation for a "holy" Roman Empire. Islam bought into this lie whenever the vision of the Qur'an was replaced by the political ambitions of caliphs or sultans. Judaism has had to wrestle with this lie since the inception of the State of Israel in 1948.

Any religious renewal in our time must reject the "Big Lie" and enunciate clearly the dichotomy between the ideology of empire and the program of God's reign. It is often the children of our world who remind the emperor that he has no clothes. The prophets of our time proclaim the essential evil of the ideology of empire, which deceives people into believing that they are waging wars for God or shoring up clerical control to achieve divine purposes in the world.

REFLECTIONS

1. How does metaphor function at different levels of consciousness?

2. What beliefs or practices in Judaism and Christianity today directly or indirectly support the "Big Lie"?

3. How do Jews and Christians share the basic fourfold message of God's reign? How can we work together for a common renewal of faith?

8

Continuity and Discontinuity

"Don't think that I've come to discard the Torah and the Prophets. I have not come to discard but to complete." (Matt. 5:17)

LB

Jeshu did not see himself as the founder of a new religion, but as a teacher of Jewish renewal. He strove to "sing unto God a new song," as the psalmist advocates. Our traditions must be continually reexamined, reenlivened, reinterpreted, and renewed so that we can successfully and meaningfully apply the ancient, unchanging teachings to new circumstances and new contexts. In this way the Torah is completed, never once and for all, but always and again in a dynamic process. Questioning, struggling with ambiguity, wrestling with God (the word "Israel" means "one who wrestles with God"), and challenging corruption (whether individual or institutional) are part of the Jewish way.

> "Until this present universe passes away, not the smallest letter or even one stroke on a letter will be removed from the Torah until everything written there comes to pass." (Matt. 5:18)

LB

Jeshu suggests that the effort to understand the many layers of Torah will go on until heaven and earth pass away—until the end of time as we know it. Then, when "everything written there comes to pass," when "the wolf shall dwell with the lamb," when "nation shall not lift up sword against nation, neither shall they learn war anymore," when the world "shall be full of the knowledge of the Lord as the waters cover the sea" (Isa. 11:6, 2:4, and 11:9), God will roll up heaven and earth like a Torah scroll.

> "For unless your God-centeredness exceeds that of the Torah scholars and Pharisees, you'll never enter God's reign." (Matt. 5:20)

LB

This reign of God region is tricky territory, indeed. We are told that it is approaching (Matt. 4:17) and that it is available to the spiritually receptive (Matt. 5:3) and to those who are persecuted for being God-centered (Matt. 5:10), as well as to those who observe and teach the commandments (Matt. 5:19). But those who fail to fulfill some of them and teach others to do the same still have a place in the kingdom; they are, however, called "least." Now we are told that one has to be *more* God-centered than the Torah scholars and Pharisees in order to gain entrance at all.

Is this a commentary on the general *lack* of righteousness (or God-centered behavior) among those in positions of authority? If so, the level of corruption must have been extreme. To put *all* the scribes and Pharisees into one corrupt category is an unfair accusation. Perhaps this is Middle Eastern hyperbole, not to be taken literally. Surely there were some righteous Pharisees leading God-centered lives and teaching Torah with integrity and *kavanah* (purity of intention, an inward attentiveness to the Divine). The implication that *none* of them is entering the kingdom is disturbing. It speaks to a clubby "in versus out" mentality (they are out, and if you want to be in, you had better be more righteous than they are), a holier-than-thou sensibility that does not suggest enlightened consciousness, and therefore does not seem to me to be of Jeshu. The life-world of this text is almost certainly Matthew's community in the 80s.

RM

Before my dissertation defense, I spent three days responding to written and oral exams on topics related to my doctoral program. I can still remember one of the questions I was asked in the oral examination: "Comment on the continuity or discontinuity of Jesus with Judaism."

Almost thirty years have passed since I was asked that question and yet it continues to challenge me. On the one hand, there are those who believe that Jeshu rejected his Judaism and purposefully set out to found Christianity in its stead. Scholars call this "replacement theology." This continues to enjoy popularity in many Christian circles but finds little support among serious scholars of the Christian Testament.

The scholarly consensus is that Jeshu lived and died a Jew. He had no intention of founding another religion. At the same time, he did have a "lover's quarrel" with Judaism and had hopes of renewing it. Like the prophets before him, Jeshu called his contemporaries to turn back to the source, the purest current of divine revelation flowing in the Jewish tradition. But whatever he taught was an implementation of that tradition, not a rejection. Although the words of the gospel in this section stem from the community that produced this text in the 80s, they reveal a direction of thought not incompatible with the renewal program of Jeshu himself. Jeshu would certainly have agreed that his purpose was not to discard the Torah and the prophets. He clearly stands in continuity with his tradition, especially with its scriptural canon.

What, then, is discontinuous with his tradition? Only the level of consciousness at which he understands it. All religions are understood and implemented at different levels of consciousness. Our world is plagued today by fundamentalists of all stripes (Jews, Christians, Muslims, and Hindus) who often understand and implement their sacred tradition at a level of tribal instinct, distorting that tradition to fit their own dichotomous worldview of good people (the true believers) and bad people (the demonic "other"). One might ask whether this very judgment does what it condemns. In other words, am I demonizing the fundamentalists? I would argue that fundamentalists are not evil in this schema. They simply tend to operate at a tribal level of development. But acting from that level of development can and does have evil results in the world.

There are also people in all religions who generally understand and implement their respective traditions at a level of rational understanding. They are capable of tolerance and dialogue. They are evolved enough to enact compromise and negotiate peace. They are able to listen and learn from those who at some level disagree with them.

And then there are the mystics. They regularly understand and implement their respective traditions at a level of nondualistic consciousness. Their identities cannot be confined to what the Sufi poet Rumi called "a coffin of words." They live and move at the center to which all religions lead, a center of compassion and wisdom, a center of harmony and peace.

What was discontinuous in Jeshu's message was the difference between his understanding of Judaism and the understanding of most of the people around him. They were still operating on a tribal level of consciousness. This is a way of looking at the world in terms of sharp dichotomies between good and evil, us and them, the right way and the wrong way. The Romans were evil and the Jews, as God's chosen people, were righteous. From this perspective, the god of the Jews was a tribal god who would punish the evil Romans and reward the "chosen people."

In addition to this fundamental dichotomy between Jew and Gentile, there were further dichotomies within Jewish life for many of Jeshu's contemporaries. Those who lived more observant lives were more loved by God. Being created male, enjoying health and affluence—these were signs of God's blessing. Women, the sick and disabled, the homeless beggars, the prostitutes and tax-collectors—these were people far from God's blessing and light.

What Jeshu rejects is not his tradition but a tribal understanding of that tradition. What he accepts and teaches is still that same tradition, but from a consciousness of unity and peace. The point is that Jeshu would have experienced discontinuity with any tradition in its tribal form. Mystics always create problems for the simple reason that most of us don't live at their level of understanding and experience. But the discontinuity of the mystic actually represents the deepest continuity possible with the received tradition.

REFLECTIONS

1. What are some examples of how my own tradition is understood at different levels by different people?

2. What is tribal in my own understanding of my religion? Which of my religious views might be called rational? Which of my religious sentiments might stem from a consciousness of unity?

3. How can this discussion of levels of consciousness play a role in the ongoing dialogue between Jews and Christians?

9

Anger, Adultery, and Divorce

21"You've heard how it was said to people long ago, 'You shall not murder; and whoever murders shall be brought to trial.' 22And now I tell you that whoever is angry with a fellow human being shall be brought to trial, whoever insults a person will answer to the Sanhedrin, and whoever says to someone 'God damn you!' deserves a hell of fire." (Matt. 5:21–22)

LB

Jeshu makes the important connection between anger and murder—highlighting the inner mental state that leads to irrevocable acts of great harm. As a teacher of *kavanah* (a Hebrew word conveying the heart's intention; what Jewish theologian Martin Buber called "the mystery of the soul connected to a goal"), he emphasizes inwardness and self-control. He understands that thoughts are powerful instigators for our actions, and, like the Buddha, he knows that afflicted mental states matter. He and the Buddha would agree on this statement from the *Dhammapada:* "Our lives are shaped by our minds; we become what we think." While the corollary between murder and being brought to trial is clear to our rational minds, Jeshu extends the consequence to anger itself, since anger does away with (murders) compassion for the other.

Jeshu then takes the matter beyond anger to insults: an angry, agitated mind produces abusive words. In Jewish tradition, *lashon hara,* or "evil talk" (literally, "evil tongue"), be it gossip or insults, is much frowned upon. Shaming someone publicly is regarded as akin to murder (the talmudic rabbis connect it to the shedding of blood: first blood comes into the face—one blushes—then it leaves the face in a ghostly, deathlike pallor). Is Jeshu actually suggesting that insults be punishable by a court of law ("the Sanhedrin") or is he speaking metaphorically? I would presume the latter, or an already overloaded court system would topple under the weight of so many cases.

I wonder about the "hell of fire" as a consequence of saying "God damn you!" (or "you fool" in other translations). Is this another instance of the Middle Eastern hyperbole found elsewhere in the Gospel—for example, in Matthew 19:24, "A camel might have a better chance of getting through the eye of a needle than a rich person has of entering God's reign"? Certainly, one suffers from inflicting angry words and insults on others, and if Jeshu is comparing that suffering to hellfire (rather than saying "You'll burn in hell"—literally), I can accept the warning. That burning, hellish experience of rage and depreciation can be a useful catalyst for the necessary *teshuvah* ("repentance"), which helps us discipline our minds and tongues on future occasions. Before Yom Kippur (the Day of Atonement), Jews are advised to seek out anyone we may have offended in the preceding year, to apologize and ask for forgiveness. When taken seriously, this is a powerful practice.

> 27"You've heard the commandment not to commit adultery. 28And now I tell you that the man who looks at a woman and starts making plans to sleep with her has already committed adultery with her in his heart." (Matt. 5:27–28)

LB

Once again, guilty as charged! This Jewish teacher of *kavanah* stresses that what we think, feel, and dwell upon inwardly counts, is felt, and impacts ourselves and the world. The separation between inner and outer is not so distinct. Here, the difference between Aramaic thought and Greek understanding (reflected in the two languages) is relevant. In Aramaic, the line between inner and outer is blurred; in Greek, the division is sharp. Jeshu is teaching that our boundaries are permeable—the inner life of thoughts and intentions touches and affects the outer life of action in the world. If we think lustful thoughts, our desire grows, as does the likelihood of acting on that desire.

The implication of Jeshu's teaching is that training our minds and purifying our thoughts are an essential part of spiritual practice. The teaching is holistic—make your inner life accord with your outer actions; let body, mind, and spirit be unified. The impact of such unification is a powerful, laserlike concentration of energy. When our consciousness is split, the disunity weakens us, and we are far less effective in our actions. When consciousness is unified, unwanted thoughts can be dismissed and disempowered (not repressed). This leads to an ability to be one-pointed, our mind fully focused on the matter at hand, rather than scattered by daydreaming, lusting, worrying, or obsessing. With one-pointed attention we are in charge of our thoughts rather than at the mercy of them.

> ²⁹"If your right eye is an occasion of sin, pluck it out and throw it away. It's better to lose one eye than to have your whole body thrown into hell. ³⁰And if it's your right hand that is the occasion of sin, cut it off and throw it away. It's better to lose one limb than to have your whole body thrown into hell." (Matt. 5:29–30)

LB

These hyperbolic statements of Jeshu are jarring and destructive if taken literally. Scripture is not for the mentally unbalanced or the metaphorically challenged (or for those who read poetry as prose). On the spiritual path, we have to know what to tear out and what to cleave to, what to lose and what to gain. The eye and the hand that are "the occasion of sin" are metaphors for the sensate world that can so easily lead us astray with its glitter and false promises. We need to cut ourselves off from that temptation, to see beyond phenomena with our spiritual senses (our third eye) if we are to enter the kingdom of heaven that opens its gates within. To be "thrown into hell" is to mistake the material, socialized world (which operates on the surface) for the whole, missing the deeper reality that is our center, our purpose, our life's meaning. Jeshu is using these extraordinary rhetorical statements to convey the message that it is worth losing anything at the periphery to reach the center, where God resides.

> ³¹"It has also been said that any husband divorcing his wife should give her an official notice. ³²And now I tell you that the husband who divorces his wife, except in the case of her unfaithfulness, is guilty of making her commit adultery if she marries

again, and the man marrying such a woman commits adultery as well." (Matt. 5:31–32)

LB

Jeshu is both a product of his time and place and well ahead of it. He is part of a very patriarchal society, where women were regarded as chattel and had no socioeconomic recourse outside the protection of a male. He is attempting to put a stop to the practice of men divorcing women for frivolous reasons and leaving them destitute. This concern for women's well-being and the inequities of a patriarchal world makes him a feminist in the context of the times. But he stops short of allowing a woman to initiate divorce proceedings when her husband has been unfaithful (or abusive). Those would have been welcome words.

In spite of his good intentions, the rigidity of these stipulations for divorce has done a lot of harm. This kind of cut-and-dried decree does not take into account the nuances and subtleties in a marriage— the many facets of intimacy that would allow a couple to break up for reasons other than adultery, and the possibility for both partners to find happiness with others without having the relationships labeled "adultery." Obviously, this is a more modern sensibility, and perhaps it is unfair to expect it of Jeshu. In his time, a woman had no freedom of movement or association, and no means of supporting herself— wife or prostitute were the basic choices. For Jeshu to advocate against divorce except in extreme cases was a compassionate position in support of women.

33"You've also heard how it was said to people in the past: 'Don't perjure yourself; perform whatever you have sworn in the sight of the Lord.' 34And now I tell you not to swear at all. Not by heaven, since that's God's throne, 35nor by the earth, since that's God's footstool, and not by Jerusalem, since that's God's city. 36Don't even swear by your head, since you can't make a single white hair black. 37Just say 'yes' or 'no'; anything more than that stems from the Evil One." (Matt. 5:33–37)

LB

Jeshu advocates a kind of honesty in speech that makes swearing oaths unnecessary. Your word is your character, your reputation, and your good name. It should stand on its own merits and not need to be backed up by heaven or earth or Jerusalem. This higher consciousness has a purity that reserves no place for deviousness or deception. Truthfulness in speech is essential to living with integrity.

RM

Jeshu takes us to the level of "what is going on in what is going on." Most of us live, operate, and make our choices on the level of what is going on. Joe was caught in bed with the woman next door. Sally murdered her husband. Sam and Edna are getting a divorce. Therefore, Joe, Sally, Sam, and Edna have sinned; they are sinners.

This superficial reading of behavior is not where Jeshu takes his stand. He looks at not merely what is going on, but also what is going on in what is going on. In other words, he reads the language of the heart. Perhaps Joe will never commit adultery because he's too lazy or too afraid of being caught, and yet he is obsessed with finding a way to be unfaithful to his wife. Perhaps Sally will never murder her husband, but what if she deals with him abusively day in and day out, telling him how fat and ugly he is, what a poor provider he is, how sexually inadequate he is, and how she hopes that he will die a painful death? And what if Sam and Edna decide not to get a divorce? They choose instead to live in a state of bitter and mutual loathing. They poison themselves and their children with the toxic air they pump into their home day after day, year after year.

Seeing life at this level goes beyond the adequacy of laws and conduct systems. We are in the realm of the deeper consciousness that was Jeshu's milieu. At this level, intentions shape the world as much as words and deeds do. If one achieves a purity of life at this level, no external norms or legal codes are necessary. But if one's consciousness is muddied at this level, no external constraints are relevant. This is the territory Jeshu challenges us to explore within ourselves.

REFLECTIONS

1. What are ways in which we catch ourselves judging people simply by observing what is going on, with no awareness of what is going on in what is going on?

2. How has this level of judgment been harmful to Jewish-Christian dialogue? Have I heard Jews described as "Christ killers"? Have I heard that Christians drink anti-Semitism with their mothers' milk?

3. How can this exploration of consciousness deepen the dialogue between Jews and Christians?

10

Opposing Evil without Emulating It

"You've heard it said: 'An eye for an eye and a tooth for a tooth.'"
(Matt. 5:38)

LB

The reference to "an eye for an eye and a tooth for a tooth" (Exod. 21:24, Lev. 24:20, Deut. 19:21) unfortunately contributes to the gross misunderstanding of this verse in the Hebrew scriptures. This was never understood literally by the rabbis, but was always interpreted as requiring monetary restitution for the lost eye, tooth, hand, or foot (as Exod. 21:24 goes on to include). It is a plea for equity, not vengeance, and for compensation, not punishment. It advocates restraint, not retribution. The Talmud points out the moral absurdity of interpreting this law literally—no eye is like any other eye. Rather than constituting a harsh, punitive law (reflecting a vengeful God) the halachic (legal) requirement of monetary compensation was a move away from the cruel, retaliatory actions of other societies; it constitutes a more compassionate response.

> 39"And now I tell you not to go toe to toe with the person doing evil to you. If anyone slaps the right side of your face, let that person slap the left side as well. 40And if someone takes you to court to sue you for your shirt, let that person have your coat as well. 41And if someone forces you to carry his gear one mile, carry it two miles." (Matt. 5:39–41)
>
> *LB*

Jeshu is now advocating an entirely different approach to injury. He moves beyond dealing with the external consequences in the form of monetary compensation to an internal shift of consciousness. Rather than going "toe to toe" with the oppressor, he suggests a more psychologically subtle form of resistance. These three verses are laden with subversive wisdom and subject to much conventional misunderstanding. The teaching is, again, one of *kavanah*—an approach to conflict and harm that potentially shifts the ground of conciousness completely because it aims to convert the hearts of both the injured and the injurer. Jeshu is describing what would become Gandhi's *satyagraha*—a "soul force" that literally means "holding on to truth" (*sat* means "that which is").

Turning the other cheek is not submission, but an assertion of equality, because striking someone with the palm of the hand on the left cheek (the turned cheek) was done only to those regarded to be of equal status in Roman society. The gesture of turning the cheek therefore subtly implies equality, dignity, and freedom, as opposed to the initial slap (with the back of the hand on the right cheek), which is the contemptuous mark of a superior toward an inferior.

For a destitute peasant, giving a coat as payment for a debt to a wealthy landowner would leave the giver basically naked (having already lost his shirt). This physical exposure opens the taker to an awareness of the inappropriateness of the deed. It makes possible a deepening of consciousness from one's own greed to the other's human need. The injustice becomes manifest in the debtor's nakedness.

Similarly, the extra mile alters the relationship between the Jew who is carrying the gear and the Roman soldier who orders him to carry it. In occupied Palestine, there was a mandate requiring any Jew to carry a soldier's pack one mile if so requested. So this first mile marks the relationship of slave to master. However, the second mile is done voluntarily as a free man. Perhaps a dialogue would ensue, or at least a seed could be planted in the soldier's consciousness. Might not the Roman soldier be provoked to ask "why?" during this second mile of the Jew's bearing his burden?

Truth and nonviolence define these responses to oppression. Such strategies assert the humanity, God-centered identity, and essential freedom of the oppressed, and make possible the transformation of the oppressor. Embodying these qualities also serves as a vital reminder to the consciousness of those who are mistreated, converting them from helpless victims to empowered defenders of their humanity. In each case, the injustice of the situation is opposed without physical force, anger, or malice. What's more, respect is maintained for the dignity of the oppressor as another human being, who is also created in God's image.

The applicability of such nonviolent strategies in relation to the most intractable hearts and minds is particularly challenging in the face of powerful, hate-infused opposition. Would *satyagraha* have had any impact on a Nazi mentality whose goal was not just subjugation of a people but genocide, a mentality that saw Jews as subhuman, as actual vermin whose extermination would benefit society? Is the Nazi mentality different only in degree from that of the British (who also depreciated and dehumanized the Indians, but did not, on the whole, murder them), or is it different in kind? When dehumanization and hatred reach genocidal proportions, is a conversion of the heart possible?

The Rosenstrasse prison demonstration in 1943 was a rare example of nonviolent protest against Nazi rule. There, an impromptu gathering of more than six thousand women, the "Aryan kin" of thousands of Jewish men arrested by the Gestapo on a Friday in February (largely Gentile wives and some mothers), managed to free their loved ones by Sunday through nonviolent confrontation outside the detention center in Berlin. These women did not go toe to toe with the evildoers; they resisted by putting their lives on the line and going heart to heart with the Gestapo. Tragically, the demonstration, which succeeded in saving the lives of thousands of Jews, did not become the movement that might have altered the course of history. The women were leaderless, untrained, and could not follow up on their remarkable success. But as Michael Nagler makes clear in his compelling book, *The Search for a Nonviolent Future*, this event "showed that sometimes just risking pain, which involves the mastery of one's fear, can be extremely effective."[1]

RM

Stop hitting your sister," screams the father as he strikes his little boy. "Learn the importance of life," shouts the judge as he pronounces the death sentence. Jeshu's teaching sheds light on these confusing and inconsistent areas of human behavior where people get caught up in the very structure of violence they claim to be opposing.

Just a few days after 9/11, I heard Elie Wiesel speak at a synagogue in Chicago. Holocaust survivor and storyteller—here was a man who had experienced the worst the world has to offer. What was his message in response to the new threat to civilization? Oppose terrorism, but be careful that in the process you don't become terrorists. Not to defeat terrorism is a tragedy. To be converted to terrorism is a worse tragedy.

This is the insight that lies at the heart of Jeshu's teaching. He did not support the guerrilla tactics of the "hawks" of his day who attacked Roman soldiers and murdered Jewish collaborators. But neither did Jeshu support a capitulation to the Roman Empire and its ideology of oppression. Nonviolent resistance represented a middle way, a strong witness to God's reign in the face of Caesar's propaganda.

Martin Luther King Jr. used these tactics in his response to American racism, just as Mahatma Gandhi had used them in opposing British colonialism. It was the strategy that led to the success of the Rosenstrasse demonstrations that Laura cited. This vision inspired Nelson Mandela in his struggle with apartheid. We sense this same spirit in the resistance to a group of male clerics electing the new pope, a process that entirely excludes women.

Does nonviolence always work? No, but what does? Is it always the best strategy? I'm not certain. If I were to absolutize anything, it would be justice. The Qur'an reminds us that fighting is better than oppression. Even the Amish are willing to restrain harmful intruders until the law enforcement officers arrive. There may be times when the use of force is necessary to correct an injustice.

Some would make a distinction between force and violence. The latter seeks to harm the other; the former does not. This difference in intentionality can apply to the suicide bomber climbing onto the school bus to blow up innocent children as opposed to a missile attack on a weapons cache resulting in the unintended death of innocent bystanders.

What seems clear is that the willingness to accept force on any level places us on a slippery slope to the kind of culture of violence that Jeshu opposes. If force seems to be the only viable alternative in a situation where injustice prevails, then so be it. But let it be with a clear awareness that at some level there has been a failure either in courage or in imagination.

REFLECTIONS

1. How can we, as Christians and Jews, better comprehend the level of violence inflicted on Jews by Christians in the past two thousand years?

2. How can Jews and Christians examine the use of force or violence by the United States and Israel in today's world?

3. How can we effectively discuss the culture of violence characterizing our movies, television shows, video games, and magazines?

11

The Most Challenging Practice

43"You've heard it said: 'Love your neighbor and hate your enemy.' 44But what I am telling you is to love your enemies and pray for your persecutors." (Matt. 5:43–44)

LB

Nowhere in the Hebrew scriptures is one exhorted to "hate your enemy." However, the Dead Sea Scrolls unearthed in 1947 contain some fifty references to hating enemies. Since Jeshu may have been part of this community at an earlier point in his life, the reference probably comes from this source. It is important to emphasize that hating your enemy never became mainstream Judaism, and that such hatred is *not* advocated in Jewish teachings.

The primary issue here is the attitude one is to take toward an enemy. As usual, Jewish teachings portray a diversity of opinions on this matter, ranging from jubilation when the wicked perish (Prov. 11:10) to the admonition that God mourns the loss of His children even when they are evildoers. Thus, when the angels tried to sing songs of praise at the Red Sea, God silenced them with a poignant question: "My handiwork, my human creatures are drowning in the sea and you want to sing a song of praise?"[1] The subtlety and sophistication with which this talmudic teaching conveys compassion for the enemy's suffering is striking—it is none other than Pharaoh's army that God is mourning.

Jeshu is offering us ways to practice this commandment in those situations where it is hardest to love. His is subversive wisdom at its most radical (that is, down to the root of the matter). In telling us to love our enemies and to pray for our persecutors, he is effectively eliminating the category of "enemy" from our human experience. As Ron comments, "This command moves us to the very highest kind of spiritual consciousness."[2] Once an antagonist is loved—that is, deeply known and understood, appreciated as bearing the image of God, deserving of respect, like oneself—she ceases to be an enemy. A transformation has occurred in the consciousness of the one who initially perceived an enemy.

"Love your enemy" is not then merely lofty rhetoric; it is a profoundly practical teaching with critical implications for our contemporary world. To dismiss it as unrealistic or utopian is to ignore the three great liberation successes of the last century, the leaders of which espoused the full humanity of the oppressor and refused to give in to enemy-driven tactics: Gandhi in India, Martin Luther King Jr. in the United States, and Nelson Mandela in South Africa. The love they practiced is not the sentimental variety; it is a tough love that boldly criticizes injustice but refuses to demonize the unjust. It is love that embodies the spiritual vision of a more just and loving world because it becomes a mirror in which oppressors might recognize themselves. This is love that sees all humanity as one interconnected unity, love that takes into account the well-being of the entire planet and all its inhabitants. Without it, we are exposing ourselves to tragedy of unprecedented proportions, as weapons of mass destruction become more available alongside the chemical and biological warfare that threaten to turn the earth into a wasteland. Spiritual consciousness is the field in which the next great human transition must come about so that we do not destroy ourselves with anger, hatred, selfishness, and greed made monstrous by our advanced technology.

Jewish teaching supports the holistic view that harming others harms ourselves. The talmudic warning, "Whoever takes vengeance destroys his own house" (Babylonian Talmud, *Sanhedrin* 102b) would change the fabric of the Israeli-Palestinian conflict if it were taken seriously. The human race does not lack spiritual wisdom; we lack spiritual practice in applying that wisdom. The very words "Love your neighbor as yourself" in Leviticus are preceded by "You shall not take revenge nor bear a grudge against your people" (literally, "the children of your people"—Lev. 19:18), another routinely disregarded precept. Of course, one has to ask, Who is "your neighbor"? Who are "your people"? The rabbis had varying views on these questions, ranging from narrowly tribalistic to universalistic, but in the twenty-first century CE we need the answer to be: *anyone* in the human community.

I maintain that Jeshu is well within the boundaries of Jewish thought and morality in these critical teachings. The brilliant second-century talmudic debater and scholar Bruriah (the only woman's name recorded in the Talmud as a teacher of Torah) instructed her husband Rabbi Meir not to pray for the death of a gang of hoodlums tormenting their neighborhood. His justification for the prayer was a verse from Psalms, "Let sins be obliterated from the earth" (104:35). She responded, "Is it written 'sinners'? The verse says 'sins.' Look further to the end of the verse: ' ... And the wicked will be no more.' Since all sins will be obliterated, then of course 'the wicked will be no more.' Therefore, pray that these hoodlums repent and they will not be 'wicked' anymore." The Talmud reports that Rabbi Meir prayed for them as his wife suggested, and they indeed repented and changed their ways.[3]

RM

Jeshu often seasons his teachings with a touch of humor. The idea of loving our enemies hits us like the punch line of a joke. Enemies are precisely those people we don't love. So loving our enemies means losing them as enemies. But then we don't have any enemies? Aha!

At a tribal level of consciousness, this is clearly nonsense. We define ourselves at this level by our distance from others whom we demonize and despise. Kill the Krauts, the Japs, the Commies, the Gooks, and the Towel Heads! I once heard a Ku Klux Klan leader on television exclaiming, "What good is being white if it don't mean that you're better than ... " I don't think I need to use the word with which his statement ended. This is classic tribal language, and you can fill in the blanks for a hundred other categories of "the other." What good is being a man if you're not better than women? What good is being straight if you're not better than gays?

What is buried in all this rhetoric, of course, is the obvious need to alleviate one's own lack of self-esteem by finding another category of people definitely inferior to you and your enclave. Thus, even when you're at your worst, you can find consolation in being better than the other group at its best. The worst American soldier in the field is still better than the best Iraqi. The worst Christian saved by the blood of Christ is nonetheless better than the most pious and observant Jew.

The exhortation to love our enemies cuts away the safety net for our insecurity and low self-esteem and has the potential to jump-start us into a higher mode of consciousness. Thinking about your enemy as yourself, someone who nursed at his mother's breast, was excited about his first day of school, and wants to be happy just like you do, can begin to change our relationships with those we want to demonize.

But what about Adolf Hitler? I am moved when I see the surviving photographs of him as a baby, looking out at the world with eyes as innocent as any of the world's children. How did he come to miss so profoundly everything our deepest human nature entails? Can I possibly love Hitler? Can I acknowledge that he, too, was made in the image and likeness of God? Can I recognize that his essential nature is the same divine reality that is my nature? As with Laura's recounting of Bruriah's comment, if Hitler's sins were obliterated (i.e., if he no longer did evil), then the "wicked" Hitler would not continue to exist.

But can we separate the sin from the sinner? We have to if we wish to discuss the divine image in every human being. The sin, after all, is a missing of the mark, a way in which a person fails to achieve the human potential for wisdom and compassion. It is precisely this tragic lack that writes the most horrible chapters of our shared human history. But that lack, that tragic wound, does not eliminate the essential goodness of the being in whom that lack resides.

Love, as Thomas Aquinas defines it, means to will the good of the other *(velle bonum alterius)*. When I separate the lack (i.e., the sin) from the sinner, then I am able to respect and affirm the other person and wish for her all the growth and fullness of which she is capable. In that case, I am truly loving my enemies because I am finding within them that depth of being where they are not enemies at all but humans like myself.

Laura rightly points out the necessity of making this challenging practice an integral part of our personal and societal growth. We can no longer demonize the other. While responding to behavior that diminishes the worth or dignity of any human being, we are reminded to meet the other as someone who is essentially all that I am. All saints have a past; all sinners have a future.

REFLECTIONS

1. How has demonization of the other played a role in the shared history of Jews and Christians?
2. What individuals or groups do I tend to categorize as "the enemy" in my own life-world?
3. How can Jews and Christians embrace this challenging practice in their interactions with one another and with the larger world as well?

12

The Lord's Prayer

9"This is how you should pray: Our heavenly Parent, may your Name be made holy. 10May your reign come and your will be done, on earth as in heaven. 11Give us today our bread for the coming day. 12Forgive us our failings, as we forgive those who fail us. 13Don't let us be tested beyond our strength, and save us from every evil." (Matt. 6:9–13)

LB

Addressing this pivotal Christian prayer as a whole, my first reaction is that I find nothing about it that in any way contradicts or fails to resonate with Jewish tradition. In addition, Jeshu was advocating two thousand years ago what members of the contemporary Jewish Renewal movement are presently advocating in relation to prayer: reduce the number of words, whose sheer volume can be an obstacle to perceiving God, and focus instead on meaningful kernels of liturgy recited or chanted with *kavanah*—that inwardness, devotion, and concentration that allows the words to live and breathe. Chanting select phrases from the morning liturgy, letting each word penetrate deeper into consciousness as it is repeated musically, is a powerful, meditative form of prayer currently practiced by many Jews in the renewal movement.

"Our heavenly Parent, may your Name be made holy." (Matt. 6:9)

LB

This line is laden with pieces of Jewish liturgy. The High Holiday prayers have repeated reference to *Avinu malkenu*—our Father, our King. God is depicted metaphorically as a heavenly Parent (traditionally "father," given the patriarchal nature of the times), throughout Jewish teaching and prayer. Reference to "our Father in heaven" is found in the *Kaddish Shalem* (one of several versions of the *Kaddish*, a central Jewish prayer extolling the greatness of God and recited in Aramaic at every prayer service; the mourner's *Kaddish* is recited at funerals and when remembering the dead).

"May your Name be made holy" comes straight from the *Kaddish*, which begins "Magnified and sanctified [or "hallowed"] may His great name be" (in Aramaic: *Yitgadal v'yitkadash sh'mei rabah*). Recognizing the sacred character of God's holiest name is basic to Jewish theology and practice. While there are many Hebrew names for God, the four-letter tetragrammaton (containing the Hebrew letters *yud, hey, vav, hey*) is considered too holy even to pronounce and is referred to as the Ineffable Name, or simply *HaShem* ("the Name" in Hebrew). Many Jews substitute Adonai (or Lord) when the unspoken Name appears in scripture or liturgy. During the Second Temple days (the time of Jeshu), it could be pronounced only by the high priest on Yom Kippur in the holy of holies; since the destruction of the Temple in the year 70, it has not been pronounced by anyone. The great insight here is that the Infinite cannot be defined or contained in a name (let alone in an image) that is within our human grasp. In thus hallowing God's Name by not pronouncing it, we bow to its inherent mystery.

"May your reign come and your will be done, on earth as in heaven." (Matt. 6:10)

LB

Again, the *Kaddish* is evoked: *v'yamlich malchutey* can be translated as "may His kingdom come," "may He cause His sovereignty soon to be accepted," or "may He rule His kingdom," among other possibilities. Surely Jeshu was drawing from this ancient prayer and from Jewish tradition, which views God's reign as a metaphor for the way the universe works: God is the sole, supreme creator, sustainer, and ruler of the world. God's way is the Tao or the grain of the universe. What needs to "come" is our alignment with that reality, with that goodness, justice, compassion, and consequence that permeates the cosmic grain. When we are in harmony with God, the kingdom (or queendom) is immediately available.

Just as Jewish mysticism maintains "as above, so below," Jeshu refers to the intrinsic correspondence between heaven and earth, light and form, spirit and matter: "on earth as in heaven." If God is the source and substance of all that is, there is nothing that is not God. And yet, paradoxically, ungodly behavior and attitudes abound, since the Divine contains the possibility to oppose divinity. Thus, the human family is often out of alignment with God's grain (or will), with its own true nature, and with nature itself.

"Give us today our bread for the coming day." (Matt. 6:11)

LB

"Our bread for the coming day" evokes the manna that God provided the children of Israel during their forty years of wandering in the desert. Poignantly aware of their dependence on God and their extreme vulnerability, they could collect only enough manna for one day's use (except on the day preceding Shabbat, when they were given a two-day supply, so as not to have to work on the Sabbath). Trust in God's providence is felt in these words; they contain satisfaction in having enough for each day, with no need to hoard or experience anxiety about the next day's nourishment.

"Forgive us our failings, as we forgive those who fail us." (Matt. 6:12)

LB

Asking God for forgiveness is an important motif in Jewish liturgy. The High Holiday rites of Rosh Hashanah (the Jewish New Year) and Yom Kippur (which means "Day of Atonement") are laden with supplications for forgiveness, as are the ten Days of Awe that fall in between the two High Holidays. Among the eighteen benedictions of the regular daily service recited three times a day (also known as the *Amidah*, or "standing prayer," because the congregation stands while reciting it) is a prayer for pardon that begins, "Pardon us, our Father, for we have sinned." The benediction ends with the words, "Blessed are You, *Adonoy* [Lord], Gracious One, who pardons abundantly."[1]

Significantly, the prayer for repentance—*teshuvah*, or a return to God-centered awareness—precedes the *Amidah* prayer for forgiveness. Repentance implies present regret for past misconduct and firm resolve for correct conduct in the future. Sincere *teshuvah*, even for the worst of sinners, results in divine mercy. God's desire is for penitence, not punishment, as the prophet Ezekiel proclaims: "As I live—declares the Lord God—it is not My desire that the wicked shall die, but that the wicked turn from his [evil] ways and live" (Ezek. 33:11).

What is striking in Jeshu's prayer is the correspondence between our being forgiven and our willingness to forgive others who have done us harm (or failed us). While this correspondence is not unheard of in Jewish tradition—the Talmud reminds us, "Whose sin does God forgive? He who forgives sins"[2]—it is given less prominence than Jeshu gives it in this verse. Jewish liturgy and writings strongly encourage repentance in order to be forgiven by God. The steps to *teshuvah* that the great medieval philosopher Maimonides outlines are as relevant today as they were in the twelfth century: awareness of our wrongdoing, verbal confession of the sin, an expression of deep regret, the resolution not to repeat the offense, and an offering of restitution when possible to those we have harmed. Repentance is complete when we encounter a similar situation and manage to respond differently. Thus, *teshuvah* is a complex process that requires hard work and much soul-searching to achieve. But where *teshuvah* is genuine, God's forgiveness is assured.

I wonder whether Jewish philosophers and theologians have been short-circuited in their efforts similarly to expand and expound upon human forgiveness (as they have upon repentance) precisely because of its association with Christianity, on the one hand, and Christianity's historic unwillingness to extend it to Judaism, on the other. The unjust charge of deicide has been used repeatedly as a weapon against Jews, alongside blood libels (accusations of ritual murder—that Jews murder non-Jews and drink their blood) and other outrageous charges. But what Christianity has seemed to find most unforgivable is Judaism's steadfast refusal to accept Jeshu as its Lord and savior. Judaism's insistence upon maintaining its own path to God and its own integrity has been a thorn in Christianity's side for which forgiveness has not been forthcoming. Two millennia of being denigrated, oppressed, persecuted, villainized, tortured, and murdered by so-called Christians have left Jews understandably wary of forgiveness as practiced by a tradition that has shown them so little mercy. The church has not practiced what Jeshu preached.

> "Don't let us be tested beyond our strength, and save us from every evil." (Matt. 6:13)

LB

Most translations portray Jeshu asking God not to put us in the position of wrestling with temptation in the first place ("And lead us not into temptation" or "And do not bring us to the time of trial"). Just as we are advised not to test God (Deut. 6:16), Jeshu asks God not to test us; temptation is a test of moral fortitude as well as faith. Yet tests of faith and moral temptations are part of our human condition. We cannot be alive for long without encountering some form of "sin crouching at the door" (Gen. 4:7).

Therefore, I prefer Ron's translation, which acknowledges this reality and asks not that we not be tested, but that we not be tested beyond our strength and endurance. Such challenges exercise our moral muscles; they show us what we are made of and where we still have room to grow. They encourage us to become larger (witness the trials of Abraham, especially his being asked to sacrifice Isaac), and even when we fail to meet them, they lead to the possibility of *teshuvah*, atonement, and deepening. For Jeshu to ask God not to give us more than we can handle is fitting for the spiritual journey on which obstacles and suffering are inevitable. When we are given experiences that produce growth, we are strengthened against evil, both internal and external.

RM

If there is one common denominator for Christians of almost any stripe or persuasion, it is their love for the Lord's Prayer. You will hear it in virtually every Christian liturgy. One of the most ancient texts on church order, the Didache, or Teaching of the Apostles, recommends that Christians pray this prayer three times a day: morning, noon, and night.

What is surprisingly ironic about this prayer is the fact that, despite its being so quintessentially Christian, it could easily be incorporated into the liturgy of the synagogue or the mosque. Laura understandably points out that she finds nothing in this prayer that is inconsistent with her Jewishness. The reason is quite simply that this prayer reflects the religion *of* Jeshu more than the religion *about* Jeshu. The rift that is our subject matter for this book stems from the latter, not the former.

The wounds of two thousand years do not heal easily. It is understandably difficult for Jews to accept Jeshu's Jewishness as readily as Hindus can accept the Buddha's Hinduism. There was a Jewish woman in one of my classes who always knitted. She told me once that she could knit contentedly as I talked about the Buddha and Muhammad, about Krishna and Lao Tzu. But as soon as I mentioned Jesus, she inevitably dropped a stitch. Somehow a discussion of Jesus made her feel disloyal to her Judaism, almost disrespectful of all the Jews killed in his name.

Jeshu's name has so long been connected to Christianity that the two have become inseparable. It is virtually impossible to distinguish Jeshu the Jew, his life and teachings, from all the crimes perpetrated in his name—from blood libels and pogroms to inquisitions and massacres. This is why it is so crucial to study Jeshu's life and teachings apart from the subsequent history of Christianity, a history containing both legitimate examples of what Jeshu taught and blasphemous denials of everything for which he stood.

The first book I wrote in my study of the historical Jeshu was *Wisdom of the Carpenter*. This offers a teaching of Jeshu plus a brief commentary and prayer for every day of the year. What has given me special satisfaction about this book is the frequency with which it is used by Jews, as well as by Christians. Several rabbis have endorsed it as a fruitful source of daily meditation. Jeshu, like the Buddha and so many others, is a universal teacher of spiritual wisdom, and he belongs to everyone.

REFLECTIONS

1. How can the Lord's Prayer be used in Jewish-Christian dialogue?
2. How can Jews and Christians study their history together in such a way as to separate Jeshu from the many crimes committed in his name?
3. How might Jews and Christians make the study of Jeshu's teachings a bridge to mutual understanding?

13

True Treasure, True Vision, and True Worth

¹⁹"Don't pile up treasures on earth, where moth and rust take their toll and thieves break in to steal. ²⁰Lay up your treasures in heaven, where neither moth nor rust can do them harm and thieves will find nothing to steal. ²¹For your heart will always be wherever you keep what you treasure." (Matt. 6:19–21)

LB

These words evoke the teachings of Hillel (a generation before Jeshu) in the *Pirkei Avot* (Wisdom of the Sages, the earliest part of the Talmud): "More flesh, more worms; more possessions, more worries ... more servants, more thievery. However, more Torah, more life; more learning, more wisdom; more counsel, more insight; more good deeds, more peace" (*Pirkei Avot* 2:8). As both Jewish sages make clear, a preoccupation with material things leads to anxiety, frustration, and disappointment at their inevitable loss. The finite, physical realm is to be enjoyed but held lightly and released easily, for by definition, it is not lasting. The tighter we grasp it, the more unhappiness we experience when it decays and disappears, like trying to cling to youth. This awareness is particularly relevant to our contemporary consumer culture, where buying more products has become a badge of patriotism and owning more luxury items a mark of prestige. We confuse our actual worth with our bank accounts and stock portfolios, overlooking the hidden treasure that is eternally ours. No wonder depression is rampant, insecurity is rife, thievery operates unchecked in corporations as well as in slums, and fear and mistrust predominate.

Heaven and earth are states of consciousness here, rather than geographic locations; they could be understood as awareness of what is infinite versus what is finite. "Treasures on earth," such as money and all it can buy, prestige or power, profit or pleasure, are consumed by time, whereas "treasures in heaven" last forever and cannot be stolen from us. Love, compassion, insight, patience, devotion, awe, wisdom, generosity, and humility—these are qualities that constitute the treasure of a heart that is centered in God. They contribute to the peace and joy that make life worth living, and they link us to what outlasts the physical dimensions of life. When we unify all our desires into one overriding desire to recognize God within ourselves and in all of creation, then we have found our eternal treasure.

22 "The eye is the body's light. If it's healthy, the whole body will be illumined, 23but if it's diseased, the whole body will be in darkness. And if the light in you is dark, what a darkness that will be!" (Matt. 6:22–23)

As Ron points out, since Jeshu speaks of "the eye" in the singular, he appears to be referring to what the Hindu tradition calls the "third eye."[1] This is the eye of insight, or sixth chakra, an energy center located between the eyebrows. This creative, intuitive realm of seeing leads to knowledge that is based on a reality deeper than what the senses can perceive. When this eye is healthy, it is open to the unity of all life—the unchanging reality beneath the world of change, and the potential within each of us to unite with and serve that reality with our own special gifts and talents. Then we are radiant with light, filled with energy that does not become depleted because it is continuously replenished by our capacity for selfless service and joy. The very term *enlightenment* as the apex of spiritual development relates to the opening of this third eye of wisdom (in conjunction, of course, with an open heart).

The Hebrew scriptures encourage us to experience our love of God as "a reminder between your eyes" (Deut. 6:8); thus, the wearing of *tefillin,* or phylacteries, while praying. This "reminder" (also translated as "band," "frontlets," "ornament," "emblem," or simply left untranslated as the Hebrew word *totafot*) takes the form of a small leather box containing verses from scripture that pertain to it. It is worn on the forehead (right over the third eye) and held by a strap around the head. A second box is strapped to the arm, because of the words "bind them as a sign upon your hand" (Deut. 6:8); the strap continues down the arm to be wound around the hand and fingers, a form of betrothal to the Divine. The Pharisees were advocates of this practice of loving and remembering (which continues among observant Jews to the present time), so Jeshu would have been very familiar with it. Perhaps he practiced it.

"You can't serve two masters at once. You'll either hate one and love the other or be loyal to one and despise the other. You can't serve both God and wealth." (Matt. 6:24)

LB

Jeshu makes the point here that we must be one-pointed in our devotion to God. The great twentieth-century Jewish philosopher Abraham Joshua Heschel put it another way: "God is of no importance unless He is of supreme importance."[2] Serving divine reality is an all-encompassing proposition that includes every aspect of our being—every thought, word, and deed is part of the process. Character, conduct, and consciousness all enter the picture. We cannot compartmentalize our lives into spiritual, business, political, and relationship segments, for example, because integrity demands that the spiritual permeate all facets of our life. From this perspective, decisions about livelihood and business are not separate from our deepest values and longings. How we treat our spouse or friends, or how we raise our children, are not separate from our highest aspirations. Whom we vote for is consistent with how we understand enlightened leadership. Our financial choices—how we make and spend our money, both personally and societally—are matters of spirit. When we live in a society that gives tax cuts to the wealthy, that budgets a hundred times more for weaponry than for education or feeding the hungry, that economically favors huge corporations that exploit people and ravage the environment, we are making a communal statement about which master we serve and what we value.

This dire situation is creating a call for reformation and renewal in our spiritual traditions that address the malaise on a societal level, as well as on an individual and a communal level. Michael Lerner, a rabbi in the Jewish Renewal movement, speaks of "Emancipatory Spirituality" as a means of "changing the bottom line of society from an ethos of selfishness and materialism to an ethos of love and caring."[3] He suggests that we redefine our understanding of productivity, rationality, and efficiency to include awe and wonder at the universe, love and solidarity with others, and ecological sensitivity toward the planet Earth (just as Ron redefines what it is to be "successful" in his translation of the Beatitudes). These are realistic, not utopian, concerns, for our very survival depends on them.

Voices in the progressive Christian community such as Bishop John Shelby Spong and Beatrice Bruteau are similarly inclined. Bruteau calls for a holistic shift away from our old domination paradigm to one of radical egalitarianism ("the communion paradigm") in which we perceive ourselves as mutually indwelling one another, affirming one another, nourishing one another. In this way we serve God, the one Master, by literally being children of God who have inherited our Divine Parent's nature: loving unconditionally and incarnating the creative process. As Bruteau points out, "This will include all types and levels of our human activity, our economic and ecological arrangements, our social relations, our scientific and technical exploration and invention, our artistic expressions."[4] Indeed, the entire world is the canvas for the "Great Work" that needs to be done.

"Look at all the birds flying around in the sky. They neither farm nor fill barns, and yet your heavenly Parent provides nourishment for them. Aren't you worth more than those birds?" (Matt. 6:26)

LB

This verse speaks of God's unconditional love for all of creation. Our very existence makes us worthy. We do not need to prove ourselves or compete at one another's expense. We are each a unique, incomparable manifestation of divine reality and therefore infinitely valuable. Thus, the Talmud teaches that "whoever destroys one life is considered by the Torah as if he destroyed an entire world, and whoever saves one life ... as if he saved an entire world" (*Mishna Sanhedrin* 4:5).

> "Don't be all worked up about tomorrow. Let tomorrow worry about tomorrow. You've got enough to concern you today." (Matt. 6:34)

LB

This reminds me of a Yiddish proverb: "If you are alive, trouble is plentiful." This is somewhat akin to the first noble truth of the Buddha: life has *dukkha* (an unsatisfactory quality, sometimes translated as "suffering"). Jeshu focuses on "today," an existential perspective that orients us to the present moment, which is always filled with sufficient challenge; we need look no further for opportunities to grow. The trouble of the day—its frustrations, disappointments, irritations, and fears—is valuable compost for spiritual growth. A Buddhist proverb advises us: "Spread your manure on the field of *bodhi* [the awakened place] and seeds of enlightenment will sprout." Our challenge is to be not only alive, but also awake to the possibility of transformation in each moment. When we practice patience with those who frustrate us, empathy with those who annoy us, and detachment from selfish preoccupations, we strengthen our will and move toward wisdom. Harshness softens into generosity and anxiety about the future diminishes, as trust in the sufficiency of today blossoms.

The shared wisdom of our sacred traditions reminds us that the world we live in is defined by our thoughts. We cannot swallow reality raw without first digesting it through our interpretations. In the first of his famous Duino Elegies, the poet Rainer Maria Rilke notes that animals, which operate on instinct, often sense the discomfort of human beings who live in a translated or interpreted world, a world filtered through a grid of thoughts. For us, to see is always to see as. The animal's experience seems to be unmediated by this process that somehow marks us as human beings.

We hear a great deal today about how persons or events are defined or framed in public discourse. A political analyst predicted during the 2004 presidential election that the winning candidate would be the one whose party most successfully defined both the candidates and the major issues. "Staying the course," "flip-flop," "tax cuts," and "a safe America" emerged as winning definitions of our present state of affairs and of the presidential race that was in progress. And that election did indeed follow the most successful definitions.

The CEO of an advertising firm pointed out to me once that you don't sell a product. You sell the consumer's self-definition. If you think of yourself as a person of sophisticated taste, then you will be inclined to buy clothes, cars, and liquors that advertising presents as suitable for sophisticated people. Machines turn out men's underwear identical in every respect, except for the fact that one gets a Calvin Klein label and one gets a Fruit of the Loom label. Since the labels match a certain kind of self-definition, the Calvin Klein underwear can be sold for a great deal more than the underwear labeled Fruit of the Loom.

The teachings of Jeshu in this chapter contain some of his most defining language about true treasure, true vision, and true worth. The golden thread running through these definitions is God and God's reign. In all the concerns and struggles of our daily life, Jeshu invites us to step back and consider the matter under the light of God's reality and God's reign.

This movement of consciousness is an expansion, an opening up to a larger vision, a more textured reality. Perhaps I have been turned down for a position after a job interview. I feel devastated. But as I bring this disappointment to a quiet space of prayer, I come to realize that my life is larger than this job. I try, then, to focus on what next step I can take to find employment, recognizing that my life looms larger than the ways in which I make a living.

Maybe you have just received the news that a good friend has been diagnosed with a particularly virulent cancer. You feel a confusion of emotions: sorrow for your friend, anger with the cancer attacking her, frustration with your own inability to alter the situation. Gently bringing this welter of emotions to the quiet center of your being, a place you have cultivated through regular meditation, you begin to open yourself up to a larger reality. Your worries become prayers—prayers that your friend may be healed and that God's will may be done in her. You gently locate your life and the life of your friend in a broader context, where death is the opposite of birth, not of life.

This process is not easy, nor does it work like a magic formula or panacea. But the practice of opening up to the scope of Jeshu's teachings brings our experiences into a larger world, one defined not by the confining slogans of our culture but by the expansive words of a deeper wisdom.

REFLECTIONS

1. What are some of the areas of constricted definition in my life that could be expanded through these teachings?

2. What are some of our shared cultural slogans that could be replaced with larger definitions?

3. How can our awareness of "true treasure" contribute to Jewish-Christian dialogue?

14

A Golden Rule and a Narrow Path

"Treat others the way you want them to treat you. That's what the Torah and the Prophets are all about." (Matt. 7:12)

LB

Here is Jeshu's Golden Rule, his incisive commentary on Leviticus 19:18: "Love your neighbor as yourself." What enormity is packed into those three Hebrew words of Torah *(v'ahavtah l'reicha camocha)*! Jeshu translates the precept from Leviticus into its positive formulation—what we should do—as opposed to how Hillel (the Jewish sage a generation prior) reminded us of what we are *not* to do: "What is hateful to you, do not do to your neighbor." Together, they give us a profound blueprint for behavior that requires a lifetime of practice to carry out. As Hillel added, "This is the essence of Torah. All the rest is commentary. Now go and learn."

Whether or not Jeshu ever met Hillel is unknown, but that the two spiritual geniuses saw eye to eye—and that Jeshu took it upon himself both to go and learn and to go and teach what he learned about this central formulation of Torah—is clear. The core of Jeshu's teaching is commentary on how to love: the art of love, the practice of love, and the radical transformation that ensues when we love wisely and well—these themes are a warm, persistent current that flow throughout Jeshu's authentic teachings.

Like Hillel, Jeshu makes it clear that he derives his Golden Rule from the biblical tradition. It is a curious misperception on the part of many Christians that this teaching is somehow unique to Jeshu. Alongside the centrality of Torah's "love your neighbor as yourself" are the many teachings of fairness; regard for the poor and other marginalized segments of society; and concern for the widows, orphans, and strangers among us. The prophets make such concern their central tenet, proclaiming again and again in the most impassioned language that God desires mercy, not sacrifices; God seeks justice, not elaborate feasts and empty rituals. Jeshu is utterly in keeping with this prophetic tradition of his heritage, decrying hypocrisy and insisting upon justice and compassion. The spiritual deepening that Jeremiah prophesied comes to all who follow this golden rule: "I will put my Teaching into their inmost being, and inscribe it upon their hearts" (Jer. 31:32). Jeshu was a zaddik—a master of Torah imbued with pure righteousness, inseparable from the teachings and, like all mystics, inseparable from God. To the extent that this law becomes written in our hearts, we become capable of loving and valuing all life as we love and value our own.

13 "Enter through the narrow gate, for the wide gate and the easy path lead to destruction, though most people choose to enter

that way. [14]But it's the narrow gate and the hard path that lead to life, and there aren't many who find it." (Matt. 7:13–14)

LB

All traditions speak of the rigors of the spiritual path. Wisdom teachers point the way, but as the Buddha tells us, "It is for you to swelter at the task." Like a birth canal, the passage is narrow; as Ron notes, there is room for only one at a time.[1] And one labors to go down it, to pass through its gate. Each path is individual and idiosyncratic, so that even as we journey in community with others (a central ingredient of spiritual life), we nonetheless, in some critical ways, walk alone: our daily decisions, our life choices, our commitments, our birth, and our death are uniquely our own. But also like a birth canal, a spiritual path leads to life and is worth all the challenges it requires of us. Gandhi put it well:

> I know the path: it is straight and narrow.
> It is like the edge of a sword.
> I rejoice to walk on it.
> I weep when I slip.[2]

RM

Both of these passages have added fuel to the fire for Christian exclusivism, which claims it is Jeshu alone who teaches compassion and love. The Jews (and there is always the implication that Jeshu is not really Jewish) demand justice, insisting on the letter of the law and their "pound of flesh." Those who believe in Jeshu have found the narrow path to life; all others travel the broad road to destruction. Only the true believers will be saved; all others are doomed to perish in hell's eternal fires.

What Laura's commentary makes abundantly clear is that these teachings, far from contradicting Jewish tradition, celebrate it and embrace it. Jeshu's formulation of the Golden Rule parallels not only the teaching of Hillel but also an element found in virtually all of the sacred traditions of the world. These words provide a point of convergence, not a mark of division.

The narrow path, far from being a reference for Christian exclusivism, is a commonplace of all religious practices. Spiritual growth seldom occurs in the football-stadium environment of the megachurches. The seeds of the spirit grow in the soil of an individual soul, when we have made that soil ready through prayer and practice.

And an integral part of that practice is to treat people as we would like to be treated. This does not mean that we do to them or for them what we like for ourselves. Tastes can differ. Not everyone will be delighted by a season's seat at the opera. But just as we like to have people respect us and our needs, so, too, do others appreciate the same kind of consideration from us.

REFLECTIONS

1. What relevance do these two central teachings have for my own life and practice?

2. How can these two teachings be used to establish a common ground for Jewish-Christian dialogue?

3. How might this dialogue find expression in some kind of shared liturgy in which Jews and Christians might join?

15

Teaching with Authority and Healing

28When Jeshu had finished these teachings, the crowd was amazed at the way he taught. 29For unlike the Torah scholars, he taught with authority. (Matt. 7:28–29)

LB

What does it mean to have authority? We speak authoritatively about what we have experienced. Knowledge gained from even the best books or the wisest teachers cannot replace the lessons of our own lived experience. The Buddha is known to have told his disciples to test his teachings and see for themselves their truth and value. We can read a hundred books on meditation, but without the experience of meditating, our appreciation remains superficial and intellectual. It does not become integrated into a holistic sense of ourselves; it does not transform us.

As an enlightened master, Jeshu had become one with the teachings he espoused. He was a zaddik, a living Torah scroll, so saturated with God's word as to be inseparable from it. His commentary on scripture flowed from him like living waters and did not require frequent reference to chapter and verse. Instead, he embodied the teachings and implemented them so that to watch him was to see Torah in action, a mirror to God. There is a well-known story of a spiritual seeker who sought out a famous hasidic teacher and later remarked, "I didn't travel all that way to hear him teach, but to watch him tie his shoelaces." To behold this degree of authority, of virtue in every action, is a revelation that inspires wonder and radical amazement.

> ¹Large numbers of people crowded around Jeshu, following him as he came down from the mountain. ²A leper stepped forward, knelt before him, and said, "Lord, if you want to, you can heal me." ³Reaching out his hand, Jeshu touched him and said, "Of course I want to. Be healed." Immediately the man's leprosy disappeared. ⁴Jeshu then said to him: "Don't talk about this to anyone until you have submitted yourself to a priestly examination and offered the sacrifice Moses commanded. Then your witness will be valid for everyone." (Matt. 8:1–4)

LB

Our awareness of the connections among body, mind, and spirit has been a shifting one. In biblical times, it was believed that some bodily ailments were a direct result of being morally "unclean" (thus, in the traditional translation, the leper asks Jeshu to make him "clean"). Skin diseases in particular, a number of which were called leprosy but included various other curable conditions, were considered a sign of sin. Social sins, such as *lashon ha-ra,* or gossip (literally, "evil tongue"), were thought to manifest in this bodily way. Thus, someone who had such a skin condition was in need of moral cleansing—*teshu-vah*—in order to be physically healed.

For hundreds of years, our modern Enlightenment mentality, with its purely rationalistic mind-set, eschewed such thinking, but more recently we are rediscovering that indeed a mind-body-spirit connection *does* exist. Medical science has found explicit relationships between stress levels and a wide variety of diseases. Emotional and spiritual well-being have been found to impact the immune system. Prayer has been shown to have a beneficial effect on illness.

None of this is to suggest that we should stigmatize physical suffering with the label "unclean." Indeed, AIDS and, to a lesser extent, cancer have been tainted with social stigma, adding insult to injury. When we are ill we need compassion, not judgment. But to recognize that a physical ailment may be a signal of imbalance in our lives—whether a sign that we need to slow down, move in a different direction, or change unhealthy habits—can be critical in our efforts to heal. Our bodies are often eloquent barometers of our soul's dis-ease.

In these verses a leper, the most marginalized member of society, recognizes in Jeshu a healing capacity. Perhaps Jeshu's transparency to the Divine shone in his demeanor, as well as in his words. The leper's receptivity to this healing presence suggests the opportunity for transformation that affliction provides. In this sense, our illnesses, our vulnerabilities, our flaws could be regarded as potential openings to a deeper reality and, therefore, as gifts. Often bad news becomes good news in the context of consciousness evolution.

Miraculous healings occur in the Hebrew scriptures as well. Both Elijah and Elisha restore life to individuals who have died (in 1 and 2 Kings, respectively), and Elisha heals a man from leprosy (2 Kings 5:8–14). They, too, are recognized as holy men—prophets and healers who have an especially intimate relationship with God and can channel divine energy to those who are receptive. Jeshu is part of this tradition.

Curiously, Jeshu now seems loath to further his reputation as a healer. Earlier we are told that he is curing diseases and sicknesses throughout the Galilee, garnering fame and attracting great crowds (Matt. 4:23–25). Yet here, he instructs the man not to tell anyone, but simply to show himself to the priests and offer the customary sacrifice as a sign that he is now clean. Jeshu neither wants credit for the healing nor is interested in changing the halacha, or law, regarding this purification ritual. It would appear that he prefers to deemphasize what could be viewed as the supernatural aspects of his ministry, in favor of the down-to-earth teachings that set him firmly in the human realm. I am reminded of a modern retelling of a story about the Buddha's encounter with a holy man whose disciples excitedly point out his ability to walk across a body of water after many years of diligent practice. "Well done," the Buddha remarks, "but did you know that for a nickel you could take the ferry?" Perhaps Jeshu's reputation as a miracle man has made him uncomfortable. He wants people to act on his teachings, which reflect the will of God, not to imitate his "deeds of power" (see Matt. 7:21–23), which could be misconstrued as magical or even demonic.

So why does Jeshu heal at all? His heart is touched by compassion when the leper kneels before him—this most marginalized of men, disfigured and judged by his disfigurement to be morally lacking. Yet in his extreme vulnerability, shunned by the rest of society, this leper knows something: "If you want to, you can heal me." He powerfully states an existential reality—you can do this if you so choose. Perhaps Jeshu is moved by the man's depth of knowing (which could be called faith) and his simple statement of the truth. He responds in kind: "Of course I want to. Be healed." By stretching out his hand to touch the leper, he does what most others would consider repulsive (and becomes ritually impure by doing so). Like Gandhi's insistence two thousand years later that no one be considered an "untouchable," Jeshu breaks through social and religious barriers to restore this child of God to health.

RM

Jeshu's authentic teaching and his gift of healing are often used by Christian apologists to prove Jeshu's divinity. Such arguments, of course, are baseless. As Laura points out, these gifts characterize spiritual adepts in virtually all of the sacred traditions. The Qur'an acknowledges both Jeshu's teaching and his healing without drawing any inference to divinity, recognizing instead his status as a true prophet.

As someone who has taught for some forty years, I recognize two ways in which I teach. Most of the time I am explaining a text, as I am doing in this instance. This is my favorite type of teaching—working through a classic text line by line and even word by word, unpacking the levels of meaning contained there. Occasionally, however, I teach in a distinctively different way. I put the text aside and speak from my own experience. At that point, I'm drawing on something learned directly from my own life's journey.

Most teaching revolves around an explication of the text. The job of the rabbi is not to wax eloquent on her own experience but to tap the depth of meaning in every word of Torah, to share the wisdom derived from centuries of commentary by the great students of the text. What is clear from even the most superficial contact with Jeshu's teaching style is that this is not the way he teaches. Jeshu tends to begin with the observation of something in the world around him— delicate spring flowers blooming on the hillside, women bent over as they prepare loaves of bread to bake in outside ovens, fishermen trudging home tired but happy with their haul, shepherds anxiously running around in search of lost sheep. Using this palette of experience, Jeshu paints metaphors that propel us from these quotidian experiences to the deepest parts of our own relationships to God, self, and others. Jeshu's teachings plunge us into the white-hot center of life.

His healing serves the same purpose as his teaching. He is not interested in setting up a medical clinic in northern Galilee for the treatment of human diseases. Healing energy, like the energy of true teaching, transforms hearts, turning his hearers to their divine center. And that is Jeshu's purpose, helping people turn to the powerful reality of God's reign in their lives. He needs neither higher accreditation to do this nor footnotes to validate it. This is where he lives, what he knows, who he is. He speaks of it with authority, an authority that few can match.

REFLECTIONS

1. What are some of my most profound experiences of being taught or being healed?
2. What are some of my most profound experiences of teaching someone else or being a healing presence for someone else?
3. How can Jews and Christians examine their respective faith communities in terms of the vitality of teaching and healing transpiring there?

16

Those Wonderful Romans!

⁵When Jeshu came into the city of Kapharnahum, a Roman officer came to him, asking for his aid. ⁶"Lord," he said, "my boy is laid up at home, paralyzed and in a great deal of pain." ⁷Jeshu replied, "I will come and make him better." ⁸But the officer remonstrated: "I am not worthy, Lord, to receive you in my house. If you just say the word, my boy will be healed. ⁹I am a man used to authority, with soldiers under my command. They come and go when I say the word; they do things because I give the orders." (Matt. 8:5–9)

LB

Jeshu now seems eager to heal—he says of the Roman officer's boy ("servant" in other translations), "I will come and make him better." He makes no distinction between Jew and Gentile here, even though later on he is loath to heal the Canaanite woman's daughter (saying,

"I was sent only to the lost sheep of the house of Israel"—Matt. 15:24). His sense of mission and identity is in flux. To heal or not to heal? To heal only Jews or to extend his ministry to Gentiles? To incur fame for miracles or to keep this capacity under wraps?

But here (as in the later example), he learns something from the encounter with the Gentile world. The centurion expands Jeshu's awareness of the nature of his healing capabilities. He has the authority (given by God) to heal from a distance, using word and intention. This is the same conclusion that physician Larry Dossey and other researchers have come to recently regarding the effectiveness of healing prayer: healing at a distance is possible. To quote Dr. Dossey, "After much research I have been unable to find a single authority who will claim that the degree of spatial separation of the praying person from the subject is a factor in its effectiveness."[1] In the first century, Jeshu discovers that healing can be a nonlocal event. In the twenty-first century, we are still grappling with the mystery and marvel of this discovery: "If you just say the word, my boy will be healed."

> When Jeshu heard this, he was amazed, and, turning to the people around him, he said, "Believe me, I've not found this kind of trust among my fellow Jews." (Matt. 8:10)

LB

Was Jeshu amazed primarily at the extent of the centurion's faith, or was it the Roman's awareness of the nature of authority that so astounded him? This officer knows that Jewish authority does not permit Jews to enter Roman homes that have idols (statues of the gods). But he also understands that Jeshu operates under a higher authority—Divine mandate—that gives him leave to heal by speaking the word. He intuits this based on his own authority as a commander of soldiers and slaves who do his bidding.

Still, it seems an exaggeration to say, "in no one in Israel have I found such faith" (the New Revised Standard translation). Either this is more Middle Eastern hyperbole characteristic of the culture, or it reflects Jeshu's exasperation that even his own followers lack faith on occasion ("you of little faith" becomes an ongoing critique). But surely those Jewish disciples who have been willing to drop everything, leave their families, and follow Jeshu could not be accused of lacking trust. So one has to suspect the authenticity of this statement, particularly considering the clearly ungenerous and un-Jeshu-like comments that follow.

> ¹¹"I've got to tell you that many people are going to come from east and west to sit down at table with Abraham, Isaac, and Jacob where God reigns, ¹²but the children called to that reign will be thrown outside into the darkness, where they will weep and grind their teeth in despair." (Matt. 8:11–12)
>
> *LB*

The vision of the messianic banquet in the world to come (where the righteous sit down to feast with the patriarchs and other assorted celebrities) derives from the Jewish midrashic tradition. But this account smacks of replacement theology, with "the children called to that reign" (in other translations, "the heirs of the kingdom")—in other words, the Jews—excluded from the table. Not only do we not get invited to the party, but we're also doomed to be thrown into the outer darkness, weeping and grinding our teeth (a phrase we will hear repeatedly, like a mantra, in verses to come). This kind of vengeful talk is unworthy of the enlightened consciousness of Jeshu, and I am convinced he never said it. It is a product, rather, of the gospel writer's polemic, from a later time and from a narrow place of anger and vindictiveness.

RM

Any Sherlock Holmes fan remembers the mystery in which the clue to solving the case was the dog that didn't bark. As the Christian story about Jeshu spreads to the Greek-speaking world of the larger Roman Empire, there is a huge dog that doesn't bark. Despite the cruel oppression of the Roman rule, there is no criticism of the Romans in any of the four gospels. On the contrary, when Romans appear, especially the officers whose presence dots the gospel landscape, they are invariably exemplary human beings, as in this story of a truly remarkable centurion.

Like the first tremors often preceding a full-blown earthquake, this story reveals early traces of the spin that will soon evolve into an eruption of anti-Jewishness. This gospel, whatever purposes it served within the local community that produced it, was written in Greek so that it could "mainline" into the larger Greco-Roman world. Criticism of Rome would be counterproductive to the vast marketing enterprise on which Christianity was embarking.

For this purpose, Romans, and especially Roman officials, must be decent and honorable people. But in that case, why was Jeshu arrested, tortured, and executed in one of the world's most barbarous forms of capital punishment? In seesaw fashion, the onus of guilt swings to the only other available party, the Jews. That's why this healing story is interrupted so that Jeshu can break into a monologue, pointing out how superior the faith of the Gentiles is to that of the Jews, culminating with the announcement that the Jews have been totally banned from God's reign. The boy's healing seems almost insignificant after the hate-filled rhetoric of the monologue.

Laura correctly discerns the venom in this language, words that certainly do not come from Jeshu himself. What we have in this passage is the angry voice of the late-first-century Christians when the emerging rabbinic community threatens their legitimacy. We hear the theme of replacement theology played for one of the first times in what will become a symphony (or, more accurately, a cacophony) of voices proclaiming Matthew's community as the true Israel and the recalcitrant Jews as an evil community, rejected by God and rightfully despised by true believers.

The hopeful news in all of this lies in the fact that as scholarship discloses the spin put on Jeshu's ministry and the historical circumstances leading to that distortion, we can begin a new path of healing and dialogue. But the less hopeful news is that large numbers of Christians, because of their belief in the doctrine of biblical inerrancy (that the scriptures are totally without error), are constrained to believe that every word attributed to Jeshu in the gospels was really said by him. Stuck with a text whose context they are unable to acknowledge, they are caught in the meshes of an anti-Jewish theology from which there is no exit.

Jews need to be aware that there are two kinds of Christian conversations in which they are challenged to participate. The conversation with conservative Christians does not include a distinction between words probably said by Jeshu within his life-world in the 20s and words attributed to Jeshu that reflect the concerns and issues of the 80s. This conversation hobbles with the handicap of a purportedly inerrant text. There is therefore little chance of reaching a level of real dialogue. But the conversation with progressive Christians who accept the contributions of historical scholarship may, in fact, lead to a dialogue capable of bringing Jew and Christian alike to a transformed understanding.

REFLECTIONS

1. As I read the story, what can I make of the shift that takes place through the insertion of the acerbic comments attributed to Jeshu?

2. How can I better understand the two different kinds of Christian communities that develop through those who do or do not accept historical criticism of the received text?

3. How can this difference provide a focus for Jewish-Christian dialogue?

17

Redeemer or
Reminder?

¹⁴Jeshu then went into Rock's [Shimon's] house, where he found Rock's [Shimon's] mother-in-law burning up with fever. ¹⁵He touched her hand, and the fever disappeared. She immediately got up and began to wait on him. (Matt. 8:14–15)

LB

Again Jeshu heals, this time with a touch on the hand. By now, we are not shocked that this happens. We are getting the message that humans imbued with the divine imprint (who are all of us), intimate with God's authority (who are some of us), and profoundly aware of the unity of all life (who are fewer of us) can heal what is sick. What is noteworthy here is the mother-in-law's response to being healed. No sooner does the fever leave her then she gets up and begins to wait on Jeshu, to minister to his needs.

The healing of this woman's body has been a resurrection of sorts, in the interior sense of being given new life, and the awareness of her real nature as "Spirit incarnated." I am drawing here from the wisdom of Beatrice Bruteau in *The Easter Mysteries*.[1] Knowing she is both mortal and immortal, the mother-in-law's desire is immediately to serve, to be a vehicle of God's will. Thomas Merton describes this unification with God's will in simple terms: "sincerely trying to do what He seems to ask of you. And of course by that I mean simply what is called for by the obvious needs of the moment."[2] This is what Bruteau calls "the second sense of resurrection"—the returning to the world imbued with the knowledge of one's immortality in order to work in the world as a life-giving spirit—"that God's will may be done on earth as it is in heaven."[3] This urge to serve is what happens when we discover experientially our divine nature.

> When it was evening, neighbors brought to Jeshu many persons who were possessed, and simply by giving a command, he expelled the evil spirits and healed all those who were sick. (Matt. 8:16)
>
> *LB*

What does it mean to be "possessed" with "evil spirits"? Assumedly, this referred to mental illness of various kinds—psychosis, schizophrenia, and other emotional disorders. Any behavior that was bizarre, irrational, violent, or unpredictably eruptive could have appeared demonic. The convulsions of epilepsy and other seizure disorders may have been understood this way as well. It is noteworthy that this category of imbalance was amenable to healing "simply by giving a command." It suggests to us that our contemporary demons of depression, crippling anxiety, obsessive compulsive disorder, and addiction are also capable of being influenced by healing prayer. We understand that such conditions are complex and the result of many factors—some physiological, some psychological, all intertwined with the spiritual. And while total cure may be beyond our reach, alleviating the intensity of suffering that these conditions incur is a worthy goal.

> In this way the oracle of the prophet Isaiah was fulfilled: "He took our infirmities upon himself and carried all our illnesses." (Matt. 8:17)

LB

This verse (Isa. 53:4) demands exploration. It is from the "suffering servant poems" of Second Isaiah (50:4–11 and 52:13–53:12). Most biblical scholars conclude that the book of Isaiah is a composite of at least three prophets from differing historic times: before, during, and after Babylonian captivity. These suffering servant fragments, preserved from a lost, larger work, are an anomaly in Jewish tradition in that they suggest a form of vicarious atonement—that the suffering of the servant brings healing and restoration to the larger community. Jewish commentary usually understands the "servant" as representing exiled, idealized Israel—the faithful remnant—humiliated and despised in Babylon, but ultimately returning in dignity and glory to Jerusalem. The theological premise of a person or group of persons bearing another's sins found no subsequent acceptance in Judaism.

RM

Two issues challenge us in this passage. First, that this anomalous text about vicarious suffering is used at all and, second, that it is used not in reference to Jeshu's suffering and death but in relation to his ministry of healing.

Vicarious suffering becomes absolutely central to certain forms of Christian spirituality. That is why it is so important to realize that the whole theme of one human being doing something instead of or in place of someone else (a *vicarius* is literally a substitute, a deputy, or a proxy) is by no means a commonplace in the Hebrew scriptures. A sacrificial animal can play that role, but definitely not another human being.

The Jewish tradition was wise to marginalize this notion. It can lead all too readily to forms of spiritual infantilism in which someone else does your spiritual work. This is precisely what has happened in many forms of Christian practice where Jeshu does everything instead of us. In such a scenario, the individual Christian is called to confess a condition of total sinfulness, complete alienation from God, abject helplessness, and lack of self-esteem. This leads to some of the most severe forms of Christian dysfunctionality in the contemporary religious landscape.

The second issue revolving around vicarious suffering concerns its apparent mislocation in a context of healing rather than of sin. This may simply involve an implied logic on the part of the gospel writer. Since humans are viewed holistically, physical and spiritual dis-ease are seen as one. Since the subsequent narrative of Jeshu's death will be interpreted as an atoning sacrifice for sin, then even these earlier healings are affected through that future act of redemption. Jeshu saves us from our sins, and in the context of his time, healing was a forgiving of sin as well.

A growing number of Christian theologians are either rejecting or radically reinterpreting both the theology of original sin and the doctrine of Jeshu's atoning death. Bishop John Shelby Spong is one of the driving forces of this emerging theology. If our "original sin" is simply our condition of not being fully evolved spiritually, then there's no need for anyone to redeem us by dying for our sins. We need wisdom, guidance, and assistance to grow spiritually, but we do not need anyone doing anything in our stead. And there is certainly no angry God demanding an atoning sacrifice, either from Jeshu or from anyone else.

From this perspective, Jeshu emerges less as a redeemer and more as a reminder (a thesis argued at least thirty years ago by the Christian theologian and prolific writer Matthew Fox). The favorite fundamentalist question "Are you saved?" becomes meaningless in this context. What we need to be saved from is our lack of spiritual growth, spiritual insight, and wisdom.

REFLECTIONS

1. What are the theological consequences of seeing Jeshu as reminder rather than as redeemer?
2. Are there any ways in which I find the metaphor of Jeshu as redeemer meaningful?
3. How does understanding Jeshu as reminder affect the conversation between Jews and Christians?

18

Sin as Paralysis

[1]Jeshu took the boat back across the lake and came to his own city, [2]where some people brought him a paralyzed man lying on a stretcher. Jeshu recognized the trust of the people who carried the paralyzed man to him, and he said to him, "Have courage, son, your sins are forgiven." (Matt. 9:1–2)

LB

The trust Jeshu recognizes is in the man's friends who are carrying him (and perhaps in the paralytic as well; this is not clear). Being surrounded by people of faith can be as critical as having it ourselves. Thus, healing prayer can be effective for those who lack faith, if those who pray for them have it. In fact, some suggest that faith follows prayer rather than precedes it. One of the "universal principles" taught in Rabbi Douglas Goldhamer's book on healing prayer is "do it and faith will follow."[1] The nonlocal or distance healing cited in Larry Dossey's book *Healing Words* also suggests that faith is not necessary in the one being healed (or even awareness that healing prayer is being administered) for healing to take place. This corporate character of human existence is a phenomenon that would benefit from more study; our knowledge of it is just beginning.

What is also striking here is Jeshu's attitude of compassion ("Have courage, son") and his offer of forgiveness for the man's sins. He regards the man with parental tenderness and care (reminiscent of the Buddha's call to feel for all creatures the love and protectiveness of a mother toward her only child). The man is like Jeshu's son. And he sees the man holistically—body, mind, and spirit are not separate entities but different manifestations of the one entity—he sees the underlying wholeness. This is mystic awareness, not judgment of the man's sins. Offering forgiveness to the spirit will affect the body as well, just as healing the body will have spiritual consequences.

> Hearing this, some of the Torah scholars standing around said to one another, "This is blasphemy!" (Matt. 9:3)

LB

How quick we are to pass judgment on what we do not understand. Just as in the previous episode when the townspeople want Jeshu out of their neighborhood (see Matt. 8:28–34), here the scribes are frightened by Jeshu's demonstration of a very human power—the power to forgive, the power to heal. This is reminiscent of the controversy occurring now in the medical profession and some theological circles regarding research into healing prayer. The charges of blasphemy on the religious end and medical heresy on the scientific end show the fear and reluctance of some to be open to new ideas regarding our healing capacities (and this is two thousand years *after* Jeshu!).

> ⁴Jeshu, however, knowing them inside out, said to them, "Why do you fill your minds with so much evil? ⁵Do you think it's easier to tell him that his sins are forgiven or to tell him to get up and walk?" (Matt. 9:4–5)

LB

Like other intuitives, Jeshu has the capacity to look deeply into people's hearts and minds and perceive their thoughts. He also knows his actions are likely to be controversial among the religious authorities. As soon as religion becomes institutionalized, questions of "who has the authority to do what" arise with regularity, such as today's differences of opinion over who is qualified to hear confession or administer communion in Christianity, and over the role of women in all faith traditions. In the Second Temple era, forgiveness was entrusted to the priests, who were responsible for offering sacrifices to God in order to attain it. In extending God's forgiveness to the paralytic as a means of healing, Jeshu is overstepping the established bounds of institutional authority, and empowering others through his example. But this empowerment is threatening to the religious power structure, which never wants to see its authority undermined. When religion clings to its own authority rather than serving as a vehicle to God, it begins to worship itself, which is a form of idolatry. Thus, Jeshu speaks of "fill[ing] your minds with so much evil" when he is accused of blaspheming.

> ⁶"Just so that you know, I have authority on earth to forgive sins," (here he spoke to the paralytic): "Get up now; take your stretcher and go home." ⁷And the former paralytic did just that. (Matt. 9:6–7)

LB

We do not know what sins the paralytic has committed, but Jeshu sees into his heart as only mystics can, and we must assume that this man was a repentant sinner. Jeshu also perceives the connection between the man's paralysis and his need for forgiveness. He operates in the more holistic framework of the times, when physical, mental, and spiritual phenomena were understood to be of a piece. As an enlightened being, he reads the man's longings and yearnings, and offers him what he needs for healing. Where does he get the authority to perform such an act? From his transparency to the Divine, which, while rare, is available to all. It is what the good news of the kingdom of God is all about: we have within us this capacity for unity consciousness, for seeing all aspects of life (and all lives) as one interconnected whole.

> The people watching all this were overwhelmed with a sense of awe, and they praised God for giving this kind of authority to human beings. (Matt. 9:8)

LB

It is awesome to apprehend what marvels we are capable of when we allow divine energy to flow through us. Here the crowd is confronted with the wonder and mystery of our dual nature—human and divine. Appropriately, they did not bow down and worship Jeshu; rather, "they praised God," the author of such awesome authority. As Heschel beautifully states: "The awe that we sense or ought to sense when standing in the presence of a human being is a moment of intuition for the likeness of God which is concealed in his essence ... something sacred is at stake in every event."[2]

The almost facile way in which Jeshu moves from spiritual to physical healing startles us. We live in a compartmentalized world in which your doctor does not concern herself with your spiritual life any more than your spiritual director prescribes pills. But in Jeshu's life-world, a paralysis suggests a state of being, not simply a physical disability. Paralysis manifests at every plane of existence.

Although I resist a New Age tendency to blame people for their diseases, there is little doubt today that our mental state and our physical condition are connected. Thirty years ago we might have spoken of ulcers or allergies as psychosomatic, a word combining soul *(psyche)* and body *(soma)*. Today, however, one would be hesitant to deny a psychosomatic component to any physical disease or disability.

But what about physical injuries? Even there a link lurks. For twenty years I passed through the door connecting the kitchen to the garage. But once, while under severe psychological pressure, I pulled the door shut on my finger, causing myself excruciating pain. Was that accident unrelated to my mental state? Hardly. In a very real sense, our soul is not in our body; our body is in our soul. At one level, our body is an interpretation of our soul.

Jeshu grasps the holistic nature of paralysis. We know that bodies can be paralyzed, but so, too, can minds and souls. Sin is not so much a presence as an absence, a lack of harmony, of proper orientation, of connection. This circle of paralysis can be entered through different doors: the body, the soul, the mind, the environment, the circumstances. Master that he is, Jeshu enters by a path leading most directly to healing and wholeness, to total transformation, his intended goal.

REFLECTIONS

1. How can I reflect on my own life in terms of areas of paralysis, stiffness, or rigidity?

2. How is paralysis manifested in religious institutions or clerical bureaucracies?

3. How can healing be brought to the paralysis that inhibits a better flow of communication between Jews and Christians?

19

The Wrong Sort of People

¹⁰Later, when Jeshu was having dinner inside, many tax-collectors and people lax in Torah observance joined him and his disciples at the table. ¹¹Seeing this, some Pharisees said to his disciples, "Why does your teacher eat with tax-collectors and unobservant Jews?" (Matt. 9:10–11)

LB

It's a valid question. How many religious authorities today sit down to eat with those who are considered sleazy? Our human and cultural tendency is to avoid association with "disreputable" elements of society, to eschew people we disapprove of. Eating is a time of sharing both food and camaraderie, and conventional wisdom dictates that we're more comfortable doing that with people we think are more like us. We may attribute this to a desire for shared values, but it more often translates into similarities of economic class, race, and religion.

Jeshu is once again our teacher of subversive wisdom, the breaker of conventional boundaries—he enjoys table fellowship with "sinners" (the traditional translation). If we want to model ourselves after our heavenly Parent whose rain falls and whose light shines on the just and the unjust alike, this opens up new possibilities for our guest list. Breaking bread with others is a time-honored way to deepen relationships—to explore commonalities, discuss differences, and correct distortions. When all goes optimally, we share more than physical nourishment—we share experiences and empathy; sometimes our very souls mingle.

The boundary between saint and sinner is often blurry in its practical application to our own lives. Most of us are a mixture of both, trying to move in a direction of healing and wholeness. We nourish and are nourished by our companions on the path when we eat together without judgment.

Overhearing this question, Jeshu said to them: "It's not the strong and healthy who need a doctor, but the sick and infirm." (Matt. 9:12)

LB

The King James translation refers to those who are "whole" (in place of "strong and healthy"), a word I like because it implies coming into our fullness or completeness as human beings. Wholeness is much more than physical soundness, or not being actively sick. It is a state of shalom, a Hebrew word that suggests fullness (thus its translation as "hello," "goodbye," and "peace"—a full circle of meanings). Our state of shalom is the measure of our well-being, and that is a mind-body-spirit matter. Thus, traditionally, when a Jew prays for another's healing, she asks for *r'fuah shleimah* (the latter word comes from the same root as shalom), "complete healing."

Jeshu makes the point that his ministry is for those who recognize in themselves some incompleteness ("blessed are the poor in spirit" or "you're successful if you're spiritually receptive") and seek wholeness. The already fully enlightened (whose numbers are not overwhelming) are not in need of his services. The sick at heart, the weary souls, the embattled bodies, the conflicted or tormented minds, the frightened among us—they (we) are hungry for his teachings.

> "Go and find out what the passage in scripture means that says, 'I want compassion, not animal sacrifice.' For I have come for the unobservant, not for those who are properly religious." (Matt. 9:13)

LB

"Go and learn" (the traditional translation, rendered here as "go and find out") has echoes of Hillel, the great talmudic sage who lived a generation prior to Jeshu (see Matt. 7:12). He used the phrase to refer to the lifetime of study and practice we must undergo if we wish to weave spiritual principles into the fabric of our being (such as loving our neighbors as ourselves).

While specifically quoting Hosea (6:6), Jeshu is delivering the central message of all the great Hebrew prophets. Caring for the poor and imprisoned, the widows and orphans, the sick and the stranger is God's desire: make right, not rites. The Hebrew word for mercy (here translated as "compassion") is *chesed*, which is a many-faceted word, as is *shalom*. It can mean "goodness" or "kindness," especially as extended to the lowly and needy among us. "Loving-kindness" is another translation, especially when used as a characteristic of God (*chesed* is one of the ten kabbalistic attributes of God, or *Sefirot*). God's *chesed* is depicted as an abundant, everlasting flow of beneficence: Psalm 118 says repeatedly, "His steadfast love [*chesed*] is eternal."

When applied to the human realm, however, *chesed* is a particular kind of love, perhaps best translated as "covenant love." This is an attitude of loyalty to God. Much more than a sentimental emotion, it is our fidelity to the agreement to carry out the *mitzvot* (commandments), which brings us back to caring for the needy among us. Such behavior is commanded of us; it is merciful and compassionate; it also demonstrates covenant love to God. Indeed, one must "go and find out" to understand and embody such *chesed*.

Jeshu drives home the point with the final comments regarding his call to the "unobservant" as opposed to "those who are properly religious" (read "sinners" in the traditional translation, as opposed to "the righteous"). While I understand Ron's discomfort with the word "sinners" (and all the baggage it carries), I think it speaks better to Jeshu's wake-up call than does "unobservant." To whom would this call not apply? Who has not repeatedly missed the mark, whether subtly or grossly? Who does not struggle with the effort toward righteousness (including the effort to eliminate self-righteousness)? The tax-collectors and obvious "sinners" wear their wrongdoing on their sleeve; most of us wear our errors more hidden in our hearts. In designating the categories of righteous and sinner, Jeshu is in effect doing away with them, and suggesting that the religious authorities stop judging others and examine their own hearts. This suggestion applies equally to all of us. As the psalmist recognizes, "my sin is before me always" (51:5). To transform sin into God-centeredness is the great task. Then, with the psalmist, we can also proclaim: "I have placed the

Divine Presence before me always" (16:8). It is an ongoing, lifelong task that requires that we humbly and devotedly "go and learn."

RM

Parents regularly admonish their children to avoid bad company. I often tell my first-year students that the friends they make during the early months of school will largely determine their college experience. Jeshu and his disciples not only associate with the wrong sort of people but also seem to belong in some ways to that category themselves, especially in their lack of concern about the people they eat with and their lax observance of the prescribed times of fasting.

I appreciate Laura's preference for the normal translation of "sinners" to describe the disreputable people with whom Jeshu so frequently associates. I use "unobservant" because I want to stress the fact that these people whose dinner invitations Jeshu so readily accepts were ostracized by the more observant community precisely because of their laxity in regard to fasting and the dietary laws. I'm not so sure that Jeshu would have been as comfortable around people who were regularly beating their wives or molesting children.

We need to keep in mind the distinction in any religion between moral laws and religious rules (sometimes called holiness codes or church laws). Practitioners of a religion don't necessarily focus on this distinction. Preparing for my confession as a young Catholic, I didn't divide my failings into these two categories, separating my disobedience to my parents from my eating meat on Friday. At some level, I knew the difference. So when the Second Vatican Council said that Catholics could eat meat on Fridays (except for those during Lent), I didn't hold my breath wondering whether the prohibition of stealing or murder would soon follow.

When a moral law is broken, someone is hurt. Thus, disrespecting parents, cheating customers, and slandering innocent people are violations of the moral law. But when religious rules are broken by a Catholic eating meat on a Friday during Lent or by a Jew enjoying pork ribs, no one is hurt. The damage in this case is to the integrity of the religious community, the ways in which it chooses to self-identify. Muslims put special value on the Friday afternoon prayers; Jews, on the Sabbath; Christians, on Sunday. These are differences in religious rules, not moral differences.

Most of the people to whom Jeshu seemed to be especially attracted were those who were lax in religious observance or who were seen as second-class citizens because of their religious status— women because of menstruation, lepers because of their disease, the poor who could not afford to buy animals for sacrifices in the Temple, and the homeless who ate so seldom they could hardly concern themselves with dietary rules or observe regular times of fasting.

The tax-collectors are an exception. Because of their regular exploitation of the poor by requiring of their fellow Jews far more than they needed to hand over to their Roman masters, these men could certainly be charged with stealing, clearly a moral offense. At the same time, however, their employment by the Romans made them social outcasts as well. This was more than likely the reason Jeshu was criticized for accepting invitations to dine with them. And it is probable that their desire to have Jeshu as a dinner guest reflected an awareness that they were wrestling with their own immorality.

Jeshu radiates a consciousness that melts societal barriers. The divine center of every being lies open to his gaze. This doesn't mean that he is unaware of the poor choices people make or of the myriad ways they devise to inflict pain on one another. But Jeshu's whole ministry entails touching people whom society considers untouchable and healing sick people whom society considers incurable, either physically or morally. Just as we expect the people in the doctor's waiting room to be sick, so does Jeshu expect those who are drawn to him to be aware of areas where they are in need.

REFLECTIONS

1. What criteria do I use in judging people as the right or wrong sort?

2. What are legitimate situations in which I might avoid certain people because of the adverse effect they have on my spiritual growth—chronic complainers, no-sayers, gossips, and the like?

3. How can this whole theme of acceptability be a topic for conversations between Jews and Christians in terms of their respect for moral laws and religious codes?

20

How New Is This Wine?

16"No one uses a piece of new cloth to patch up an old coat. The patch would just tear away from the coat, and the hole would be bigger than ever. 17By the same token, you don't put new wine that's still fermenting into old winebags. If you did, the brittle winebags would burst open, spilling the wine and ruining the winebags as well. When you have new wine, you put it into new winebags, and then both are kept safe." (Matt. 9:16–17)

LB

Jeshu is calling for an institutional overhaul that is more than cosmetic. While this could be interpreted (and has been) as replacement theology, it could also be understood as a call for radical renewal in an institution top-heavy with bureaucracy, sick with official corruption, and insensitive to the needs of its rank and file members. These are familiar concerns, pertinent to Christianity today, and to organized religion everywhere.

The notion of re-creating Judaism is as old as the Hebrew Bible. The Psalms exhort us to "sing unto God a new song," and every historical period has its reworking of the tradition through new commentary, midrash, and interpretation of laws.

Jeshu lived in a particularly turbulent time of Jewish history—a time of cruel Roman occupation, a time of bitter poverty, struggle, and class warfare. The vast majority of Jews (90 percent) were unhappy peasants, oppressed not only by the Roman occupiers but also by some of their own people—the priesthood (called Sadducees) and the wealthy Jewish landlords. These were few in number, but as upper-class collaborators with Rome, they were heavy in influence, and thus largely despised by the peasant class. The high priest was actually appointed by Rome. The highest Temple authorities were quislings, utterly offensive to the Jewish population at large; even the ritual vestments were kept under lock and key by the Romans.

The priesthood controlled Temple sacrifice, which involved both the purchase of livestock and the money exchange required for this purchase, as foreign coins had to be exchanged for shekels. The poor pilgrims were thereby doubly charged money they could ill afford in order to participate in Temple worship and sacrifice and receive forgiveness for sins, while the priesthood profited and lived well. Jeshu's critique of Temple practices put him squarely in the Jewish majority of peasants who fervently disliked the status quo.

Was Jeshu calling for a new religion in these verses? Most certainly he was not. The new coat, the new wineskin containing fresh wine, is exactly what happened to Judaism after the destruction of the Temple in 70 CE. The priesthood was dissolved, animal sacrifice was disbanded, and rabbinic Judaism became the new format, with prayer replacing sacrifice as the primary vehicle to God. The locally based synagogues became the places for prayer and study, replacing the centralized Temple in Jerusalem. Yeshivas became training centers for rabbis, and the oral tradition became written, as the Talmud assumed a pivotal place in Jewish learning, even attaining the status of a second Torah. Fresh wine in new wineskins is by no means too extreme a metaphor to describe this radical Judaic transformation.

But even cloaked in new garments, Judaism remained Judaism, with the Torah as its guidebook, the prophets as its moral compass, and the one God as its absolute center. And Jeshu was not advocating otherwise. He wanted Torah teachings to be implemented, not abandoned, the prophetic tradition to be heard, not ignored, the reign of God to be now, not later. It is Judaism's ability to grow and evolve, to be innovative and flexible while staying true to its essence that has enabled it to survive more than three millennia, in spite of almost unending persecution. An appreciation for controversy and diversity of opinion (alongside an actual distrust of unanimity) has been part of this growth process from the beginning. Judaism rightly celebrates the effort to arrive at truth through impassioned disagreement and dialogue. Jeshu's voice is an important part of this ongoing dialogue, and his advocacy for Jewish renewal is as relevant today as it was two thousand years ago.

RM

Like most Christians, I grew up with the notion that Jeshu rejected his Judaism as stagnant and legalistic, establishing in its place the spiritual community of which I was a part. An opposite view maintains that Jeshu lived and died a Jew and that any discrepancies with his Judaism occurred after his death through those who claimed to be his followers. Laura and I hold a middle view, seeing

Jeshu's program as both an acceptance of and a challenge to his Jewish tradition.

At its deepest level, Jeshu's new wine does not pertain so much to a discussion of religion as to what lies beyond religion. Religion remains of secondary importance to Jeshu, while what is of supreme importance is God. The failure to recognize their secondary status leads most religions to stray from their deepest calling to be vehicles, not idols. Self-idolatry remains the besetting sin of religion.

The prevalence of religious exclusivism today and its alliance with a lust for political power constitutes a severe threat to planetary peace. The face of fanatic fundamentalism looks very much the same on Christians, Muslims, Hindus, and Jews. Dogmatic exclusivism and political dominance make a wicked team, whenever and wherever they are found. It is this combination that leads people to believe that they are invading countries, bombing civilians, or blowing up school buses because it is God's will.

Jeshu's message, in the final analysis, is not about Judaism, not about Christianity, and not about religion. It is a message about God and God's reign. Organized religion, like family and the socialization process, often opposes our connection with God more than it promotes it. This awareness is the heady wine Jeshu offers all of us, whatever our religious affiliation or lack thereof.

REFLECTIONS

1. What role does religion play in my life?
2. How does attachment to religion affect people I know, as well as the larger world community?
3. How can this theme of religion as vehicle inform Jewish-Christian dialogue?

21

Good News?

Jeshu continued through all the towns and villages, teaching in their synagogues, announcing the good news of God's reign, and healing every kind of disease and illness. (Matt. 9:35)

LB

Apparently, Jeshu decides to throw caution to the wind—if he is going to be accused of being in league with the devil (as in the previous verses), so be it. His is a healing ministry, and healing is symbolic of the good news that wholeness and fulfillment are available here and now. Such is the essence of the kingdom that ordinary Jews, oppressed by Rome and undermined by their own leadership, have lost sight of. Again, the gospel writer tries to distance Jeshu from his Jewish brethren by saying "their" synagogues (see Matt. 4:23).

And whenever he looked at the crowds of people around him, he was filled with compassion for them, since he recognized how worried and anxious they were, like sheep without a shepherd. (Matt. 9:36)

LB

The sheep/shepherd image is familiar in the Hebrew Bible, notably in Psalm 23 ("The Lord is my shepherd; I shall not want") and Isaiah 53:6 ("All we like sheep have gone astray"). The patriarchs were all shepherds, as were Moses and David. To use this metaphor as the prototype of a great leader who has compassion for his people is in keeping with Jewish tradition. There is a midrash that suggests God chose Moses to be the liberator of the Jewish people when He observed Moses rescuing a lost kid that had wandered away to seek water, tenderly carrying the weary animal back to the flock: "Because you showed such mercy, you will tend my flock Israel" (*Exod. Rabbah* 2:2).

37At one point, Jeshu said to his disciples: "How rich is this harvest and how few the workers. 38You must ask the owner of these fields to send workers out for the harvesting." (Matt. 9:37–38)

LB

The gospel writer switches to a farming metaphor. The crowds of people are like an abundance of grain or grapes ready to be harvested, but "how few the workers"—sound, spiritual leadership is a rare and precious phenomenon, then as now. To view ourselves as God's nourishment (in this metaphor, God is the owner of the fields and we are the harvest) is to understand the mutuality of the Divine-human connection. We are longing to be gathered to God, but often lack direction and discipline; thus, we wither on the vine. If we are fortunate and persevere, however, we find spiritual teachers ("workers") and communities that lead us toward the supreme goal of unification with God.

> Jeshu called his twelve disciples to himself and gave them authority to cast out unclean spirits and to heal every kind of disease and illness. (Matt. 10:1)
>
> *LB*

Again, it is clear that "authority" to heal is not peculiar to Jeshu, but available to all who walk a spiritual path with sincerity and devotion, whose lives are imbued with spiritual values. The Baal Shem Tov and some of his disciples in the hasidic movement of the eighteenth century are later examples of this phenomenon, as spiritual and physical healing was part of their ministry. The number twelve recalls the twelve tribes of Israel that stemmed from the twelve sons of Jacob in the book of Genesis.

> 2The names of those twelve apostles are as follows: first, Shimon (called "Rock") and his brother Andri; the sons of Zebedee, Jacob and his brother Jochanan; 3Philip; Bar-Tolmai; Toma; Mattiyah, the tax-collector; Jacob, the son of Chalfai; Taddai; 4Shimon the Zealot; and the traitor, Judah Iscariot. (Matt. 10:2–4)
>
> *LB*

What stands out here to Jewish ears is "the traitor, Judah Iscariot." He seems to be the only one with a surname, and in the traditional translation he is given the only Jewish-sounding name of the twelve (since the usual list includes Hellenized names like Peter, James, and John, rather than Ron's Hebrew version).

Judah is an important figure in the book of Genesis. As the fourth son of Jacob and Leah, he represents one of the original twelve tribes of Israel. The southern kingdom, which contained Jerusalem, bore his name. It is Judah who persuades his brothers to sell their younger brother Joseph to a caravan of traders, rather than shed his blood out of jealousy toward him. This could be perceived as both betrayal (at Judah's instigation they sell Joseph into slavery for twenty pieces of silver) and salvation (the alternative was to slay him). Of course, sending Joseph to Egypt is subsequently seen as God's plan for saving his entire family from famine years later, ensuring the survival of the Jewish people. Judah receives his father's deathbed blessing of leadership, with the added suggestion that the messianic line will stem from his seed (as indeed it does; Judah, through his son Peretz, is a progenitor of King David). Judah and Jeshu could be regarded as related by the Davidic line (at least as midrash).

So it is noteworthy that *this* name is given to the one who will betray Jeshu. One has to question the historical existence of this most Jewish-sounding traitor and the fact of the betrayal itself. Both suggest a midrashic product of late-first-century polemic, when the need to exonerate Rome and the desire to cast Jews in the role of villain were intense preoccupations. In his excellent book *The Sins of Scripture*, Bishop John Shelby Spong dedicates an entire chapter to Judah as a product of Christian imagination.[1] Judah becomes the prototype for perceived Jewish villainy for the next two thousand years. Innocent Jews have paid the price of this tragic misperception millions of times over.

> [5]It is these twelve that Jeshu sent out after giving them the following instructions: "Don't go into the territory of the Gentiles nor into any Samaritan towns. [6]Go rather to the lost sheep that belong to the house of Israel." (Matt. 10:5–6)

LB

Despite his prior experience with the Roman officer (Matt. 8:5–10), Jeshu's original sense of outreach is to his fellow Jews, not to the Gentiles. It is to these "lost sheep of the house of Israel" that Jeshu is drawn—those who have fallen away from the Torah, who are discouraged by the corrupt priesthood, disheartened by the oppression and brutality of Roman occupation, and embittered by their harsh, marginalized existence. Many of these Jews were poorer than the poor. Having lost their land, they were destitute, barely able to eke out a living as day laborers and homeless wanderers. To maintain faith in God under such deprived circumstances and without adequate spiritual leadership would be challenging to most.

"And announce to people along your way that God's reign is very close to them." (Matt. 10:7)

LB

The nearness of God's reign is the message here, a proclamation that is eternally true. Jeshu is reiterating the same message Moses gave the children of Israel at the close of Deuteronomy: "For this commandment that I command you today [to love God, to walk in His ways, to choose life] is not beyond your understanding nor is it far away. It is not in heaven ... Neither is it beyond the sea ... For the Word is very near to you, to carry it out with your mouth and with your heart" (30:11–14).

The teachings have been provided, the guidebook—the Torah—is at hand, and we are its subject. Its content is none other than our own life on earth and our relationship with God and one another. We have only to open our eyes (especially our intuitive third eye) and both our inner and outer lives in order to encounter divine reality, to discover the truth of Torah and its relevance to every facet of our existence. We carry the word with us in our capacity for speech, for communication with others, for interpretation. We carry it in our heart in our capacity for understanding and compassion, for lovingkindness and forgiveness. In an intimate, covenanted relationship with God, we are commanded to choose life and to love, that we may be blessed and prosper. This is good news.

> "Heal the sick, raise the dead, cleanse the lepers, drive out the demons. Give away free of charge all that has been given to you free of charge." (Matt. 10:8)

LB

The mission is one of healing, resurrecting, cleansing, and purifying. God's reign is the land of the living—a place where all that is fragmented and diseased in us can be made whole and healthy, all that is dead can be regenerated, all that is contaminated by our baser inclinations or possessed by our untamed fears and distortions can be cleansed and transformed. What a message of hope and faith in our human potential to heal and be healed!

It is noteworthy that the capacity to serve as a vehicle for such transformation belongs not only to Jeshu but also to all who walk an authentic spiritual path. The apostles are representatives of flawed humankind, individuals with doubts and fears, ego issues and petty grievances, who nonetheless are striving to lead God-centered lives. What miracles can be accomplished when ordinary people devote themselves to God-realization!

The connection between receiving and giving is made manifest in this verse. When we recognize all that we have received unconditionally ("free of charge")—the bounty of life itself, its opportunities for love and growth, for awe and wonder, for service and blessing—the desire to give unconditionally is kindled. The deepest form of giving is that which enhances the well-being of another and asks for nothing in return but the opportunity to go on giving. The Talmud reminds us that the reward for a mitzvah (a good deed) is the opportunity for another mitzvah.

RM

The word *gospel* means "good news." Good news should be the ultimate content of every religion and sacred tradition. Unfortunately, Christianity has all too often shown itself to be bad news: for Jews and Muslims, for women and homosexuals, for indigenous peoples and goddess worshipers. What stems from Jeshu himself, of course, is indeed good news; the bad news inevitably derives from the corporate egos and institutional ignorance of various organizations self-identifying as Christian.

It is important to separate Jeshu from the crimes committed in his name. What is even more important, however, though vastly more difficult, is to separate Jeshu from the spin added to his story by the writers of the Christian Testament. In other words, the very persona of Jeshu in the Gospel of Matthew carries the virus of anti-Jewishness. Christians of almost any persuasion can join in seeing the abuses of the Inquisition, the Crusades, witch hunts, blood libel trials, ghettos, pogroms, and persecutions. But we are far from unanimity in the Christian community regarding the criticism of the sacred text itself, a text that many consider to be inspired and some consider to be inerrant.

Biblical inerrancy and biblical literalness negate the entire project of historical criticism. As long as people hold to the belief that the text is without any kind of error and that Jeshu literally said everything ascribed to him in the gospel stories, the deepest root of anti-Jewishness will never be eliminated. For Christians caught in this unfortunate dogmatic trap of inerrancy, there is no alternative but to affirm the hate-filled distortions that are part of the gospel story and that even cross the lips of Jeshu himself.

How do people move beyond this pernicious dogma of biblical inerrancy? Only an open-minded confrontation with the text itself can make this possible. This, of course, is precisely what Laura and I are trying to offer our readers in this book. Seeing the way Matthew's gospel heightens the anti-Jewish elements inherited from Mark can lead anyone with an open mind to the obvious conclusion that the anti-Jewish spin stems from the life-world of Matthew's community in the 80s and not from the life-world of Jeshu in the late 20s of the first century.

REFLECTIONS

1. How can I understand and articulate the arguments for rejecting the doctrine of biblical inerrancy found in conservative Christian circles?

2. How can I extrapolate from what I'm learning in reading the text of Matthew to other books of the Christian Testament, especially the Gospel of John?

3. How might an examination of both the good news and the bad news in the gospels facilitate a Jewish-Christian conversation?

22

Enemies at the Door

¹⁷"Be on your guard! Your enemies will drag you into courts, flog you in their synagogues, ¹⁸haul you before governors and kings—all on my account and so that you can witness both to them and to the Gentiles." (Matt. 10:17–18)

LB

It is absurd to imagine that Jeshu would speak of his fellow Jews as "enemies" or refer to "their" synagogues. The disputes that arose about a variety of issues were Jewish disputes, in-house debates and arguments that grew increasingly fierce in the decades following Jeshu's death (an incredibly turbulent period in Jewish history, which included the destruction of the Temple, Rome's increasing suppression of all Jewish resistance, and persecution of the budding Christian communities). Undeniably, the Christian Testament includes many polemical texts; the task is to find ways to address them. Most importantly, we need to put them into their appropriate first-century context.

How can we contextualize this verse about flogging in "their synagogues"? By the time this gospel was written in the 80s, the relationship between the Jewish followers of Jeshu and the majority of Jews who did not choose this path was horribly strained. Indeed, some early "Christians" were probably flogged in synagogues as the animosity grew intense (Paul was a self-professed persecutor of the Jeshu sect before he became a follower). What was this animosity about?

Jews strongly resented the Jewish-Christians' insistence that they were the "true Israel," and that their unfolding story was the only correct version—that Jeshu was not only the Messiah but also the Son of God, that a covenant mediated by him replaced the covenant at Sinai, that this new covenant obviated the need to follow the *mitzvot,* or commandments of God in the Torah. As far as most Jews were concerned, the Messiah had clearly *not* come, the increasing deification of Jeshu constituted blasphemy, and Torah observance remained the way to God.

By the mid-80s, Matthew's community, which initially had seen itself as a Jewish sect, was growing increasingly resentful of rabbinic Jews. As time went on they became more and more perturbed at the refusal of most Jews to join the new movement, at their insistence on the integrity of Torah and Jewish tradition—the Jews' inability to see what they saw, to believe what they believed. Such passionate differences are primarily a matter of experience, not intellectual profession, and no one can dictate the content of another's faith encounter. Increasingly (with the acceptance of Paul's teachings), this new vision involved a redefinition of religious identity. An evolving shift was emerging, from an emphasis on Torah as the vehicle to the

Divine to an emphasis on the death and resurrection of Jeshu as a new, primary, and exclusive vehicle.

But these differences of opinion, experience, and belief would not have resulted in nearly the same degree of animosity had it not been for the backdrop of fear and brutality stemming from the Roman occupation, which stained first-century Palestine like a plague of blood. This period could be likened to the Nazi occupation of countries in Europe during World War II. It was a time of political humiliation, immense physical suffering, cruel retribution for any resistance (political prisoners were regularly crucified), and tremendous anxiety, as dissatisfaction and unrest grew ever more unbearable. Jews had some legitimacy in this precarious environment as long as they begrudgingly paid the exorbitant Roman tax and kept quiet. In exchange, they were allowed to practice their religion, albeit in a compromised form, given that the high priest was appointed by Rome and the highest Temple authorities were also complicit with the occupiers. Multiple rebellious Jewish movements kept springing up in the forms of bandits, revolutionaries, and guerilla fighters protesting the status quo (this sometimes involved murdering wealthy Jewish landlords who were hated for their collaboration with Rome). These resistance fighters were routinely captured and crucified. Messianic figures also arose, as the longing for redemption from the Romans intensified in every Jewish mind and heart. They, too, were killed under torture by the powers that be, which regarded them as a political threat (remember that *mashiach* means "anointed king"—see commentary on Matt. 1:1).

This, then, was the first-century backdrop for early Christianity. Jews who were not part of this movement were understandably wary of yet another upstart group that might threaten their shaky legal status in a dominant culture that largely despised them. After the Jewish authorities excommunicated the Jeshu communities, those communities had no legal status in the empire, and they were subject to imprisonment, torture, and death at the hands of the Romans. The two groups were ultimately pitted against each other in a struggle for survival.

It is out of this ambience of fear and privation that Jews sometimes flogged their religious rivals as a punishment for apostasy. Such harsh measures arise out of insecurity, self-doubt, and despair. They are, of course, entirely unproductive, as they only create more animosity and suffering. You can no more flog a person into believing what you believe than you can create love from acts of hatred. Sadly, the Christians did not learn from their experience as victims and, once given power, went on to become some of the worst perpetrators of religious violence the world has known (witness the Crusades, the Inquisition, the burnings at the stake, and indirectly but inexorably, the Holocaust). That such violence is the antithesis of all that Jeshu taught is an ongoing tragic irony.

RM

Laura rightly discerns how obviously this passage matches the lifeworld of the 80s. When the Romans destroyed the Jewish Temple in 70 CE, biblical Judaism was over. Animal sacrifice had been a part of Jewish worship since the days of the patriarch Abraham in the second millennium BCE. The later offering of a bull every morning and evening in the Temple in Jerusalem (first built by King Solomon in the beginning of the first millennium BCE) constituted an everlasting sacrifice to God. Anyone in the environs of the Temple could see the fire by night and the clouds of smoke by day, eternal signs of the covenant between God and Israel.

But now all of that was gone and the Temple, one of the seven wonders of the ancient world, lay in ruins. The priests could no longer offer sacrifices to God. What could replace these sacrifices to mediate Israel's covenant with God? There were two competing answers to this question, emerging at the same time from the womb of biblical Judaism like rival siblings, twins of the same mother, struggling with each other with their first gasping breaths. One of these two answers came from the Pharisees, who were soon to be known as the rabbis. The other answer stemmed from the followers of Jeshu, who would soon be known as Christians.

The Pharisees, who numbered some six thousand in a worldwide Jewish community of some seven million, were a reform-minded, theologically innovative group of conscientious Jews, organized into intentional communities of table fellowship, prayer, and study. It was clear to them that the animals sacrificed had meaning only as symbols of dedication to God expressed by the one making the sacrifice. The gift of heart and soul to God constituted the real sacrifice all along. Consequently, the Pharisees were able to teach that times of prayer could replace the daily sacrifices, just as the table in every Jewish home could assume the sacredness of the altar in the former Temple. Thus began rabbinic Judaism, the essential form of all the denominations of Judaism to this day.

The followers of Jeshu had another way of understanding the destruction of the Temple and the cessation of animal sacrifice. Jeshu's life of total dedication to God and his martyr's death constituted the quintessential sacrifice, obviating the need for any new sacrifice of any kind. This sacrificial metaphor developed dramatically because of the Temple's destruction. As Christians continued to meditate on Jeshu's execution, the blame began to move gradually from the Roman imperial system to the Jews. And the destruction of the Temple became less a crime committed by the Romans and more a justified punishment of the Jews by God for their rejection of Jeshu as the Messiah.

By these diverse paths of interpretation, both communities found a way to live beyond the Temple's destruction, but enmity grew between them because of the incompatibility of these two interpretative paths. Each claimed to be the legitimate successor to the mantle of biblical Judaism, and each denigrated the other as illegitimate and bastardized. A rift was created that has not been healed to this day, a rift that grew wider with each passing century as new forms of polemic and persecution developed.

REFLECTIONS

1. Where do I see the clearest examples of the way the struggle for legitimacy colors the telling of the story of Jeshu?

2. How might the shared history of Jews and Christians have developed differently after the year 70 CE?

3. How can this tragic polemic of two thousand years be converted into a dialogue of respect and even mutual enrichment?

23

A Challenging Kind of Peace

"Don't think that I've come to bring the world an easy peace. What I bring is much more like warfare than that kind of peace." (Matt. 10:34)

LB

Some of Jeshu's statements sound like Buddhist koans when placed beside other seemingly contradictory teachings. Put the above verse (especially in the traditional translation: "I have not come to bring peace, but a sword") next to "Blessed are the peacemakers ..." (Matt. 5:9) or "Put your sword back into its place; for all who take the sword will perish by the sword" (Matt. 26:52), and your rational mind will hit a wall. This verse, when unpacked, speaks of the subversive wisdom that is Jeshu's defining tone and ethos.

Jeshu's teachings are like a sword—sharp, dangerous to the

status quo of power and oppression, capable of inflicting lethal wounds on our ego agenda. Like the Buddhist term *prajna,* or discriminating awareness, also depicted as a sword (double-edged for maximum effectiveness against ignorance), Jeshu's words have a bladelike quality. They cut through falsehood, hypocrisy, and greed; they slice through conventional wisdom, revealing its bankrupt shadow and empty promises. They are challenging and can be painful, but like a skillful surgeon's scalpel, they remove what is dead or diseased and promote healing. Our complacency in the face of corruption, injustice, and violence must be cut to shreds if we are to undergo the radical transformation Jeshu calls for. The Hebrew prophets demand no less: "Your hands are full of blood. Wash yourselves; make yourselves clean ... seek justice; rescue the oppressed, defend the orphan, plead for the widow ... but if you refuse and rebel, you shall be devoured by the sword; for the mouth of the Lord has spoken" (Isa. 1:15–17, 20).

35"My coming sets sons against fathers, daughters against mothers, daughters-in-law against mothers-in-law. 36You won't have to look beyond your own family members to find your enemies." (Matt. 10:35–36)

LB

Business as usual is not an option, as Jeshu sets patriarchy on its ear and disrupts the family power structure. The typical authority allegiances of the time (sons allegiant to fathers, daughters to mothers and, when married, to mothers-in-law) do not apply in the egalitarian society Jeshu envisions. He is reminding us of the higher authority that prevails over our man-made pecking orders and renders them null and void, particularly when they violate divine laws of fairness and compassion. We owe ultimate allegiance to one Parent, the Mother-Father-God of our mothers and fathers.

Whether Jeshu intended these words metaphorically (teacher of inwardness that he was) or was pointing to an external reality, or both, they are provocative and disturbing, especially given the context of households split apart by ideological division and its resulting accusations and hatred. This is gut-wrenching territory, the shadow side of "love your enemies and pray for your persecutors" (Matt. 5:44). Family members are your foes here (if they are operating in opposition to God's will), and while you are instructed to love them, you are also to be set against them.

There is a precedent for this in the Hebrew Bible. Abraham is told by God to leave his father Terakh's house (midrash tells us Terakh worshiped idols) and start fresh in a new land. Was there strife between him and his father? Midrash provides the tale that Abraham smashed the statues in Terakh's shop (selling idols was the family business), blaming the chaos and destruction on one club-wielding, angry idol. This explanation caused Terakh to protest that statues have no such power, giving Abraham the golden opportunity to point out, "Yet you bow down and worship them." Did this endear him to his father? Probably not. Abraham both loves his father and is set against him. Taking a stand for what our heart tells us is true and right may alienate those closest to us. This will bring conflict, not peace, in the short term, but it is the only way to ultimate harmony, to *tikkun olam,* which is our guiding light.

Still, Jeshu's language of swords and foes is open to misunderstanding and misinterpretation that becomes dangerous in fanatic, fundamentalist hands. Our sacred texts are full of ambiguous language that must be wrestled with, unpacked, and always held up to the light of wisdom and compassion, lest the words become weapons of darkness and destruction. The sword must be balanced against the love that Jeshu proclaims as primary, if it is to be used judiciously. Otherwise, it becomes an instrument of violence rather than one of discriminating awareness. A Jewish mystical analogy is found in the *Sefirot,* the ten God attributes that must operate in balance with one another or great harm results. Specifically, *Chesed*—the flow of unconditional love—is placed opposite *Gevurah,* which is more like the sword—strength, power, limit setting, necessary boundaries, or tough love. When these two qualities work together optimally, the result is a third attribute, *Tiferet,* or harmony, beauty. But woe to us if *Gevurah* gets the upper hand. This is what has happened repeatedly in Christianity's violent history of the Crusades, the Inquisition, and pogroms.

So just as "love your enemies and pray for your persecutors" must be held in our hearts alongside this verse about foes in our own household, so should we also balance this verse with the prior teachings about anger and insults toward our fellow human beings (Matt. 5:21–26). Controlling our temper, holding our tongue, seeking reconciliation, and seeing our own part in disputes frees us from the prison of our ego. Detachment from our cherished opinions enables us to cherish those who disagree with them. Such loving behavior is the necessary *chesed* that balances the *gevurah* behind our values and beliefs so that they do not become rigid, dogmatic, and violent.

> 37"You're not worthy to be my disciple if you prefer father or mother to me; you're not worthy to be my disciple if you prefer son or daughter to me; 38you're not worthy to be my disciple if you're not ready to take up your cross and follow me." (Matt. 10:37–38)

The emphasis on "me" is suspect here (again, Jeshu was not into self-promotion) and smacks of later editorial revision. Loving God is the point (the traditional translation uses "love more than me" in place of "prefer"), not preferring Jeshu to family members. And Jeshu is (to use a Buddhist metaphor) the finger pointing toward God. We should not confuse the two, although mystical awareness does blur the distinction between God and ourselves. As Rumi plaintively cries out, "You, the One in all, say who I am; say I am You!"[1]

The issue is having only one absolute, and centering our lives in that truth. Putting God at the center enables us to love those around us—parents, children, friends, and enemies—wisely and well. When our central allegiance is to God rather than to narrow self-interest, we behave lovingly. We resolve disputes; reconcile differences; control anger; withhold insults; and are altogether better parents, children, friends, and citizens (see Matt. 5:21–26). Our worthiness expands when we take that central commandment of Judaism as our raison d'être: "Love the Unnamable your God with all your heart and soul and strength" (Deut. 6:5). Loving God with this completeness enables us to be radiant with love. Thus, this commandment works hand in hand with Leviticus 19:18: "Love your neighbor as yourself" (as Jeshu will make explicit later on; see Matt. 22:36–40). Since God is present in every one of us, we best express our love of God by the way we treat one another.

Here again the word *love* (alongside *God*, one of the most misused words in the English language) must be understood not as some superficial romantic encounter, as Madison Avenue and popular culture would have us believe. Nor is it unquestioning obedience to authority figures or becoming a doormat to abuse. Real love is patience when irritated, respect when provoked, loyalty and fidelity when tempted, forgiveness when injured, compassion and kindness when tested, and firmness when necessary. It may require opposition to our loved one's endeavors (witness Abraham and his father, Terakh, in the above verse). This is love worthy of the name and the Unnamable.

It also seems unlikely that Jeshu spoke of "taking up your cross"—this sounds like post-crucifixion language. The cross became associated with Jeshu only after his death, and the "not worthy to be my disciples" is highly un-Jeshu. The main message in this verse, however, comes directly out of his teachings. We cannot know joy if we do not also embrace necessary suffering, for the two do not operate separately. Taking up the cross is a striking metaphor for accepting what comes on a spiritual path, be it illness, loss, relinquished comforts, or even persecution and revilement. At the very least, old age with its diminishments awaits us if we live long enough, and eventual death is a certainty. In some cases, accepting what is means giving up our physical lives for a God-centered path, as have martyrs in every tradition across the ages. Putting our ego to death is a necessity for fullness of spiritual life. That is usually an excruciating process, but one that paradoxically results in profound peace and great joy.

RM

Every virtue has a closely related vice. Compassion lives close to what the Buddhists call "idiot compassion." Would you give a gun to a madman, a case of bourbon to an alcoholic, money to a drug addict? We easily recognize these behaviors as distortions of true compassion. But what if we are complacent in the face of injustice, passive in the face of sexual abuse, silent when confronted with corruption or prejudice in the workplace? Can we not rightly call this "idiot peace"?

The biblical tradition assures us that peace is the fruit of justice. Where people perceive themselves as being treated fairly, peace usually reigns. In my years as dean of students at Lake Forest College, I found that students were generally happy campers if they felt they were being dealt with fairly, whether in the classroom, in the judicial system, or in the determination of housing. In this context, justice is the goal, the absolute, and peace is the means, something relative. In other words, if justice can be achieved only by force, then force may be necessary.

If Jeshu had seen a Roman soldier dragging a Jewish girl into an alley to rape her, would he have walked by indifferently? Of course not. Would he have intervened? Certainly. Would he have used force if necessary to protect the girl? I believe so. Might he have wrestled the sword from the Roman and used it on the Roman if necessary? Perhaps. There is a relativity regarding the means Jeshu might have used but an absoluteness about the goal of protecting the girl. If he fails to make every effort to protect the girl, how could Jeshu claim to love his neighbor as himself?

But is the Roman soldier not Jeshu's neighbor, too? And even if he is an enemy in this situation, has not Jeshu exhorted us to love our enemies? And wouldn't Jeshu be loving the Roman by allowing him to rape the girl? The question answers itself. Loving someone means calling that person to live in truth, and truth entails respect for others. Jeshu would not be loving the Roman by allowing him to live in a world where it was all right for him to rape people. That would be allowing the Roman to live a lie, the false notion that the Jewish girl did not deserve his respect. Love comes in many forms, and restraining evil is one of them.

REFLECTIONS

1. Has my own commitment to peace as the fruit of justice ever involved the use of force? Would I make a different decision now, either to avoid force or to use it where I previously hadn't?

2. Is there a difference between force and violence? Does it have something to do with intent? Explain.

3. How does this topic of peace as the fruit of justice lend itself to contemporary Jewish-Christian dialogue?

24

Mixed Messages

¹²"From Jochanan's time until today, God's reign has been sub-jected to violence, and the violent have claimed it. ¹³For until you come to Jochanan, all of the scriptures are prophecy. ¹⁴And if you're ready to accept that prophecy, you know that Jochanan is the Elijah whose return the scriptures promise. ¹⁵Those of you who are ready for this teaching will understand it." (Matt. 11:12–15)

LB

Now comes the direct assertion that Jochanan is Elijah, fiery prophet of the Hebrew Bible (who lived more than eight hundred years before Jochanan and Jeshu), whom Jewish tradition maintains will return to announce the Messiah's arrival and the coming messianic age. He will also perform a final miracle of reconciling the hearts of parents and children (Mal. 3:23–24). This vision of reconciliation and peacemaking is a far cry from the bloody, contentious reality of first-century Palestine, where bitter upheaval characterizes families, communities, and society at large (remember Jeshu's prediction of interfamilial strife?—Matt. 10:35–36). By Jewish criteria, Jochanan (whose life ends violently when he is beheaded by Herod) is no Elijah, nor is it likely that Jeshu thought so; this is another text from a later time and sensibility.

Jeshu's kingdom of heaven moves far beyond Jochanan to a consciousness that emulates God by loving enemies, not wreaking vengeance on them, by praying for persecutors, not cursing them, by forgiving those who harm us, not damning them to hell. He knows us to be capable of such a consciousness. This is an altered emphasis from the Hebrew prophets' condemnatory tone; it leads us by a different route to an exalted awareness of what it is to be truly human. It is a necessary complement to the Hebrew prophets—those amazing, agonized witnesses to human outrage and divine retribution. The prophets cried out for justice and repentance with a ferocity that excoriates humankind for its crimes and a luminosity that reveals a suffering God's pathos in participation with our plight. Jeshu holds us no less responsible, but he offers us a different facet of our humanness and our godliness as inspiration on our path toward *teshuvah* and transformation. By emphasizing what we could be—nonviolent, compassionate, generous, whole—rather than what we've been—belligerent, grasping, indifferent to suffering, fragmented—Jeshu holds out renewed hope for a transformed humanity. As Ron points out, "Jeshu realized that the whole conversation about God's reign had heretofore been saturated in a commentary of violence. Now that was all going to change."[1]

Indeed, Jeshu's consciousness changed, but collectively we have yet to catch up with him. The prevalence to this day of "shouting televangelists, promising a sweet revenge when the godless fall into the hands of a wrathful God,"[2] alongside the accumulated horrors that have been perpetrated in Jeshu's name over the centuries, suggest that change is painfully slow in coming. The radical transformation of consciousness that Jeshu embodied and taught has yet to become a widespread reality, in part because his teachings have been so contaminated with conflicting—even completely opposing—convictions and sensibilities woven into the gospel text.

These mixed messages have allowed for so much misinterpretation that Jeshu's nonviolent agenda was turned into the bloody Crusades. His invitational stance became the coercion of the Inquisition. His egalitarianism has been twisted into church hierarchies fostering patriarchy. And his deeply Jewish passion for intimacy with God and for an inclusiveness of that intimacy has degenerated into dogmatic exclusivity, catapulting all other faiths directly out of the kingdom into the darkness, and leaving his fellow Jews particularly despised and even demonized. Jeshu can only be weeping and gnashing his teeth at this ongoing *shonda* (Yiddish for "enormous disgrace") of the last two thousand years.

The significant move toward *tikkun olam* that Jeshu's teachings represent must be rescued from ongoing efforts to thwart it by turning it into its opposite. Luminaries of the last century, such as Gandhi, King, and Mandela, have managed to see beyond the distortions (as have multitudes of mystics, scholars, theologians, social activists, and uncelebrated others) and have used the inspiration of Jeshu courageously and creatively. Nonviolent resistance has become a blip on the radar screen of consciousness in some circles. Loving one's enemy (the antithesis of proclaiming an "axis of evil"), while not a popular point of view, has its proponents also. We are seeing the beginning of a new way to address conflict, which, if taken seriously, could bring about a messianic age: a time when war has become archaic; when nonviolence has become an organizing principle of our society and our world (*satyagraha,* to use Gandhi's term; "truth and reconciliation," to use Nelson Mandela's application of it); when loving our neighbor (who is anyone who crosses our path) as ourselves (whom we recognize as a manifestation of the Divine, like our neighbor) is the rule, not the exception.

It is up to those of us who are ready for this teaching and understand it—who have ears to hear and a third eye (the wisdom chakra) to see—to work with all our heart and soul and strength to implement it. This entails responding with respect and compassion to those who vehemently disagree with us, who dismiss us, scorn us, and damn us to hell. If we can meet arrogance, hatred, and fear with humility, love, and courage, there is hope of finding some common ground. That is our empowerment. The truth is that all of us long for lives that contain joy and fulfillment, that are meaningful and rich with loving relationships, that can thrive in a context of peace and justice. Working together to create a world that supports this truth is the ticket to *tikkun olam* and the key to God's reign.

RM

Every Sunday school student knows the story of Elijah being taken to heaven in a fiery chariot. In the Jewish tradition, his return comes to be linked to the advent of the Messiah. If Jeshu is indeed to be the Messiah, he must have his Elijah. It is against this backdrop that the story appears in our text.

Only a thin veil separates us here from a Jewish-Christian conversation taking shape in the latter decades of the first century CE.

The members of Matthew's community claim that Jeshu is the Messiah, snatched from his ministry by his execution but raised from the dead now and poised for his glorious return, or *parousia,* the Greek word for the triumphal entrance into a city by a conquering hero.

But if Jeshu is indeed the Messiah, then the members of the rabbinic community want to know why Elijah did not return to announce his arrival. What we have in the text is the response by Jeshu's followers that Elijah has indeed returned in the form of Jochanan the Immerser. Those who are ready for the teaching will understand it, the implication being that the rabbinic community will not be ready for it and will therefore not understand it. This, of course, is a clever way of making it impossible for your adversaries to disagree.

Laura's comments open a wonderful door to dialogue. While Jews and Christians may disagree about both the messianic identity of Jeshu and the legitimacy of seeing in Jochanan Elijah returned, there can be renewed conversation regarding the image of God's reign, which so powerfully dominated Jeshu's consciousness.

So many people, then and now, smack their lips in anticipation of the coming of God's reign, fully expecting a punitive God to wreak his vengeance on all the evildoers, while exalting and rewarding the true believers. And yet the message of Jeshu cuts through this kind of dualism. We are all made in God's image, bear God's stamp, and carry God's life as our deepest being. To be open to God's reign is to be open to this profound experience of God and all that it entails for the way we live in the world. Just as there is nothing punitive in Jeshu's God, so there can be nothing vengeful or vindictive in those who truly understand his message.

REFLECTIONS

1. What are my initial thoughts when I hear the phrase "God's reign"?

2. How is God's reign depicted in our media and pop culture?

3. How can this theme of God's reign and *tikkun olam* be a fruitful topic for Jewish-Christian dialogue?

25

Jeshu the Lawbreaker?

¹Around this same time, Jeshu and his disciples were walking through some wheat fields on the Sabbath. Being hungry, the disciples were picking the tops of the grain to eat. ²Some Pharisees saw this and said to Jeshu, "Look at your disciples; they're guilty of violating the Sabbath." ³He replied, "Haven't you read what David did when he and his companions were hungry? ⁴Going into God's house, David ate the special loaves kept there in God's presence, bread that neither he nor his companions had the right to eat, since they were reserved for the priests.

⁵"Or haven't you read in the Torah how the priests in the Temple regularly violate the Sabbath and yet are without guilt? ⁶Are you aware that someone greater than the Temple is here? ⁷If you understood the scriptures that tell us how God wants compassion more than ritual sacrifice, you wouldn't be condemning people who are without guilt. ⁸For it is the Lord of the Sabbath who is here with you." (Matt. 12:1–8)

Jeshu is pointing to one of the most insidious problems in organized religion—its tendency to worship itself. When religious rules and ritual practices take precedence over compassion and alleviating suffering, God's greater law is being violated. This awareness is in keeping with, not contrary to, Jewish understanding, as Jeshu's example of David illustrates, and the reference to the prophet Hosea reinforces. David, hungry and on the run from King Saul, requests and is given the holy bread to eat by the priest, bread that would be off-limits under normal circumstances (see 1 Sam. 21:4–7). Hosea states the larger principle: "For I desire mercy [*chesed*] and not sacrifice, and the knowledge of God rather than burnt offerings" (Hos. 6:6). Ritual, including Sabbath observance, should not take precedence over dire human need. The wandering homeless and destitute need to eat on Shabbat as well as the other days of the week. By Jewish law, they are guaranteed the gleanings that farmers are required to leave around the corners of their fields. Shabbat, a day of joyful recognition of God's blessings and abundance, a day dedicated to "the knowledge of God," should not be a fast day for the poor and hungry.

Thus, something greater than the temple, the church, the mosque, or the ashram is always at stake when dogma or ritual conflict with existential urgency. In the pressing demands of the moment, love and mercy override narrow legality. *Chesed,* translated as "mercy" above in the quote from Hosea, also means "steadfast love." This is what God desires. Knowledge of God is a deeply felt, intimate knowing—an inwardness—and all our actions, ritual and otherwise, should serve to deepen that knowledge further. Jeshu's comment that the priests in the Temple break the Sabbath (they labor when performing their priestly duties) brings to mind the stirring words in

Exodus: "You shall be to me a kingdom of priests and a holy nation" (Exod. 19:6). We are all commissioned to be priests in the kingdom of God, which means knowing when to follow the letter of the law and when to forego the letter for the spirit of the law. Rigid adherence to law can become an obstacle to knowing God.

The "Lord of the Sabbath" comment makes good Jewish sense if the phrase "Son of Man" (the NRSV translation reads, "For the Son of Man is lord of the Sabbath") can be understood as referring to all humankind. Jewish tradition teaches that the Sabbath was created for humanity's sake, not the other way around; similarly, Shabbat is not for the sake of the weekdays; the weekdays exist for the sake of the Sabbath. This "climax of living," as Heschel puts it, is a time of celebration and gratitude, of restoring our souls before and after the workweek. It is a time of sensual delight, gratitude, joy, and camaraderie with family and friends. Shabbat offers us a taste of eternity; it is a microcosm of the perfected world to come. What's more, the Sabbath is often depicted as a queen or a bride (especially in mystical circles) whom we joyfully welcome into our homes and our hearts. It is thus in keeping with Jewish awareness to see ourselves as lords and ladies of the Sabbath, a royal retinue around the Queen who presides in this holy palace in time.[1]

9Jeshu went on from there and entered their synagogue, 10where he encountered a man with a crippled hand. Some people who were looking to find fault with Jeshu asked him whether or not it was permitted to heal on the Sabbath. 11He responded, "Who among you, if you had just one sheep, would not pull it out of a pit it fell into on a Sabbath? 12A human being is worth a lot more than a sheep, so of course it's permitted to do good on the Sabbath." 13Jeshu then said to the man, "Put out your hand." And when he did, it was just as good as the other one. (Matt. 12:9–13)

The disputation over the letter versus the spirit of the law continues here with regard to healing on the Sabbath. A withered hand is not a life-threatening condition, so some would maintain that the healing could wait a day (to sustain a life, such Sabbath healing would be completely permissible). The parable of the fallen sheep contains a surprising fallacy, however, according to Ned Rosenbaum in *Jesus Through Jewish Eyes:* "Sheep die if not watered every day, whereas a man with such a condition could wait one day more."[2] Ron points out that Jeshu is using this parable ironically to suggest that the economic value of the sheep should carry less legal weight than the suffering of a human being.[3] This implies that monetary concern, not compassion, might have motivated a departure from the law and thereby saved the sheep.

But Jeshu is emphasizing the value of relieving suffering, and the good of doing good, even if it constitutes "work" in the technical sense. As Rosenbaum adds, "Is doing the 'good' of a 'good work' sometimes more important than avoiding the 'work' required to do it? … Extending the idea of release must be the real reason for Joshua's [Jeshu's] argument."[4] Such release from life's painful grip, part of the Sabbath's implicit purpose, would constitute a compassionate extension of its boundaries regarding work. As Heschel maintains, "The Sabbath comes like a caress, wiping away fear, sorrow and somber memories."[5] Jeshu is saying, in effect, "Let's rule on the side of mercy, not judgment, in such a matter." Rabbi Hillel, "Judaism's model human being," who was well known both to hold and to inspire a similar bias, would do no less. A talmudic tale describes him climbing to the roof of the *beit midrash* (house of learning) one Shabbat winter night to listen to the teachings of the learned rabbis through the skylight (being too poor to afford the entry fee). When the rabbis discovered him the next morning covered in snow atop the skylight, they hastened to carry him, bathe him, and anoint him (all technical prohibitions of Shabbat), then set him by the fire, proclaiming: "This man deserves that the Sabbath be violated on his behalf."[6]

RM

Just as we saw Jeshu loose about religion but tight about God, so now we find him lax about religious rules but strict about the moral code. As we saw earlier in our discussion, religious rules (holiness codes) pertain to a community's identity and integrity, but moral laws affect people, protecting them from harm and fostering their well-being. I hear a poignancy in Jeshu's response: "A human being is worth a lot more than a sheep." Isn't this the same man who said that human beings are worth more than many sparrows (Matt. 10:31)? So much of Jeshu's teaching centers around the value, the holiness, and the infinite worth of each human being. No other law is needed for one who has internalized and deeply understood this truth. Is there any evil under the sun that cannot be traced to its neglect? From Cain's murder of Abel in our mythic past to Iraqis and Americans blowing each other up in the all-too-literal present, failure to love our neighbor has been the root of all our sin.

Jeshu's profound sense of compassion for his fellow human beings is so overwhelming that the religious rules pale in comparison, unless he judges them to be promoting the love of neighbor. Let hungry people eat, regardless of dietary rules or other niceties of observance. Let sick people be healed, regardless of what day of the week it is. For Jeshu, human needs trump all the rules of religion.

REFLECTIONS

1. How do religious rules and moral codes weave together in my own sense of spirituality?

2. How are they coordinated in the religious institutions of which I am a part?

3. How does this tension serve as a topic for Jewish-Christian dialogue?

26

Those Terrible Pharisees!

14At this point, the Pharisees went out of the synagogue to discuss among themselves how they might cut Jeshu off from teaching. 15Being aware of what they were plotting, Jeshu left that place. (Matt. 12:14–15)

LB

Here we go again. This is more spin, not truth. To repeat (because it bears repetition): the Pharisees were Jeshu's ideological dialogue partners; they were spiritual innovators (like Hillel); they were his table-fellowship comrades and friends, and the group with which he was most identified. They would not have wished to silence (or destroy) Jeshu. It was the priestly class (in bed with Rome) with whom Jeshu fiercely clashed, but since the Sadducees declined (and ultimately disappeared) after the destruction of the Temple and the Pharisees became the chief proponents of rabbinic Judaism, it was they who were pitted against the emerging Jeshu community.

The NRSV translation is much harsher than Ron's (the KJV is similarly harsh): "But the Pharisees went out and conspired against him, to destroy him." These accusations of conspiracy with the desire to kill Jeshu come out of the diatribe of the 80s, not the life-world of Jeshu in the 20s. This depiction of the Pharisees as harsh, conspiratorial, and destructive (which becomes generalized to all Jews as the gospel unfolds) is a gross distortion that cries out to be corrected. Ron, whose teaching over the last thirty years has been a valiant, eloquent effort on behalf of setting the record straight, expresses the injustice as follows: "This stain of antipharisaism, often spreading over to anti-Judaism, clearly reveals the shadow side of this gospel. In the light of two thousand years of Christian anti-Semitism, these later comments polluting the original teachings of Jeshu seem particularly obscene. It is only by eliminating them that we can disclose the 'hidden gospel' that is the goal of our study."[1]

How do we "eliminate" these polluting comments when they continue to live and breathe in every copy of the Christian Bible throughout the world? We cannot undo the damage of the past (the slights, the slurs, the hatreds, the prohibitions, the persecutions, the torture, the murders), but how can we prevent further damage from being done? What about the millions of people who read these words and know nothing of the context? What about those who use such words to incite hatred and contempt of Jews? How can the original teachings of Jeshu be rescued from this stain that sullies them, that leads people to despise instead of to love their "enemies"? What are people in church leadership positions doing to address this "shadow side" of the gospel?

This raises the knotty but necessary issue of what to do with portions of our sacred texts that come from human wound rather than divine inspiration. Virtually every spiritual tradition suffers from this problem, containing lines of scripture that would best be repented, not prayed over. Some people would advocate eliminating these lines of text completely; that is, changing our sacred documents. I recall one rabbi saying that his preference would be to take a black marker and remove all references to God sanctioning the ruin of cities, the killing of every man, woman, and child, as in Deuteronomy 2:33–35, or God urging such destruction, as in Deuteronomy 7:2: "... you must utterly destroy them. Make no covenant with them and show them no mercy." That strategy opens up the contentious dilemma over what to keep and what to remove (violence being only one out of a number of unsavory biblical categories, including sexism and homophobia).

Rabbi Michael Lerner addresses this subject in *Jewish Renewal*. He urges us to distinguish between the voice of cruelty (which comes from pain and distortion, and evokes fanaticism, intolerance, and oppression) and the voice of God (a voice of love, justice, compassion, and transcendence) in the Torah: "Whatever parts of the tradition help you to connect with the recognition of the other as created in the image of God, whatever tends to give you confidence and hopefulness about the possibility of joining as partners with God in the task of healing and repair of the universe, those are the parts of the tradition that have been revealed, that have the mark of God in them."[2]

The same criteria hold for recognizing the authentic voice of Jeshu in this gospel, as opposed to the voice of accumulated pain, anger, and retaliation. It is incumbent upon us to use all our resources—intellectual, intuitive, emotional, and spiritual—to make this vital distinction, to grapple with the text, celebrating its holiness and uncovering its shadow. This book is one effort to do exactly that.

> ²²Then a demon-possessed man who was both blind and mute was brought to Jeshu, and he healed the man, enabling him once again both to see and speak. ²³The people crowding around them were amazed, asking whether or not Jeshu might be the Son of David. ²⁴But when the Pharisees heard it, they said: "It's only by Beelzebul, the ruler of the demons, that this man casts out demons." ²⁵Intuiting their true motives, Jeshu said to them: "Any kingdom filled with internal dissent collapses; and the same thing happens with any city or town. ²⁶So if now we have Satan driving out Satan, that's a kingdom so filled with internal dissent that it could never survive. ²⁷Furthermore, if I'm casting out demons with the help of Beelzebul, how are your followers doing it? They will have to be your judges. ²⁸But if I'm casting out demons with the help of God's spirit, then God's reign is among you." (Matt. 12:22–28)

LB

Again, we encounter the blanket condemnation of "the Pharisees," the product of later times and narrower consciousness. The awestruck crowds are ready to crown Jeshu as the *Mashiach*, but those accusing Pharisees declare him in league with Beelzebul, the dung god. Jeshu's response to the hecklers (and probably there were some) is helpful for discerning the false from the true. If the healing heals (and the demons depart), then the spirit of God is at work here. Satan doesn't work against his own interests; our ego may be malevolent, but it is not stupid.

Apparently others, including those in the pharisaic community, were performing healings as well as exorcisms. There should be a natural camaraderie in the community of healers, rather than the competitiveness and fear voiced by the naysayers. Jeshu suggests that those who actually practice the healing arts will recognize the truth and goodness of his ministry, for they are all working with the same divine energy (good intentions, focused one-pointedly like a laser). He points out the absurdity of using demonic energy (or evil intentions) to defeat what is evil (or harmful or dis-eased) within us.

Those who attempt to demonize Jeshu are doing so out of fear and ego agenda. Because he does not speak the party line—in his radical egalitarianism, his table-fellowship habits, his "violation" of the Sabbath, his condemnation of hypocrisy—the powers that be are threatened by his message and his power, including his gift of healing. Some of them may have attempted to discredit him and demonize him. Tragically, this is exactly what happens to the Jews collectively by the Christian church as it becomes powerful. The stage is being set for that tragedy in this gospel.

RM

One has only to open any random English dictionary and look up *Pharisee* to find the English word *pharisaical,* an adjective describing someone who is hypocritical. We have passages like these to blame for this prejudice and resulting stereotype. After the destruction of the Second Temple by the Romans in 70 CE, the Pharisees became the rabbis (the founders of rabbinic Judaism). And since rabbinic Judaism was a rival to Matthew's community, the author(s) of this gospel rarely pass up an opportunity to decry the Pharisees. Writing in the 80s, they retroject this hostility into the 20s when Jeshu was teaching. Jeshu becomes the persona for their opposition, almost demonic in its virulence, to rabbinic Judaism.

The Pharisees dotting the landscape in Matthew's gospel are largely fictional foils, straw men set up to highlight the power and truth of Jeshu's message. The historical Jeshu did, of course, deal with Pharisees, and no doubt he sometimes disagreed with some of them. But since the gospel narratives place Jeshu so frequently at their dinner tables, one imagines that their conversations were normally friendly. For the Pharisees, the observance of religious rules was more central to Judaism than it was for Jeshu. Moral passion and mystical vision were more characteristic of this charismatic hasid from the Galilee. But there were certainly countless points on which they found agreement.

The transformation of theological sparring partners into homicidal adversaries falls wide of the mark. About that there can be little legitimate disagreement. But what can we do about it today? Laura refers to one rabbi who would like to go through all of our sacred texts with a black marker to eliminate offensive passages. While sympathetic with that idea, I believe that our received texts are part of our tradition. We learn from their limitations as well as from their insights. As Jews and as Christians, we are a people in process. As more liberal thinkers have long taught us, our tradition always has a voice, but not a veto. It provides a starting point, but never the final word.

I don't think we could find many Americans who would want to discard the Constitution. But I don't think we could find any Americans who would want to live with an unamended Constitution. The amendments are a vital part of our constitutional history. They demonstrate our growth and our legitimate progress. Our classic religious texts need amendments no less. Patriarchy should not be carried forward as a divine mandate, any more than slavery, capital punishment, or homophobia. And, most importantly for Christians, anti-Jewishness should not be clung to as though it were part of the good news Christianity claims to bring.

REFLECTIONS

1. Can I think of prejudices my parents or grandparents held that I have chosen to reject, though I continue to love and cherish them as my relatives?

2. In what ways has my own religious tradition let go of some cherished prejudices in its recent history?

3. What changes—positive or negative—would Christianity need to undergo if it ceased to be patriarchal, homophobic, and anti-Semitic? How do our responses to this question influence Jewish-Christian dialogue?

27

Jews Seek Signs

38At this point some of the Torah scholars and Pharisees said to Jeshu, "Teacher, we'd like a sign from you." 39Jeshu answered them: "This is an evil and adulterous generation that is seeking a sign, and the only sign it's getting is the sign of the prophet Jonah. 40For just as Jonah was in the belly of the monster for three days and three nights, so too will I be in the heart of the earth for three days and three nights. 41At the judgment, the people of Nineveh will stand up and condemn this generation, for when the Ninevites heard Jonah preach, they turned their lives around. Are you aware that someone greater than Jonah is here with you now? 42At the judgment, the queen of the south will stand up and condemn this generation, for she came from the ends of the earth to listen to Solomon's wisdom. Are you aware that someone greater than Solomon is here with you now?" (Matt. 12:38–42)

The wish for concrete, tangible evidence of God's providence and presence is an age-old yearning, as common as it is ultimately inadequate. Not long after the Red Sea was dramatically split (a sign, if ever there was one), the children of Israel were bemoaning the lack of food and water in the desert and pining for the fleshpots of Egypt (see Exod. 15:23–24 and 16:2–3). The initial revelation at Mount Sinai (perhaps the sign of signs) was followed by worship of the golden calf (Exod. 32). And Jeshu has been performing multiple healings, raising the dead, exorcising demons—are these not signs?

We have a human propensity for amnesia when it comes to such external manifestations of God's work in the world. That is why we are commanded to love God with all our heart and soul and strength and place these words upon our hearts (Deut. 6:5–6). It is the transformation of the heart that keeps God's presence before us continuously. In Jewish language, the heart becomes circumcised, then the words upon our uncovered hearts can drop in. And such transformation is a dynamic, ongoing experience rather than a once-and-for-all phenomenon. We build trust and reinforce our covenant with God through spiritual practice. Prayer, meditation, deeds of loving-kindness, study, spiritual companionship, and acts of social justice all feed our faith and devotion, which in turn nourishes our practice. This self-perpetuating cycle of love and commitment, of discipline and devotion, of contemplation and action becomes all the sign we need. Then we can say with conviction, *Shiviti Adonai l'negdi tamid*—"I place the Divine Presence before me always" (Ps. 16:8).

The "sign of Jonah" section suggests later editorial comment. As a metaphor for Jeshu's death and resurrection, it is potent midrash created not by him, but by his followers, as this transformation later became central to Christian belief and understanding. It was not central to the teachings of Jeshu himself, at least not in relation to his own death. Adding to the inauthenticity of these lines are the assertions by Jeshu of his superior status: "someone greater than Jonah is here … someone greater than Solomon is here." Jeshu, the "gentle and humble of heart," was not self-aggrandizing or prone to self-elevating comparisons (or comparisons at all, for that matter). His role is to be a vehicle for God and to empower others, not to point to his own greatness. These words are tributes to him, not *by* him.

RM

Writing in the 50s, Paul already spoke about Jews seeking signs (1 Cor. 1:22). This is part of a developing Jewish-Christian polemic. As Christians increased their insistence that Jeshu was the Messiah, Jews were quite understandably puzzled. The signs of the Messiah's coming should be a matter of perception, not of faith. The signs of the Messiah's coming will be believed when they're seen.

The messianic age comes with clearly visible signs, including the cessation of war, the removal of the Romans from power, and the teaching of Torah going out from Jerusalem to all the world. But even though Jeshu has come and gone, everything looks surprisingly the same. How can this be a messianic age? Christian theology develops a rebuttal, pointing out that Jeshu is a suffering messiah rather than a conquering one. Furthermore, the effects of his messianic reality are in the spiritual rather than the physical realm. Sins are forgiven and people find salvation and a promise of eternal life.

Jochanan was the new Elijah because he was Jeshu's predecessor and proclaimer. Jeshu is the new Jonah because he was raised to life after three days in the belly of the earth. Jeshu is also the new Moses because he goes up on a mountain before proclaiming a new Torah. He is the new David as well, born in David's city and recognized as Israel's true king, though the glory of his kingdom will be visible only at his glorious return. These claims leave most Jews at this time unimpressed. Where are some signs that these claims are legitimate?

Christianity develops a two-phase understanding of Jeshu's messianic mission. His first coming was in humility, but his second coming will be in glory. Our present history falls between the decisive messianic battle won by Jeshu's death and resurrection and the full messianic victory, which will be manifested at the time of his *parousia* (or glorious coming) on the clouds of heaven. For Christians who understand this language metaphorically rather than literally, Jeshu's message was messianic insofar as he was an anointed (the root of the word *messiah*) teacher of divine truth. Jeshu "returns" in everyone who attains Christ-consciousness.

The literal interpretation tends to be exclusivist—it is only through Jeshu that one attains salvation, healing, and wholeness. The transformational interpretation discerns a process available to every human being, a spiritual evolution or growing up that can take place in the life of a Muslim or a Buddhist, a Hindu or a Jew, a person of any religion or of none. And the messianic age will have fully arrived when the entire human community has attained this "Christ-consciousness," which goes by other names in other sacred traditions.

REFLECTIONS

1. What would convince me that the messianic age had arrived?

2. How has this language of messianic signs been used historically by Jews and Christians?

3. How can current theological discussion of this topic enliven Jewish-Christian conversations?

28

What Makes Us Unclean?

¹After this, Jeshu was approached by some Pharisees and Torah scholars from Jerusalem, who asked him, ²"Why are your disciples unobservant of the tradition of the elders by not washing their hands before they break bread together?" ³In response, Jeshu said to them, "And why is it that because of your tradition you are unobservant of the commandments of God? ⁴For God commanded us to honor our parents and further said that those who curse their parents are worthy of death. ⁵But you claim that those who make an offering to God of monies that are needed to help their parents are in no way dishonoring them. ⁶And yet this tradition of yours denies God's word. ⁷You mock true observance in doing this, and you fit the words that Isaiah spoke in prophecy when he said: ⁸'This people pays me lip service, but they hold their hearts far from me; ⁹their religion is ridiculous, because what they are teaching are human inventions.'"

¹⁰Then Jeshu gathered a crowd of people around him and said, "I want you to hear and understand what I'm saying. ¹¹It's not what goes into our mouths that can make us unclean but what comes out of our mouths." ¹²At this point his disciples came up to him and said, "Do you realize that the Pharisees are really upset in hearing this teaching?" ¹³But Jeshu merely said, "Every plant not planted by my heavenly Parent is going to be uprooted. ¹⁴Don't worry about those Pharisees. They're blind leaders, and when one blind person leads another person equally blind, they both end up falling in the ditch." ¹⁵Rock [Shimon] spoke up at this point and asked Jeshu to explain this parable. ¹⁶Jeshu asked, "Are you missing the point just as much as they are? ¹⁷Don't you understand that whatever goes into our mouths passes through our intestines and is then eliminated? ¹⁸But the things that come out of our mouths come from our hearts, and those are the things that can make us unclean. ¹⁹For it's in the heart that evil thoughts originate, along with murder, sexual immorality, theft, lies about other people, and false oaths made in God's name. ²⁰These are what make people unclean. But to omit washing one's hands before breaking bread—no one becomes unclean that way!" (Matt. 15:1–20)

LB

Again, Jeshu shines as a teacher of *kavanah*—inwardness, intention, and the stirrings of the heart. The hand washing referred to in verses 2 and 20 is not about cleanliness but is part of the tradition of fulfilling God's ritual commandments (which always involves the recitation of a blessing). Jeshu is firmly in the Jewish prophetic mode when he states that ritual hand washing (or any other ritual, for that matter) is less important than God's moral commandments regarding fair and loving treatment of one another. Ritual's very purpose (and religion's purpose as well) is to connect us to God's love and will. When it fails to be a vehicle to the Divine, it becomes empty and sterile and needs to be reconfigured or discarded.

Jeshu, in typical Jewish fashion, answers a question with a question (verse 3). In one sense, it is surprising that he points to the commandment to honor our parents as the one the Pharisees are remiss about, given his strong critique of parents in previous verses (see Matt. 10:35–37 and 12:48). But just as the critique of families was related to larger issues (of dismantling patriarchy, of looking beyond blood ties for spiritual community), here, too, he is highlighting the hidden trap that all religious institutions can fall into: the trap of self-worship.

For the authorities to condone the giving of money needed by one's elderly parents to Temple coffers is a serious case of mistaken priorities and a moral lapse. I question whether the Pharisees would have supported this practice, and suspect that Matthew has again confused them with the Sadducees. Isaiah's quote is apt here (Isa. 29:13), and Jeshu is speaking straight out of Jewish prophetic tradition when he differentiates between man-made rituals (whether it be animal sacrifice, donning *tefillin,* or hand washing) and the essence of Torah found in the Ten Commandments. Honoring our parents (which would include supporting them in their old age) is central to Jewish belief and practice.

I take issue with Jeshu's contention that "what goes into our mouths" is of no consequence regarding purity (or being "unclean," verse 11), although it is not the traditional laws of kashrut (or dietary restrictions) that concern me, nor the traditional meaning of purity, with its ritual rather than ethical connotation. In fact, Jeshu is mixing the two categories by saying that what goes into our mouths (in his time, largely a ritual concern regarding dietary requirements) is less important than what comes out of our mouths (always an ethical concern). In our current life-world, however, unmindful eating—with no consciousness of the suffering caused when animals are cruelly mistreated (as in the torture of calves to make veal, or the abuse of chickens to get high yields of eggs, or the misery of cows and pigs raised in factory "farms" that treat them like objects rather than living beings)—raises a serious moral issue. What we put into our mouth defiles us when such considerations are disregarded.

Eating the top of the food chain has other ethical and environmental implications. Our inordinate appetite for meat requires growing huge amounts of grain—ten pounds of plant material for every pound of animal flesh produced. This is an inefficient, wasteful use of protein that also destroys topsoil and depletes diminishing water reserves. The grazing of livestock is decimating rain forests, further harming the earth's ecology and contributing to global warming. Hungry people by the millions could be fed with the grain now given to animals, if we reduced our meat intake even by ten percent. The Jewish Renewal movement thus speaks of keeping "eco-kosher," advocating a vegetarian diet, the consumption of locally grown organic foods, and other compassionate, earth-friendly practices.[1] These particular issues were not relevant in Jeshu's life-world (and certainly food choice was not an option to the poor and the destitute, then as now), but the underlying principle of moral and mindful consumption still applies. If Jeshu were alive today, he would be talking about what goes into our mouths.

As for the Pharisees becoming "really upset" at Jeshu's effort to put ritual dietary restrictions in their proper place (verse 12), we have to be willing to offend the authorities with just critiques and perspectives on truth that make people uncomfortable. As in the practice of hatha yoga, we must learn to be comfortable in uncomfortable positions. Jeshu's response takes the larger view that what is not in accord with the grain of the universe (call it the Tao, call it God's will, call it the way things are) will not last; it will be "uprooted" by the heavenly gardener. Empires come and go, religious institutions come and go, man-made rules and rituals come and go. But God—the power that makes transformation and liberation from the past possible, the force that propels us forward in our evolutionary journey of conscious- ness—is unchanging and everlasting.

Jeshu's comment about the blind leading the blind is both help- ful and disturbing. We need to exercise discernment about whom we turn to for spiritual direction; that's good advice. But calling the Pharisees blind guides who lead the unwary into ditches contributes to the antipharisaic and ultimately anti-Jewish diatribe that does harm, not good. This is Matthew's commentary, not Jeshu's, and it has contributed to the portrayal of Jewish teaching as blind, ignorant, and dangerous. A standard feature of many European cathedrals is the depiction of the synagogue as a blindfolded woman with a broken staff.

The connection Jeshu makes between speech and heart, and their relationship to what defiles, is wonderful spiritual teaching. The importance of our inner life is paramount. Indeed, the thoughts of the heart get expressed in words (and ultimately in actions); thoughts are where our good and evil intentions originate. Jeshu again draws from the Ten Commandments—the final five that relate to human interac- tions and govern how we are to treat one another (or not to treat one another). The urge to murder, lie, steal, commit adultery, or covet all begin as far more innocent thoughts: I don't like him; I wish I had a car like hers, a wife like his, a house like theirs; she makes me sick; he's an idiot; they deserve to go to hell; I hate them! Thoughts like these (common as grass) are the insidious beginning of harmful habits of mind leading to destructive words and deeds. They pollute our purity of heart and contaminate our best intentions if we allow them free reign. The point is not to suppress or repress them, but to channel their considerable energy constructively. Anger, hatred, covetousness, and sexual urges all fuel powerful desires that can be used to heal rather than harm, to build rather than destroy.

As Jeshu emphasizes (alongside all the Hebrew prophets before him), what should concern us most is not ritual purity (the right ablution) but right relationship with one another. This is what most concerns God. Loving others as ourselves, which entails seeing the unity of all life, is the royal road to right relationship with God. What comes out of our mouth is a reflection of our heart, our intention, our *kavanah,* and our deepest desires. As with raising our consciousness regarding what goes into our mouth, monitoring our words for truth, kindness, and right purpose is a sacred task, a powerful spiritual practice.

RM

The question of ritual cleanness highlights the tension between religious rules and ethical issues. I agree with Laura that what we put into our mouths can have moral implications. Not only is this true regarding the moral issues raised by eating meat, but it also relates to the epidemic of obesity in our culture, not to mention addiction issues involving alcohol, nicotine, or other substances. If I continue to stuff myself with junk food when I am dangerously overweight, then I am not truly loving myself, despite the commandment shared by Jews and Christians alike to love our neighbor as ourself.

I remember speaking to a Methodist friend who was active in her church. She went to a regional meeting of Sunday school teachers and noticed that many of the women were so overweight that they were barely able to climb the stairs to the second floor where some of the meetings took place. Nonetheless, the dessert tables were laden with pies, cakes, and ice cream. These were committed Christians, faithful churchgoers, volunteers in the Christian education program. But the problem of obesity was never raised as a moral concern for Christians.

So I think Laura is right that Jeshu is wrong, at least if you take the words literally. But it might be argued that he's making a point with allowable hyperbole. What he's really trying to do is highlight the anomaly of paying punctilious concern to religious rules while being neglectful of deeper moral concerns. A Catholic might give up beer for Lent and then be a total pain in the neck to his family for the next forty days. A Jew may go to a kosher restaurant, being careful to observe all the laws of kashrut, but demean and humiliate the wait-staff. And everyone knows the church or synagogue volunteer who never misses a meeting but whose children are left at home and neglected.

What I find most interesting in teachings of this kind is the sense we get of Jeshu's priorities. Time and again he shows himself to be loose about religion while tight about God and God's children, God's words spoken into the world. Jeshu wants us to think about people: their feelings, their needs, their possibilities, and their infinite worth.

This is the test of moral behavior in the world. Nothing seems to hurt Jeshu more than harm done to people—especially women and children, the poor and the sick—by representatives of religion. This harm continues in our modern society: A recent headline informs us that a Catholic bishop has denied the plea of a child with a wheat allergy to receive communion with a non-wheat wafer. This bishop, caught in his small world of religious rules, lacks even a glimmer of understanding of Jeshu, someone who could have written D. H. Lawrence's short poem "Immorality":

It is only immoral to be dead-alive, sun-extinct,
and busy putting out the sun in other people.

REFLECTIONS

1. When in my life have I allowed moral issues to be put on a back burner for the sake of religious rules?
2. Where have I seen instances of such behavior in any religious institutions with which I've been affiliated?
3. How is the topic of what goes into our mouths and what comes out of our mouths relevant to Jewish-Christian dialogue?

29

Identity Issues

13When Jeshu came into the neighborhood of Caesarea Philippi, he asked his disciples, "Who do people say that I am?" 14"Some say you're Jochanan the Immerser," they answered, "but others say you're Elijah or Jeremiah or some other prophet." 15"But what about you," he said to them; "who do you say that I am?" 16Shimon Rock said in response, "You're the Messiah, the son of the living God." 17"God bless you for saying that, Shimon, son of Jonah," answered Jeshu, "for only my heavenly Parent, not any creature of flesh and blood, could have revealed it to you. 18So now I'll tell you something too: you are Rock, and it is on this Rock that I'll establish my community. No forces of hell will overcome it. 19I will give you the keys to the heavenly reign so that whatever you allow on earth will be allowed in heaven and whatever you forbid on earth will be forbidden in heaven." 20Then Jeshu gave his disciples strict orders not to tell anyone that he was the Messiah. (Matt. 16:13–20)

Did Jeshu see himself as the Messiah? Or do we encounter here the meditations of a later age? There must have been a great longing on the part of his disciples for Jeshu to be the Messiah—the one who would bring peace, justice, and compassion to a world so saturated with bloodshed, oppression, and corruption. Roman rule was cruel and unforgiving; anyone who opposed it was tortured and put to death. That God would send the Messiah now to oppose such a regime would seem a fitting, glorious response.

But Jeshu did not fit the traditional description of Messiah as king, with its political implications and its military obligations. He did not advocate the overthrow of Rome by force, for both pragmatic and philosophical reasons. He saw the futility of armed resistance against Rome's far more numerous and better-equipped army, but on a deeper level, he saw the futility of violent means to peaceful ends. His manner of resisting evil and corruption was subtle and revolutionary, involving a shift of consciousness away from hated enemies who were to be conquered and toward wounded equals who were to be transformed.

By deleting the "you're the Messiah" piece of Shimon Rock's answer, we're left with "you're the son of the living God." This is a purer reflection of the foundation of Jeshu's teachings: the issue is not his messiahship, but his status as a child of God, a thoroughly Jewish way to regard someone who powerfully conveys God's presence. To discover ourselves as beloved children in whom God dwells and delights is to be handed the keys to the kingdom. That's the message Jeshu tries to impart over and over again. He empowers his disciples by awakening that awareness: *you* have God in you; *you* can heal the sick, feed the hungry, move mountains, and walk on water if you'll only recognize who you are. That mystical consciousness is what makes living together in loving community possible—where giving to one another is receiving, where forgiving one another is being forgiven, where the death of ego (our false self) is the birth of our authentic self. From the perspective of unity consciousness, duality is overcome and heaven and earth are intricately linked.

I appreciate Ron's substitution of the word "community" for the usual translation "church" in verse 18 ("it is on this Rock that I'll establish my community"). I had wondered when reading the other translations where Jeshu would have come upon the word "church." Certainly no such word existed in his Aramaic vocabulary, nor did he see himself as establishing an entirely new religion with a new house of worship. If he were to return today, he would probably feel most at home in an Orthodox synagogue with its Hebrew liturgy and its lack of reference to him.

RM

Who was this Jeshu? Was he the Messiah? Was he God's only begotten Son? Was he the Second Person of the Blessed Trinity? Was he and is he God? The story is told of a liberal theologian called in by his bishop for questioning. "Do you believe that Jesus is God?" bellowed the bishop. "Yes," responded the theologian. The bishop seemed satisfied and the theologian turned to leave the bishop's quarters. "But do you believe that Jesus is God in any way that you and I are not?" asked the bishop. "No," answered the theologian, realizing that he was signing his own condemnation papers, but grateful perhaps that at least he would not be burned at the stake as in the "good old days."

"Do you believe that Jesus is the Son of God?" was the question directed to scripture scholar John Dominic Crossan at a conference I was attending. "Yes, and I also believe he was the Lamb of God and yet I don't think that Jesus was white and wooly," responded Crossan. How long it takes Christians—even ones in high places—to understand that religious language is written in metaphors. I was taught by an English teacher to chart metaphors. Put the subject and the metaphor on one line, and on the next line find the commonality that makes the metaphor work. My love is a red, red rose. All right, "my love" and "rose" go on the first line. But what goes on the next? That my love has thorns and petals? No. The element that belongs on the second line is beauty.

As with the symbolic language of poetry, so, too, with the metaphors of theology. God is our rock, but God is not granite. God is a king but does not sit on a throne. God is, in the words of Martin Luther, "a mighty fortress" but alas has no drawbridge. Careful study of biblical language leads us to a humility about the capacity of language to describe the mystery of the Divine. In the long run, we are bound to agree with the thirteenth-century Christian theologian Thomas Aquinas, who wrote in the seventh chapter of his *De Potentia,* "*Nemo scit plus de Deo quam de Deo nescit*"—"No one knows more about God than the fact that he does not know him." And the mystery of Jeshu's participation in the divine reality—or your participation or mine—is no less mysterious and no more capable of being adequately expressed in words.

I can affirm the language of all the Christian creeds as long as you allow me to understand that language as metaphorical. Each title—God, Son of God, and Lamb of God—captures a facet of the divine mystery manifested so clearly in this hasid from the Galilee. He is different from us in degree, not in kind. We are what he is, and he is what God is. The difference is that he has less ego in the way of that manifestation than most of us do, and it is the ego or false self that obfuscates the clarity of the divine image in us.

REFLECTIONS

1. What are some of the ways in which I think of myself as divine?
2. What meaning can I find in each of the metaphors used to describe Jeshu in the Christian creeds?
3. How can a discussion of the metaphorical nature of God language be used in Jewish-Christian dialogue?

30

Jeshu the Rabble-Rouser?

¹²Then Jeshu went into the Temple and threw out all who were buying and selling things there; he overturned the tables of those who were exchanging currency and the chairs of those who were selling pigeons for sacrifice. ¹³He said to them, "It is written in the scriptures that my house will be called a house of prayer, but you have turned it into a den of robbers." (Matt. 21:12–13)

LB

That Jeshu strongly critiqued the Temple power structure and its abuses of the poor is without question. The system of Temple officials selling animals for sacrifice alongside money changers exchanging foreign coins for shekels (since images on coins were not allowed on the premises) was a double thorn in the side of poor pilgrims, who could barely afford the pigeons, let alone the more expensive and prestigious bulls and rams, and for whom the cost of money exchange was a hardship. Price gouging added to the exploitation of the needy. The priests in charge of the operation were collaborators with Rome, and the whole process had become tainted with corruption. When organized religion fails, it fails mightily. For Jeshu to have opposed the "God brokering" and elitism of Temple policy is justified and believable.

However, I doubt that Jeshu would have forcibly thrown people out of the Temple, nor would he have overturned tables and chairs. Such hotheaded behavior would have caused a riot, and people would have been hurt and possibly killed. Roman guards were stationed within viewing range of the Temple to keep order, and they would have intervened violently. Jeshu would have been promptly arrested and taken away. Fomenting a chaotic scene like this is not in accord with Jeshu's consciousness or ethos; he is a teacher of nonviolent resistance, not a rabble-rouser or a proponent of brute force. To turn him into a conventional action hero is to lose the essence of his much subtler, more powerful message.

Such a story is in accord with the midrashic character of this chapter, which begins with Jeshu parading into Jerusalem awkwardly perched on two donkeys (a misunderstanding of the Hebrew in Zachariah, who prophesies the Messiah's arrival on a young donkey, not two donkeys), with crowds shouting hosannas and strewing branches about. It is unlikely that Jeshu would have drawn attention to himself with such a grand entrance—he put God at the center of things, not himself—nor would he have wished to alert the Roman authorities to his presence. On the eve of Passover, they were especially vigilant about disturbances, and the capital city in turmoil would have been a red alert.

I wonder why Jeshu did not oppose the whole sorry institution of animal sacrifice as an inherently flawed way of approaching God.

The Hebrew word *korban* (sacrificial offering) comes from a root that means "to draw near." The purpose of the animal offerings was to draw closer to God, to atone for wrongdoing, receive forgiveness, and thereby unite ourselves with God's presence. But a system of sacrificial service that involved bloodshed and cruelty to animals as a means of expiating our sins was sadly missing the mark, creating suffering as it attempted to alleviate it.

As Jeshu recognized and taught, the essence of our service to God—our alignment with Ultimate Reality or God's will—is giving up no less than our ego. This is the only necessary slaughter. It is an internal process. When we relinquish the chaff of our false self that thrives on the delusion that grasping at material goods, clutching hold of relationships, seizing power, or garnering prestige will result in fulfillment, then we draw near to God. The pearl of great price is the nourishing kernel of our true self, created in God's image, unconditionally beloved and capable of extraordinary love. This discovery of unity with the Divine is the essence of our service, and no further sacrifice is needed.

RM

This story is pivotal. John's gospel—different from those of Mark, Matthew, and Luke in so many ways—includes two accounts of a Temple cleansing by Jeshu. A historical event certainly underlies these multiple narratives. But what exactly did happen that day? What did Jeshu say and do? Did he act out of prophetic zeal or personal pique? And what message was he trying to communicate?

Laura may be correct in eliminating some of the violence from the scene. On the other hand, this may have been more of a prophetic sign than an instigation to civil disorder. Prophets taught by symbolic deeds, as well as by words. Turning over a moneychanger's table and letting some caged birds fly free may have been symbolic gestures. But symbols of what? We're confronted with at least three plausible explanations of what happened that day.

One explanation presumes that Jeshu has nothing against the sacrificial system per se. After all, he has come to Jerusalem to celebrate the holiday of Passover. And having one's lamb sacrificed in the Temple in preparation for the Passover meal was an essential ingredient of the holiday. From this perspective, Jeshu was responding to the abuse of the sacrificial system, not to its existence. He was responding to the injustice to the poor accompanying the system, ideas developed in Laura's commentary.

A second interpretation suggests that Jeshu chose these deeds to symbolize a more radical protest against the Temple system. This may or may not have anything to do with the respect for animal life that Laura suggests. In a world where there was very little respect for women or slaves, animal rights were clearly not at the top of any list of concerns. But it's entirely possible that a deeper critique is embedded in this scene, especially if we hypothesize (as I do) that Jeshu more than likely spent some time with the Essenes.

The whole Essene movement had begun more than a hundred years before the time of Jeshu and was led by a high priest who had been forcibly removed from office. He may indeed be the figure known by the enigmatic title "Righteous Teacher," the appellation found in several of the Dead Sea Scrolls. The Essenes saw their life of separation as a protest against the illegitimate priesthood in Jerusalem, the group that had rejected and replaced their founder. If this was part of the background of Jeshu's thoughts that day, then his problem with the Temple may have run deeper than his concerns about the social injustices involved in the priestly practices.

A third possibility is the most radical. Jeshu was signaling the coming destruction of the Temple itself, along with the system of animal sacrifices that was at its heart. The immersion ritual practiced by Jochanan may have been all that was necessary to demonstrate *teshuvah,* the desire to turn to God. And the simple sharing of bread and wine practiced by Jeshu and his disciples may be all that was necessary to celebrate communion with God. Furthermore, he may have realized that the persistent attacks of Jewish insurgents against the force of Roman law and order were leading to a showdown. He did, after all, prophesy that within the lifetime of most of his disciples, the Romans would come in full military power to destroy the Temple and shut down the entire system of animal sacrifice forever (Matt. 24:2).

REFLECTIONS

1. What are other instances of prophetic signs used by the prophets of Israel?

2. How does the street theater of current protests relate to the kind of actions we connect with this scene?

3. How is the topic of sacrifice relevant to Jewish-Christian dialogue?

31

Jews as Rotten Tenants

33"Listen to another story. There was a landowner who planted a vineyard, put a fence around it, dug a hole for the winepress, and built a watchtower. He then turned it over to some tenant farmers while he traveled to another country. 34When the right time for picking the grapes drew near, he sent his servants to the tenant farmers to get the grape harvest. 35But the tenant farmers grabbed the servants, beat one, murdered another, and threw stones at a third. 36So the landowner sent other servants—more this time—and they did the same thing to them. 37Finally, he sent his son to them, figuring that they would respect him. 38But when the tenant farmers saw the son, they said to themselves, 'This is the son; if we kill him, we can inherit the whole estate.' 39So they grabbed him, threw him out of the vineyard, and murdered him. 40What do you think the owner of this vineyard is going to do to those tenant farmers when he comes home?" 41They answered him, "He'll kill those rotten tenant farmers, and he'll rent his vineyard to other tenant farmers who will deliver the grape harvest to him at the right time." 42Jeshu said to them, "Didn't you ever read the verse of scripture that says: 'The very stone that the builders rejected has become the cornerstone; the Lord did this, and we think it's wonderful'? 43This is why I'm telling you now that God's reign will be taken from you and given to a people who will produce the right kind of fruit. 44Whoever stumbles on the stone will be injured, and whomever it falls on will be crushed." 45When the chief priests and the Pharisees heard these stories, they realized that Jeshu was talking about them. 46They wanted to arrest him, but they were afraid of the crowds, who looked on him as a prophet. (Matt. 21:33–46)

LB

Now we skip ahead at least fifty years from the many authentic and pithy parables of Jeshu (the seed, the soil, the pearl, the yeast, the hidden treasure) to one entirely lacking his distinctive voice and ethos. We move past the destruction of the Temple and into the angry, oppositional context of Matthew's emerging Christian community doing battle with the emerging rabbinic Jewish community. This parable contains the roots of replacement theology in all its ugliness.

The tenants of the vineyard are the Jews who reject Jeshu, first seizing, stoning, and even killing his predecessors, the prophets (the servants); then seizing and killing him (the son and heir to the estate). The tenant-Jews are depicted as greedy, violent schemers, utterly without redeeming qualities: "'This is the son; if we kill him, we can inherit the whole estate.' So they grabbed him, threw him out of the vineyard, and murdered him." The owner of the vineyard (God) repays them in kind. This God-owner is not about forgiveness but revenge, giving them the miserable death they deserve. Once the Jews are dispatched, new tenants (the righteous Christians) are hired to take care of the grape harvest. What a vast difference in consciousness this is from the man who taught "love your enemies."

To add insult to injury, the gospel writer depicts the priests and elders as markedly dim-witted. As if the parable were not a transparent slur on their character, they respond to Jeshu's question ("What will the owner do to the tenants when he comes home?") by indicting themselves and pronouncing their own death penalty. These sneaky, conniving Jews walk right into Jeshu's trap and only realize it after he pounds them with a quote from Psalm 118 (verses 22 and 23) about the rejected stone that becomes the cornerstone (this having been originally a reference to David, who was chosen to be king of Israel despite his father, Jesse, assuming that the crown would go to one of his other sons; David was the youngest, smallest, and least likely candidate). Here, the stone becomes a crushing instrument of their own destruction. Christianity is portrayed as replacing Judaism with a vengeance.

The relative handful of Jewish authorities who colluded with Rome (to the detriment of the Jewish people as a whole) were understandably not prime candidates for God's reign—collaborators in any occupied land lack integrity and are looked upon with contempt. However, "the crowd" that is repeatedly referred to in the gospel—the suffering majority of poor landless peasants as well as the Pharisees—were also Jews.

Although the intent of the parable is otherwise, a subversive reading could regard the suffering, steadfast Jewish majority as the new tenants who will produce the fruits of the kingdom at the proper time. Indeed, the corrupt Second Temple fell (as did Rome eventually) and the priesthood dissolved, but the cornerstone of Judaism—the Torah, the Prophets, and the Writings, and the creative rabbinic traditions that emerged from pharisaic innovation—remained intact. Despite repeated efforts at its destruction, this foundation has provided an abundantly rich harvest for two thousand years and continues to bear good fruit to this day.

RM

Does an authentic parable of Jeshu lie behind this distorted and hate-filled story? Certainly, Jeshu was critical of the religious and political leadership of his day, beginning with the Romans but including the Jewish priests and political quislings who were co-opted by the Roman ideology of conquest and control. Thus, Jeshu telling a story about the vineyard (an ancient image of Israel) being in the hands of unworthy tenant farmers would not surprise us.

But how would the story end? Jeshu did not tell parables about himself, so we can presume that it would not have ended with a message about the Jewish failure to respond to God's true son. Nor would Jeshu have seen himself as the landowner's son (i.e., God's son) in any sense that set him apart from his fellow human beings, all of whom are sons and daughters of the same heavenly Parent.

Perhaps in the original parable the landowner does finally send his son. But the son in this case is the true disciple of Jeshu, one who is humble and meek. After all, didn't Jeshu teach that the meek would inherit the earth? Why would they not then inherit the vineyard as well? So perhaps this landowner's son was someone who deeply listened to the tenants and their concerns, someone who could lead them to successful negotiations so that they would be able to deliver the grape harvest at the right time. In other words, Jeshu might have told the story of how a true Jewish renewal could save Israel both from internal disaster and from foreign invasion.

We will probably never know the original parable as Jeshu taught it. But at least the story I have suggested seems consonant with Jeshu's mind and message. Jeshu is very clear on this point: God does win in the end. The human community does eventually grow into a consciousness of God and into a conscience working for justice and peace. The landowner's son, the truly successful human being, is indeed the one who will finally inherit the earth.

This announces wonderful good news at that white-hot center where all the sacred traditions meet. The world will one day belong to those who realize, as Hinduism teaches, that they are divine. Those who, as Buddhism reminds us, are truly awake, enlightened, and compassionate. Those who, as Islam declares, strive for justice and peace. Those who, as Judaism proclaims, seek righteousness and mercy and walk humbly with God. Those who, as Christianity announces, live and love in the world as Jeshu did.

There is no uglier blemish on the face of religion than the running sore of exclusivism, filled with all the poison of religious arrogance and egotism. In the history of Jews and Christians, this exclusivism has taken the form of replacement theology, which claims that Christians constitute the true Israel. They are now God's chosen people. They alone have a true covenant with God. The Jewish story is an *old* testament (*testamentum* being the Latin word for "covenant") and the Christian story is the *new* testament. Only Jews who convert to Christianity are complete or fulfilled Jews.

I visited a nearby megachurch one recent Sunday. After being treated to an hour's fare of "Christianity Lite," I roamed around the various booths downstairs featuring the church's ministries. One booth had a sign: "Jewish Seekers." I asked the woman tending the booth what this ministry was about and she said that it led small group sessions for Jews seeking to understand Christianity. If they converted, then they joined another group called "Jewish Believers." "But what about Jews who believe and live their lives as Jews?" I asked. She paused for a moment and then responded, "Well, they would be seekers."

So by this token, the only way to be a believer is to be a Christian. There cannot be any Jewish believers or Muslim believers. Despite the impressive "Christian" music and all the state-of-the-art technology, the doctrine was the same old replacement theology, just dressed in an up-to-date outfit. There's no other way to be a believer, to be saved, to be loved by God except my way. What a sad tribal ideology. How far it seems from the inclusive compassion of the gentle teacher from Galilee.

REFLECTIONS

1. When have I encountered an exclusivist mentality ("my way is the only way") in my own thoughts, attitudes, or words about people different from me?
2. Have I seen exclusivism in any of the religious organizations with which I have been affiliated? If yes, what forms has it taken?
3. How does this discussion of exclusivism and tribalism have relevance for Jewish-Christian dialogue?

32

A Damning Diatribe

¹After this, Jeshu spoke to a crowd that included his own disciples: ²"The Torah scholars and the Pharisees are your official religious teachers. ³You should, therefore, obey and follow everything they teach. But don't imitate their practice, because they don't practice what they preach.

⁴They create heavy burdens to put on other people's backs, but you won't see them lifting a finger to help. ⁵Everything they do is for show. They make their *tefillin* broad and their *tzitzit* long. ⁶They seek out the places of honor at formal dinners and the best seats in the synagogues. ⁷They love the recognition they receive in public places when others call them rabbi." (Matt. 23:1–7)

LB

The tortured heart of this chapter is an increasingly virulent attack against some of the leadership—the scribes and the Pharisees—of

Judaism in Jeshu's time. The Sadducees, who were most responsible for Temple abuses, are not mentioned (undoubtedly because they no longer existed at the time this gospel was written). These words contain a mixture of legitimate critique of organized religion (all too relevant today), which probably stems from Jeshu, but as they intensify they take on an ugly vitriolic tone with hateful language that utterly contradicts Jeshu's sensibility and consciousness. The latter is very painful to Jewish ears; I expect it would be painful to Jeshu as well. A careful examination of the transition from his authentic teaching voice to Matthew's collective voice of wounded outrage is in order.

This first section distinguishes wise teachings from shoddy practice. Such discrepancy is the bane of all organized religion and, as Ron points out, contemporary examples abound.[1] Jeshu makes it clear that he reveres Moses and Judaism and advocates following the teachings of Torah espoused by the leadership: don't throw out the baby with the bathwater. But he warns against imitating their practice: do as they teach, not as they do. Of course, the most effective teaching is never through lofty words, but through example. Parents who tell their children not to lie or cheat, but who lie or cheat themselves, speak louder in their actions than their stated values. Priests who preach love and compassion but who sexually abuse children (and bishops who protect the priests rather than their victims) make a sham out of spiritual leadership. These are "heavy burdens" indeed, imposed upon the most vulnerable among us.

This text portrays Jeshu painting a bleak picture of the Jewish leadership of his day as lazy, perverse, corrupt, self-serving, and hypocritical. Clearly then, as now, this applied to some. But did he have no contact with enlightened Jewish teachers, such as Rabbi Hillel and his followers, whose abundant wisdom and good examples are found in the *Pirkei Avot* (the earliest talmudic teachings) and the Midrash? Or have his conversations with them simply been expunged from the record? He did, after all, eat in their homes on numerous occasions.

The warning about the gap between preaching and practicing has a particular irony in the verses that follow. We shall see how this teacher of humility, nonjudgment, unlimited forgiveness, loving neighbor and enemy alike, turns into the opposite, as the community's escalating anger creates a monster.

> [13]"Damn you, Torah scholars and Pharisees! Pious phonies! You slam the door to God's reign in people's faces. Not only do you not want to go in yourselves, but you won't even let in the people trying to enter.

> [15]"Damn you, Torah scholars and Pharisees! Pious phonies! Your proselytizing zeal leads you around the world to convert others, but you end up making them even more damnable than yourselves.

> [16]"Damn you, blind leaders! You teach people that oaths aren't binding if they're sworn by the Temple, but they are binding if they're sworn by the Temple's treasury! [17]Blind fools! Which is more important: the treasury or the Temple that makes the treasury holy? [18]You also teach that oaths aren't binding if they're sworn by the altar, but they are binding if they're sworn by the offering on the altar. [19]How blind you are! Which is more important: the offering or the altar that makes the offering holy? [20]Oaths sworn by the altar include all the offerings on it; [21]oaths sworn by the Temple include the God whose house the Temple is; [22]oaths sworn by heaven include both God's throne and the God who reigns from that throne.

> [23]"Damn you, Torah scholars and Pharisees! Pious phonies! You're so punctilious in paying your tithes on mint, dill, and

cumin, but you ignore what's most important in the Torah: justice, compassion, and trust. The tithing is fine, as long as these more important matters aren't ignored in the process. 24Blind guides! You strain out the gnat and then gulp down the camel.

25"Damn you, Torah scholars and Pharisees! Pious phonies! You scrub the outside of your cup and bowl, but what's inside them are greed and immorality. 26Blind Pharisees! First clean up what's inside your cup and bowl, then you can clean the outside, too.

27"Damn you, Torah scholars and Pharisees! Pious phonies! You're like newly painted mausoleums. From the outside they look beautiful, but inside there's nothing but the bones of dead people and pollution. 28This is just what you're like. You make an appearance of being God-centered, but inside you're phony and far from what the Torah is really about.

29"Damn you, Torah scholars and Pharisees! Pious phonies! You build tombs for the prophets and decorate the monuments of holy people. 30You tell us, 'If we had been alive in those days, we wouldn't have been part of the murder of these prophets.' 31You're admitting by your own words that you're the children of those who murdered the prophets. 32Now you're just finishing up what your parents started. 33You are snakes as well as being the offspring of snakes. How do you expect to escape damnation?

34It's for this reason that I send you prophets, teachers of wisdom, and Torah scholars. Some of these you kill on crosses; others you whip in your synagogues, chasing them from one town to another. 35As a result, the responsibility is yours for all the martyrs' blood that's been shed, from the God-centered Abel to Zecharaiah, Barachiah's son, whom you murdered between the sanctuary and the altar. 36Believe me when I tell you that the responsibility for all of this will fall on this generation." (Matt. 23:13–36)

Here we see clearly the entangled mixture of legitimate censure of religion gone awry, which comes from Jeshu, alongside a strident voice of anger and retribution that is utterly unlike him. Separating the two strands is a vital discernment, without which the beauty and power of Jeshu's teachings are contaminated and diluted at best, and turned into their opposite at worst. His litany of corrupt Temple policies, and his denunciation of the greed and immorality of the clergy, are straight out of the prophetic tradition. The pitfall for religious structures is the temptation and tendency to idolize themselves and thus impede what they should facilitate: closeness to God.

Jeshu decries the theological nit-picking over swearing of oaths and correct performance of rituals as an external emphasis that detracts from the interiority, the *kavanah,* of our actions. He rightly denounces the phoniness, the skewed priorities: "You strain out the gnat and then gulp down the camel" (with a sense of humor that is deliciously Jewish). When justice, compassion, and trust have been lost in concerns with tithing and money matters, when rite supplants right, the Temple (substitute church, mosque, or ashram) is worshiping itself. The whitewashed tombs with their gleaming facades surrounding putrefied flesh and bones is an apt image for this deterioration of godliness into deadness and decay. This is a desecration of the living God, "far from what the Torah is really about."

However, the language directed here at the scribes and Pharisees (who, it bears repeating, were Jeshu's ideological dialogue partners, not his enemies) in these scathing condemnations becomes so vituperative and mean-spirited that the prophetic message is tainted and perverted into an anti-Jewish diatribe. In addition to the "damn you" that begins each accusation, Jeshu resorts to public name-calling that is simply unworthy of him and directly contradicts all his prior teachings on human relations. (Contrast this with the language of Isa. 5, which repeats the phrase "woe to them," but never stoops to name-calling or vilification, even as he describes in detail the sins of Israel and the dire consequences that will result.) The insults move in a descent of consciousness from accusatory to disrespectful to dehumanizing and demonizing: from "pious phonies" to "blind leaders," from "blind guides" to "blind fools," and finally degenerating into "snakes" and "the offspring of snakes." Even the Pharisees' parents and ancestors are not exempt from attack and demonization, for snakes are not only subhuman but also associated with Satan.

This is not the way an enlightened teacher would speak to his adversaries, let alone his friends and dining companions. What kind of example does this set for conflict resolution, for handling anger appropriately, for engaging in dialogue, for treating others the way you want them to treat you? What does it mean to "love your enemies," to "judge not so you will not be judged" in the face of these demeaning judgments? When has consciousness ever been transformed by insults? Is this the same teacher who proclaimed, "Whoever insults a person will answer to the Sanhedrin, and whoever says to someone 'God damn you!' deserves a hell of fire" (Matt. 5:22)? Either Jeshu has developed a split personality (and Dr. Jekyll has become Mr. Hyde) or this vitriol comes not from him, but from his followers who have failed to assimilate his teachings. I vote for the latter.

This tirade has all the animosity of a political ad against a hated opponent. And indeed, by Matthew's time, the bitterness and backbiting on both sides was fierce. Rabbinic Jews (descended from the Pharisees) and Jeshu followers were battling it out, with the rabbinic Jews having the upper hand for the moment because they had legal status in the Roman Empire. Flogging in synagogues and denouncing the illicit Jeshu community to the Romans was a sad reality (in response to the Jeshu movement calling themselves the "true Israel" and berating their fellow Jews for not signing on to their version of Jeshu's program). This is the distortion and mutual nonrecognition that comes out of hatred and fear. It is the people in authority who miss the mark but are clueless regarding their own flaws who most provoke contempt; their arrogance stimulates our own egos into overdrive.

This distortion is exactly what happens here. Just when it seems that the attack on the Pharisees can't get any worse, all the righteous blood ever shed on earth (going back to the murdered Abel in Gen. 4) gets dumped onto the Jewish leaders' shoulders; they are held responsible for every such crime from the beginning of time. That such political malevolence is included in a sacred text is tragic testimony to our human woundedness and our tendency to turn pain and anger into blame and vengeance. That it is put into the mouth of the man understood as an incarnation of God is sacrilege. The tendency to turn outrage into retaliation, to fall victim to the compulsion to return ego blow for ego blow, is exactly what Jeshu was striving mightily to transform.

This segment illustrates in lurid color the double injustice that has been present in smaller doses throughout the gospel: an injustice to the Jews collectively (since they will bear the weight of these ugly denunciations) and to Jeshu himself, whose real teachings are obscured if not obliterated in the fire of this hatred. "The Jews" become seen as hypocritical, obstructionist, blind and foolish, wicked and damned, murderers and descendents of murderers, snakes and demons, responsible for all the evil in the world. Such descriptions set them up to become the ontological "other" that justifies their ongoing persecution and humiliation for centuries to come; these descriptions become the ammunition and justification for genocide.[2]

But hideous as this reality is, there is a larger, underlying tragedy at work here. This bite taken out of the heart of Jeshu's program for renewal and transformation has led to a persistent, pernicious misunderstanding and reversal of his most vital teachings. Loving our enemies (and effectively eliminating the category of enemy) becomes reviling and despising our enemies. Relinquishing judgment becomes an inquisition of judgments. Peacemaking and nonviolence become the Crusades and support for "holy wars." Egalitarianism—seeing everyone as inclusively created in God's image and treating them as brothers and sisters—becomes hierarchical exclusivity and damning to hell anyone who does not follow a strictly Christian agenda.

This undercutting of what could have been a leap in our collective human consciousness toward *tikkun olam* has been a monumental disaster on a worldwide scale. Truly, as Ron notes (quoting the Latin proverb), "the corruption of the best things is the worst kind of corruption."[3] It is incumbent upon us, Christians and Jews alike, to undo that reversal and restore the integrity of Jeshu's authentic teachings by repudiating what is false and practicing what is true. When we appreciate the universality of these teachings, that is, their relevance to all traditions, we can begin to integrate their wisdom and make them our own.

RM

The obscenity of putting some of these hateful sentiments in the mouth of Jeshu leaves us stunned. Who are the enemies of Jeshu, of what he taught and lived? The Jews, the atheists, the agnostics, the secularists, the terrorists? I think not. Jeshu has no more real enemies than the Christian authors who wrote these words and had the audacity to attribute them to Jeshu. Joining them are those Christians who, to this day, caught up in the trap of the dogma of biblical inerrancy, continue to teach that these are indeed Jeshu's sentiments and very words.

Biblical inerrancy is the dogma defining evangelical and fundamentalist Christianity. It is the pernicious doctrine that everything in the Bible is true and totally without error. Why do I call this doctrine pernicious? First of all, because it is idolatrous. Idolatry is the confusion of the relative and the absolute; by making a human text absolute, one has created a rival god. Second, because, as Bishop John Shelby Spong points out, "Sometimes the Bible is quite overtly evil; sometimes its truths are terrible."[4] Such a judgment is apt for these passages we are considering. These are, without a doubt, terrible texts.

Laura has done such an excellent job of exposing the problems in these texts that I have nothing to add except to say that it is precisely in this kind of commentary that there is hope for a better future. An honest look at the historical context of these texts will allow us one day to see and experience a Christianity that is good news without simultaneously being bad news for Jews, women, and homosexuals. But it must be stressed that this kind of progress is possible only when the dogma of biblical inerrancy has been exposed as erroneous.

Roman Catholics were saved from the trap of biblical inerrancy by the Dogmatic Constitution on Divine Revelation *(Dei Verbum)* promulgated on November 18, 1965. The council fathers rejected biblical inerrancy, stating instead that the scriptures teach without error "that truth which God, for the sake of our salvation, wished to see confided to the Sacred Scriptures."[5] In other words, we are to read the

Bible as a spiritual book, looking for the spiritual principles that are eternally true but not expecting to find inerrant truth about matters of science and geography, politics and sociology, history and etymology. In fact, Catholics are encouraged to pay attention to "the customary and characteristic patterns of perception, speech, and narrative which prevailed at the age of the sacred writer, and to the conventions which the people of the time followed in their dealings with one another."[6]

It is important to distinguish the argument that the Catholic Church and other mainline churches have with biblical inerrancy from any argument with the persons (evangelical or fundamentalist Christians) who embrace this dogma. Anyone in the mainline churches can certainly be humbled by the faith, the sense of prayer, and the genuine love of many of the Christians who accept this dogma. This argument is not with them but with an ideology that victimizes them and makes it impossible for them to learn from two thousand years of human knowledge and experience. If the inerrant truth is contained in this ancient text, then what purpose has been served by human thought since that time? Adherents of this dogma are frozen in a mind-set that accepts the subservience of slaves, the subordination of women, the excoriation of same-sex behavior, and the demonization of Jews.

Three of the most important projects for the world at this juncture may well be: the dialogue between moderate Jews and fanatic settlers, the dialogue between progressive Muslims and terrorists, and the dialogue between mainline Christians and overzealous fundamentalists. If these three dialogical projects fail—or if, as is more likely, they are never even launched—then the world is in grave peril indeed. And it is only by the abandonment of any claim to an infallible and inerrant text that these dialogues can even begin.

REFLECTIONS

1. Do I ever find myself condemning others through the language of prejudice and stereotype? What forms does that behavior take in my life?

2. Do I find these attitudes in any of the institutions with which I am affiliated? What forms does that behavior take in the lives of these institutions?

3. How can an honest discussion of the problems with the dogma of biblical inerrancy serve the goals of Jewish-Christian dialogue?

33

Christianity's Greatest Lie

¹When Jeshu had finished these teachings, he said to his disciples, ²"You know that Pesach is just two days away, and it is then that I will be handed over to be crucified." ³It was at this same time that the chief priests and the elders of the people gathered together in the palace of Kayafa, the high priest, ⁴where they plotted to arrest Jeshu secretly and kill him. ⁵But they said, "We can't do this at the time of the high holiday, or the people will riot." (Matt. 26:1–5)

LB

That the chief priests and elders—at the instigation of the Roman authorities—might have conspired to arrest Jeshu is conceivable. Jeshu's critique of the Temple system of God brokering threatened the status quo that enhanced their power and prestige. They were understandably on guard to root out any opposition to business as usual.

These corrupt few were in no way representative of the Jews collectively, who despised them as much as the oppressive Romans with whom they collaborated. Kayafa, the high priest, was appointed by Rome and was therefore a political rather than a spiritual leader. He would not have been respected by the Jewish populace.

That is why executing a Jewish freedom fighter could indeed provoke a riot among the people during Passover, a pilgrimage holiday when masses of Jews from all over the world gathered in Jerusalem to celebrate the Exodus story and make their sacrifices at the Temple. The themes of release from bondage and victory over the cruel dictates of Pharaoh (substitute Caesar) would be throbbing in every Jewish heart. The poor, powerless, and downtrodden—"the people" who would riot—were Jews, sympathetic to Jeshu's teachings, responsive to his message, and ripe for revolt. Thus, there were many groups of rebels dotting the countryside.

> [14]Then one of the twelve, the one called Judah from Kriot, went to the chief priests and said, [15]"What are you willing to give me if I turn this Jeshu over to you?" They agreed to pay him thirty silver coins. [16]And from that point on Judah started looking for a good opportunity to betray Jeshu. (Matt. 26:14–16)

LB

None of this rings true to me as fact. Jeshu, who taught in the Temple and before large crowds in the Galilee, was not an elusive figure. It would have been easy for the authorities to track him down and arrest him without the assistance of Judah. That the betrayer is the one disciple with an overtly Jewish name (meaning "the Jew," no less), and the only one to call Jeshu "Rabbi" (Matt. 26:25 and 26:49), suggests anti-Jewish midrash in the making. Putting that Jewish title in the mouth of the villain (the same mouth that will betray Jeshu with a kiss) taints the word *rabbi* with treason.

The theory that this is midrash is reinforced by the payment of thirty silver coins, which evokes two different biblical stories. One is the Joseph story at the end of Genesis. There, another Judah proposes selling his brother Joseph as a slave to the Midianites for twenty pieces of silver (Gen. 37:27). Unlike the totally despicable act of the present Judah, however, the earlier one saves Joseph's life. But that both Judahs were involved in acts of betrayal for which they were paid in pieces of silver seems more than coincidental. In another biblical story from the prophet Zechariah (11:12–13), the shepherd king of Israel was betrayed for thirty shekels of silver. Zechariah's text goes on to tell us that the money was hurled back into the Temple treasury, an action that may be the source of Judah's identical gesture in Matthew 27:5.

Judah's damnation in the mouth of Jeshu (Matt. 26:24) becomes two thousand years of tears and bitterness for his and Jeshu's Jewish brethren, who will be made to suffer mightily for this midrashic villain's misdeed.

RM

Christianity's greatest lie consists of four little words: "The Jews Killed Jesus." What we are seeing here is the mother lode from which this lie was mined. It begins with an alleged plot of priests and elders—sans Romans. It progresses with the villainy of a traitor who just happens to be named "the Jew." And it culminates with the story of a homicidal and blood-thirsty Jewish crowd calling down on their own heads an eternal curse as they profess their total loyalty to Caesar and the Roman Empire.

As Laura argues so well, the involvement of the high priest and a few community leaders (elders) is a believable scenario. What does not make sense, however, is the conspicuous absence of the Roman authorities. It's hard to believe that the Jewish religious leadership would have been exercised enough to arrest Jeshu without pressure from their Roman overlords. The high priest and his associates had surely seen more than enough Jewish death at Roman hands. There were times when the road to Jerusalem was lined with crucified Jews dying in agony. What Jew would want to see yet another crucifix?

Pontius Pilate, the Roman procurator, left his luxurious villa by the sea to reside in Jerusalem during the High Holidays as part of a crowd-control effort. A cruel and insensitive ruler, Pilate managed to insult the Jews with his every move. Surely he heard about the near riot in the Temple within hours of its occurrence. Did he then call Kayafa and some of his cronies to an emergency meeting? Jeshu's ministry was centered some sixty miles north of Jerusalem, where most of his followers lived. The Galilee was no place to have Jeshu arrested. But Jerusalem was now filled with Jews who did not know Jeshu, and his arrest could easily be arranged. This Galilean had fulminated against Caesar long enough with all his talk about God's reign.

Romans didn't like to do their own dirty work. That's why they had Jews serve as tax-collectors for their fellow Jews. So Jeshu was not to be arrested by Roman soldiers. Let Kayafa's private army arrest him late at night when most people were asleep. He certainly wouldn't be hard to find, since he was daily seen going in and out of the Temple precincts. Kayafa could bring Jeshu to Pilate the morning after his arrest. There were a couple of other freedom fighters who had to be dispatched before the holiday officially began at sunset, and Jeshu could easily be thrown in with them. It would all be over before the people knew what happened and the holiday could commence in peace, with one less headache for Pilate to be concerned about.

It was a Roman plot and it was the Roman imperial system that killed Jeshu. But from Mark's gospel to Mel Gibson's movie, history has been replaced by propaganda. The Romans are progressively exonerated. Pilate becomes a sensitive and sympathetic figure, even offering Jeshu a cup of water in the Gibson film. The Jews, however, are demonized, and a heartless Jewish crowd cries out to the Romans to kill one of their own people, a fellow Jew, a hasid whose whole ministry has been one of healing and helping the most neglected of his people. And so the terrible lie is born: "The Jews Killed Jesus."

REFLECTIONS

1. What was the context in which I first heard the story of Jeshu's arrest and execution? Who were the villains in the story?

2. Have I recently heard the story in the context of a Christian liturgy or adult educational program? Who were the villains then?

3. How can those four fateful words ("The Jews Killed Jesus") serve as a focus for Jewish-Christian conversations?

34

A Final Meal

²⁶After they resumed eating, Jeshu took some matzah, blessed it, broke it, and gave it to his disciples, saying, "Take this and eat it; this is my body." ²⁷He also took a cup of wine, blessed it, and gave it to them, saying, "Drink from this, all of you; ²⁸for this is my blood of the covenant, blood poured out for many, so that the sins of many will be forgiven. ²⁹I'm telling you now that I will not drink the fruit of the vine again until I drink new wine with you where my heavenly Parent reigns." (Matt. 26:26–29)

LB

I agree with Ron's assessment that a Jewish teacher would probably not speak metaphorically of drinking blood, given the taboo against it in Jewish law, which is deeply engrained in Jewish sensibility.[1] Blood is scrupulously avoided in the laws of kashrut; all the blood is to be drained out of an animal before it is fit for consumption. The notion of drinking blood in any form would be considered an abomination. Granted, Jeshu was a breaker of some powerful taboos—he reached out to lepers, fraternized with prostitutes, and was not alarmed by the touch of a bleeding woman. But those breaches all concerned inclusivity and egalitarianism; they are in line with his views on loving neighbor as self. Rather than saying, "this is my body; this is my blood," it is more likely that Jeshu said something like: "As this matzah is in you, I am in you; as this wine becomes part of you, I am part of you. Now nourish one another, as I nourish you." In this way, food and drink become powerful symbols of how we are to share our substance, our essence, our abundance of being with one another, and thereby become whole.

While we don't know what the wine represented at Seders in the year 30—Seder ritual evolved over the centuries—the four cups of wine have come to represent specific phrases of Torah, each being one of God's promises to Israel. The first cup signifies relief from oppression: "I will free you from the labors of the Egyptians." The second cup promises deliverance: "I will deliver you from their bondage." The third cup is for redemption: "I will redeem you with an outstretched arm" (all Exod. 6:6). The fourth cup is the promise of belonging to God: "I will take you to be My people, and I will be your God" (Exod. 6:7). The cup of Elijah is a fifth cup, poured but not drunk, representing messianic hope and the cup of *tikkun olam*.

These quintessential Jewish meanings also correspond to the kingdom of God that Jeshu proclaims. Relief from corrupt authority's oppressive grip, deliverance from bondage to Caesar, redemption from arrogant power structures, and fulfillment of the longing to be close to God are all part of his understanding of God's reign. But unlike the Exodus story, where redemption is dramatically visible in a series of external events (plagues, the parting of the sea, the drowning of Pharaoh's army, the revelation at Sinai), Jeshu is speaking primarily to an internal process of discovering God. The external events of his day and century did not promise redemption: Rome did not fall swiftly from power; persecution continued; the Temple fell; and Jewish suffering intensified.

Jeshu advocated the deliverance that is available regardless of circumstance: the relief and fulfillment of a transformed consciousness. These two teachings do not contradict one another; redemption from a cruel Pharaoh and release from the bonds of our own hatred, greed, and fear are complementary freedoms. And, of course, the Torah speaks to both. Jewish mystic that he is, Jeshu emphasizes the interior journey that God's reign requires. Relationship as mutual indwelling, as communion, is central to this journey.[2]

As for the "blood of the covenant" poured out "so that the sins of many will be forgiven," this, too, is a later addendum from Matthew's community. The leap from the communion paradigm—"I am in you and you are in me"—to spilled blood as a covenant for the forgiveness of sins is not Jeshu's leap. He may well have been anticipating his crucifixion, but that he viewed his death as an atoning sacrifice upon which a new religion should be based has no basis in his teachings or outlook. He may well have objected to animal sacrifice, but that he substituted his own bloody sacrifice in its stead contradicts his teachings. The sanctity of every human life and a passionate commitment to nonviolence are at the heart of his program. Forgiveness for sins comes from unity with neighbors (enemies and friends alike) and God—this loving, serving, mutually enhancing relationship is the essence of *teshuvah* and communion. It provides atonement through at-one-ment.

Ron speaks of Jeshu's broken body and poured-out blood as emblematic of his human vulnerability remembered in the bread and wine of communion, and that makes sense.[3] But while the way he poured out his life in loving service to others provides an essential example of how we are to live, it was not essential that Jeshu be brutally murdered for his body of wisdom to become food for our souls. Perhaps had he been granted as long a life as Moses or the Buddha, his message of how to live nonviolently and compassionately would not have been so easily co-opted and corrupted and would not be so consistently ignored two thousand years later.

RM

As long as there are Christians on this planet, there are two things they will most likely do. They will immerse in water or pour water on new members of their community, and they will share bread and wine with one another in a common meal. This communion connotes a union with God, with Jeshu, and with one another. It's a celebration, a way of giving thanks (the word *Eucharist* comes from the Greek word for thanking), and a way of blessing God in community.

From the beginning of Christianity, however, this ritual meal has been interpreted in different ways. Christians are most familiar with the interpretation that appears in Paul's writings in the 50s and then becomes a part of the tradition feeding into Mark, Matthew, and Luke. And yet, there were radically different understandings of this communion from the very beginning. The Didache, an early church manual, for example, describes a communion celebration in which there is no mention of Jeshu's death and nothing connecting the bread and wine with his body and blood. The Didache community gives thanks over the cup of wine for "the holy vine of David" made known through Jeshu, God's servant. And then the community thanks God over the broken bread for "the life and knowledge" made known to them through God's servant, Jeshu.[4]

At least two currents of understanding exist from the beginning, one viewing Jeshu as redeemer and the other seeing him as reminder. The tradition of Paul is strongly redemptive and shapes most Christian thought to this day. But the tradition found in the Didache (and in numerous other early Christian documents) speaks of a gnosis, a transforming knowledge bringing in its wake immortal life. The redemptive theology focuses on sin and its expiation and is exclusivist in viewing other religions. The gnosis tradition tends to be inclusive, grateful for all that is given through Jeshu but recognizing other ways in which the divine mystery can be mediated to humankind.

The communion meal, which should be a sign of union, can become a weapon against nonconformity. Heretics can be excommunicated, literally cut off from the communion. In certain American cities today, some Catholic priests will not give communion to any of the faithful wearing emblems signifying their support of homosexuals. Ironically, in Nazi Germany, the bishops decided that it was all right for someone to approach communion wearing a swastika. But perhaps Nazis can be more easily tolerated since they, too, are enemies of Jews and homosexuals.

Orthodox Christians (Greek, Russian, Serbian, etc.) refuse to share communion with anyone outside of their denomination, as do certain conservative Protestant groups, such as Missouri and Wisconsin Synod Lutherans. Other Christians support an open communion, as does the radical Jesuit priest, Fr. Dan Berrigan, who gave communion to Thich Nhat Hanh, a Buddhist monk. Perhaps we will never know what Jeshu intended that fateful night before his arrest and execution. But certainly those of his disciples who interpret that final meal in a spirit of love are closer to Jeshu's intentions than those who see it as a weapon of rejection and condemnation.

REFLECTIONS

1. What is my view of the communion ritual celebrated by Christians?

2. Have I observed or experienced communion rituals in Christian churches? What was my impression of those experiences?

3. How can this communion ritual serve as a focus for Jewish-Christian dialogue?

35

The Unbearable Curse

¹⁵It was the governor's custom to release a prisoner—anyone the crowd asked for—at the time of the high holiday. ¹⁶There was a notorious prisoner in jail at that time, a man named Jeshu Bar-Abba. ¹⁷So when the crowd was gathered together, Pilate asked them, "Do you want me to release for you Jeshu Bar-Abba or Jeshu who is called the Messiah?" ¹⁸Pilate asked this, knowing full well that the chief priests and elders had arrested Jeshu out of spite. ¹⁹While Pilate was sitting there as judge, his wife sent him a message: "Have nothing to do with that God-centered man; I had a disturbing dream last night about him." ²⁰Meanwhile, the chief priests and the elders persuaded the crowd to ask Pilate to free Bar-Abba and have Jeshu put to death. ²¹"Which of these two men do you want me to release for you?" asked the governor. And they answered, "Bar-Abba." ²²Pilate then asked them, "So what shall I do with this Jeshu who is called the Messiah?" They all said, "Crucify him." ²³But Pilate

asked,"What crime has he committed?" But they shouted all the more,"Crucify him." 24When Pilate saw that his efforts were useless and that there were even signs of a possible riot, he took some water, washed his hands in front of everyone, and said,"I'm innocent of this man's blood; he's your responsibility." 25Then all the people answered, "Let his blood be on us and on our children." (Matt. 27:15–25)

LB

The "custom" of releasing a prisoner at a time when the city was teeming with potentially rebellious peasant pilgrims is pure fantasy. To release a "notorious" political prisoner who would be capable of agitating a Passover crowd into protest against Roman occupation would be an incredibly poor administrative decision. Even a procurator as insensitive as Pilate might have glimpsed the similarity between Caesar and Pharaoh in Jewish minds. As Ron points out, "However unimaginative the Romans were in their rule, they were not dumb."[1] So why did the gospel writer (in this case Mark, from whom Matthew borrows it) invent such a tale?

We've been noting the steady move away from Roman culpability in the arrest and death of Jeshu, with Jewish culpability flooding in to fill the gap. Here is a story that ironically transforms Pilate—notorious for his cruelty and ruthlessness, finally removed from his post by Rome after brutally murdering a group of Samaritans (even by Roman standards he went too far), virulently anti-Jewish, adept at vicious tactics for crowd control—into the well-meaning pawn of a vindictive Jewish crowd. Side by side we have character exoneration (Pilate) and character assassination (the Jews). This is whitewashing of the merciless Pilate (whose behavior we know about from the historical writings of Philo and Josephus) into a kind, somewhat bumbling governor who tries to release Jeshu but is prevented from doing so by the malicious mob of Jews. Such distortion overlooks obvious Roman authority and substitutes Jewish guilt for the death of Jeshu. Even Pilate's wife gets into the act, with her dream warning him of Jeshu's innocence.

There is another explanation for the creation of Bar-Abba, whose name means "son of the father" in Aramaic. The name intimately connects him to Jeshu, almost like a twin. But this "son of the father" is a bandit or rebel (or freedom fighter, depending on one's perspective in the matter)—he is the prototype for the Zealots who advocated military overthrow of Rome, in contrast to Jeshu's nonviolent program of resistance. Unfortunately, it was the Zealots' military strategy that prevailed, leading to the Great Revolt against Rome in 66 and ending in the year 70 with a terrible defeat for the Jews. The gospel is written after that fact, and Bar-Abba's release in this narrative represents the fateful choice of Jerusalem, which unwisely chose armed rebellion over Jeshu's alternative of God's reign.[2] As Ron points out, shifting the political accusations entirely onto Bar-Abba leaves Jeshu as a purely religious martyr, which is more palatable to most Christians.[3] It works as midrash, but has no historical basis.

We are confronted with a chilling scenario that, despite its factual absurdity, has been widely accepted as "gospel truth," leaving a devastating legacy of hatred and violence against Jews in its wake. According to this fantasy, the chief priests and elders accomplish the Machiavellian task of convincing the crowd to insist upon the death of a beloved Jewish teacher and healer. This crowd supposedly consists of the same people who have been devotedly listening to Jeshu in the Temple, admiring his egalitarian agenda and prophetic voice, who have been touched by his compassion and awed by his healings. But we are asked to believe that the very authorities this crowd mistrusts and dislikes can produce, as if by magic, a complete change of attitude toward Jeshu so that they cry out as one body, "Crucify him!" And we are even to believe that the previously tyrannical Pilate who tolerates no dissent is here turned weak and helpless against the unruly crowd's demands—even frightened by them. Much as he would prefer to save this hapless Jew from crucifixion, he accedes to the mob's bloodthirsty wishes and washes his hands of the whole affair, putting all the responsibility squarely upon them.

This brings us to the most condemning moment in the entire gospel, a verse whose weight is almost unbearable for the suffering that it has caused, for the harm that it has heaped upon millions: "Then all the people answered, 'Let his blood be on us and on our children.'" The blood of the innocents cries out against these words. The enormity of this distortion and its impact, which puts collective guilt on an entire people and their children in perpetuity, is agonizing and almost ungraspable. This misrepresentation has led to nearly two thousand years of persecution, hatred, revilement, torture, and murder. The damage that has been done, the brutality inflicted on Jeshu's own people, who are effectively being crucified alongside him, cannot be enumerated, cannot be overstated, cannot be understood by reason or insanity. Such a curse is emblematic of the worst that human beings are capable of devising. It comes out of the imagination of those who have been blinded by hatred and fear, those whose wounds have inspired vindictiveness rather than healing. It takes the truth and beauty of a loving God and turns it into an ungodly perversion.

There is a footnote to this verse in the Pilgrim Edition of the New Testament, the King James Version, "with notes especially adapted for young Christians." A close friend who wished to convert me to Christianity at the tender age of seventeen gave this copy of the Bible to me forty years ago. His intentions were good and his concern for me was genuine. The footnote reads, "Do we not have here the reason for the suffering of the Jewish people during the last nineteen centuries?" There is no irony intended; the blood indictment is seen as a logical explanation for all the miseries Jews have endured throughout the ages at the hands of so-called Christians. There is no awareness of the diabolical distortion of this curse, put in the mouths of the Jewish people to condemn themselves and their offspring, no awareness that their nineteen hundred years of suffering comes from falsehood, no awareness that such persecution contradicts everything Jeshu lived and died for.

Ron's summation is clear and concise: "The attempt to tell the story in such a way as to exonerate the Romans is pulling Matthew into the great lie that the Jews, not the Roman imperial system, killed Jeshu."[4] The last redactor of this text could have no idea of the enormous evil this sentence would perpetrate in history. Significantly, this line appears only in Matthew's gospel, and it can be contrasted to a line that appears only in Luke's gospel, words of Jeshu just after he has been hung on the cross: "Father, forgive them; for they do not know what they are doing" (Luke 23:34). Yet because this line of forgiveness is omitted in several important ancient texts, its authenticity is open to question. Contemporary Christian scholars Raymond Brown and John Dominic Crossan suggest the line was excised because "they found it too favorable to the Jews." Crossan's extraordinary book *Who Killed Jesus?* includes Brown's reflection, "It is ironical that perhaps the most beautiful sentence in the passion narrative should be textually doubtful." Crossan adds, "It is doubly ironical, and just as significant, that no Christian copyist ever excised that 'blood be upon us' verse from Matthew 27:25."[5] God have mercy on the souls who

created this punishing line, who sustained its infamous lie, who per-
petuated its blood-soaked condemnation; God have mercy on the
community who sanctioned it and canonized it.

RM

How many Jews have been called "Christ killers" because of this verse?
How many Jews have been insulted and beaten because of this
verse? How many Jews have been killed because of this verse? This
curse leaves no Jew untargeted. Every Jew born into this world until the
end of human history is marked by this curse. How can anyone believe
that such a text is inerrant, that it is something God intended to be part
of divine revelation, something that should be accepted as literally
shouted out by a Jewish mob on that fateful day, April 7, 30 CE?

This verse and the theology behind it remained unchallenged by
Christian saints and scholars for centuries. The first major refutation
occurred as part of the Second Vatican Council. This terrible lie was
finally addressed in the document *Nostra Aetate* (Declaration on the
Relations of the Church to Non-Christian Religions) on October 28,
1965.[6] The document is flawed in many ways. Both Thomas Merton,
a Trappist monk, and Rabbi Abraham Joshua Heschel, a leading
Jewish scholar, had hoped that the council would write a separate document on the church's relationship to Jews and Judaism, since that constituted such a wounded and lengthy shared history. Instead the
document lumps Jews together with Hindus, Buddhists, Muslims, and
everyone else who is "non-Christian." Furthermore, no real spirit of
repentance breathes in the text. Nevertheless, flawed as it was, an
important milestone was reached: a corner had been turned, and a new
era for the church's relationship with Jews and Judaism was dawning.

The document first addresses the big lie, the claim that "The Jews

Killed Jesus." It states explicitly, "neither all Jews indiscriminately at that time, nor Jews today, can be charged with the crimes committed during his passion." Second, the document rejects the curse and its two-thousand-year legacy of suffering for the Jewish people: "The Jews should not be spoken of as rejected or accursed, as if this followed from Holy Scripture." Third, the document declares, "… she [the church] deplores all hatred, persecutions, displays of anti-Semitism leveled at any time or from any source against the Jews."[7]

A battle was won, but the war was far from over. A statement of sincere repentance would have been welcome, not simply the vague condemnation of anti-Semitism "from any source." A more frankly pluralistic position could have been taken, including the clear assertion that Jews are saved as Jews through their own covenantal relationship to God. In other words, Jews relate to God through the Torah and not through anything that was mediated through Jeshu. The same, of course, could have been said of Muslims and Hindus and people of other religions. But this further agenda, neglected in 1965, still remains to be addressed today.

REFLECTIONS

1. What attitudes toward Jews and Judaism and toward Christians and Christianity did I pick up as a child?

2. What attitudes toward Jews and Judaism and toward Christians and Christianity do I notice from private conversations, from religious statements, or from the media today?

3. How can this "unbearable curse" become a focus for contemporary Jewish-Christian dialogue?

36

Worse Than Liars

11While the women were on their way, some of the guards went back to the city to tell the chief priests everything that had happened. 12The chief priests met with the elders and made plans to bribe the guards 13and instruct them to tell everybody that Jeshu's disciples had come during the night and stolen the corpse while they were sleeping. 14They also told the guards that if the governor got wind of the matter, they would take care of him, and the guards would have nothing to worry about. 15So the guards took the bribe and did what they were told, and this is the story the Jews are still spreading around today. (Matt. 28:11–15)

LB

We have here the aftermath of Jeshu's agonized death, which prior to these verses included the rupture of the two communities symbolized by the ripped Temple curtain, and the mystery of his resurrection symbolized by the empty tomb. These are powerful, penetrating, and provocative images.

Now we move from the sublime—resurrection as a holy metaphor for the movement from death to life that is God's reign—to the ridiculous. When the focus is on a literal empty tomb (a later assertion, since as Ron points out, none of Paul's letters from the 50s refers to it),[1] the stage is set for the unproductive arguments of the 80s that are reflected in these verses. "The tomb was empty" is countered by "the corpse was stolen." "The tomb was guarded" is countered by "why, then, did the guards say nothing about an angel, an earthquake, and a man raised from the dead?" which is further countered by "the guards were bribed to keep quiet."

The argument defies human nature and credulity. Just as Jeshu was entirely unsuccessful in preventing people from talking about his healings, what guard would allow a few shekels to stand in the way of sharing this amazing story? It further demonizes the Jewish leadership as well, portraying them as deliberately defying God's will by subverting the truth, and it implicates all "the Jews" for believing and spreading the falsehood. Ironically, the last line could properly read, "and this is the story the Christians are still spreading around today" and have equal validity. Such polemic keeps us on the surface and prevents us from entering the deeper waters of resurrection's universal reality.

> [16]The eleven disciples went to the hill in the Galilee where Jeshu had told them to go. [17]When they saw him, they fell down at his feet, though some of them held back. [18]Jeshu came close to them and talked with them. "I have been given all authority in heaven and on earth. [19]Go and make disciples from every people, immersing them in the name of the Father, the Son, and the

Holy Spirit. [20]Teach them to obey everything that I've commanded you. And remember that I'm always with you, right up
to the day when this present world order ends." (Matt. 28:16–20)

LB

These final verses, like so much of the preceding gospel, contain a mixture of timeless truth and a particular historical community's interpretation of that truth. Jeshu's teachings and life example transformed the disciples of his day, and they continue to touch, inspire, and transform multitudes of followers to this day. He is a living presence in the hearts and minds of everyone who derives nourishment from his teachings, who takes seriously his revolutionary agenda for implementing Torah, for sharing and caring for one another in radically new ways. For his disciples to have experienced him as alive after his death speaks to the quality of unquenchable love they shared— eternal love, stronger than death, transcending finite physical boundaries. This is the kind of love that is emblematic of God's reign, where we become food for one another, where we share our deepest selves in a spiritual intimacy so complete that we become part of one another. Then we truly love one another as ourselves.

However, the depiction in these verses of the disciples falling at his feet and worshiping him speaks not of Jeshu's vision of God's reign, with its radical egalitarianism and dismantling of lordship power structures, but of the later community's wish to invest him with that mantle. Did those who "held back" see the contradiction in this behavior? Jeshu's authority is expressed precisely by his insistence on eliminating all oppressive models of authority—the domination of master over servant, the injustice of patriarchy, the inequality of all categories of social status, the violence and arrogance of empire—and substituting a new order where equality and mutuality of love and life-giving purpose reign supreme. His willingness to die for that vision of God's reign has further enlivened his presence for all who seek sustenance in his love and wisdom. Physical death is only the prelude for ongoing life, which is available both while we live and after we die.

As for the injunction to make "disciples from every people" and to baptize them in the name of the Trinity, we are hearing the later community's zeal and growing theological sophistication, rather than words that came from Jeshu himself. Certainly the "Father, Son, and Holy Spirit" language was not in his vocabulary. His intention was a radical spiritual renewal, not a new religion. I suspect he would have admired the new wine in fresh wineskins that rabbinic Judaism became as it arose from the ashes to sing unto God a new song in the centuries after the destruction of the Temple, as it struggled to reinterpret and renew Jewish worship and practice, as it produced the gems of the Talmud and the philosophic and midrashic literature, as it made way for the mystical tradition to flourish.

I know Jeshu would have been appalled at the stream of atrocities committed in his name, agonized when the mandate to "make disciples of every people" turned into a commission of evil, as followers misconstrued the word of God with the word of their own deified human ego. From it ensued the forced conversions; the brutal torture of Jews, Muslims, and "heretics"; the murderous Crusades, the Inquisition, and the pogroms; the unspeakable horror of the Holocaust. Rivers of blood wail and Jeshu is crucified again every time an act of violence and hatred, of contempt and arrogance, occurs through those who subvert his message of peacemaking and compassion, of equality and inclusivity, and twist it into its opposite.

Yet the roots of such subversion are to be found in the very scriptures that carry Jeshu's magnificent message. It has been the purpose of this volume to examine the first gospel with an eye that sees the inconsistencies, an ear that hears the discordant notes, and a heart that cries out against the injustice and harm to the man, his message, and his people (indeed, all people) when his voice is muted by the strident voice of polemic.

The historical backdrop for these distortions has been referred to repeatedly: two Jewish communities of the 80s locked in bitter hostility toward one another as they fight for the soul of Judaism under the heel of Roman occupation and oppression. When the gospels were being written, the rabbinic Jews had the upper hand and the marginalized Jeshu movement was suffering mightily under the combination of their authority and Roman cruelty. It became expedient to excuse the Romans and blame the Jews for all the ills of the day. Thus, the authors of these inspired sacred writings inserted their own prejudices, fears, and hatreds alongside the sublimity of Jeshu's authentic teachings. Revelation is from God, but interpretation is filtered through flawed, often wounded human beings and cultural contexts. None of our sacred scriptures is immune from this dilemma. As soon as Christianity became the state religion of the Roman Empire, the tables would turn with a vengeance and the Jews would become the tragic victims of this canonized prejudice.

But beyond the enormity of harm to the Jewish people is the larger harm done by contaminating and weakening the purity and power of Jeshu's program for *tikkun olam*. When "love your enemies" becomes "demonize and damn your enemies," then "pray for those who persecute you" becomes "persecute those who persecuted you." When "judge not lest you be judged" becomes "throw him into the outer darkness where he'll weep and grind his teeth in despair," then "forgive unstintingly" becomes "his blood be on us and on our children." The very heart has been removed from Jeshu's most radical and crucial teachings about the kingdom of God.

If Christians can make these kinds of exceptions to Jeshu's teachings in order to exclude the Jews, then the door opens to "holy wars" against any and all perceived opposition to God's reign. The justification of violence over peacemaking, of making war against our neighbors over loving them, has been the legacy of these distortions. The assertion that some are worthier than others, and the division into categories of saved and damned, have countered Jeshu's insistence on the absolute unconditionality of God's love and providence. It has inhibited the interfaith work toward planetary salvation that desperately needs to happen as Jews, Christians, Muslims, Hindus, Buddhists, and every other path to the center cooperate with mutual respect, each contributing its unique insights and best efforts to the well-being and healing of our precious, wounded world.

Whereas the above remarks contain an underlying plea to Christians to pay attention to the "real" Jeshu in their midst, I would like to close with a plea to my fellow Jews. Jeshu, one of our own, has been excluded from our sacred body of wisdom long enough. He has been excluded for understandable historical reasons. How could we embrace a brother whose name was invoked so regularly to produce hatred and malice against us? We, too, have been misled into misunderstanding the authentic teachings and inspired offerings of this God-saturated Jewish sage and mystic. We have blamed him for the sins of some of his misguided followers (just as we were unfairly blamed for the sins of a few of our misguided forefathers). Blame, whether fair or not, is a singularly doomed response to conflict resolution. It is time to move beyond it, to let go of resentment, mistrust, and fear and welcome back this long-lost rebbe into the fold of our most respected, revered teachers and zaddikim (holy ones).

Whether an avatar (a divine incarnation) or "merely" an enlightened sage, Jeshu has something vital to add to Jewish discourse. Jewish hearts and minds need to wrestle with what it means to love our enemies and pray for our persecutors. Most of the world has not caught on to this oh-so-Jewish elaboration of the great precept in Leviticus 19:18. Perhaps if we were to warm to it, it would catch fire and peacemaking could become a reality instead of a longed-for fantasy. Wounded as we've been, we need to examine further the deep waters of forgiveness to see what treasures we can find regarding how to love and to forgive our neighbors as ourselves. As revolutionary as Judaism is—with our God of transformation from what is to what ought to be,[2] with our mysticism that involves partnership with God in effecting social justice and cocreating a healed, transformed world—we need to look at Jeshu's revolutionary agenda for replacing domination with communion consciousness and hierarchy with equality.[3] None of these suggestions involves being unfaithful to our covenant with God, to our relationship with Torah, or to our identity as Jews. On the contrary, to love the stranger and welcome him into our midst is quintessentially Jewish. Let's pull up a chair for Jeshu at our table. Let all who are hungry come and eat.

RM

Those few words—"and this is the story the Jews are still spreading around today"—break through the life-world of the story being told about events in the 20s and thrust us into the life-world of the battles being fought in the 80s, the fiercely polemical period following the Temple's destruction. With these few words, a veil is lifted and it all becomes clear. Stories and counterstories continue to circulate for several decades after the actual events written about in this gospel. The gospel in our hands is part of that polemical exchange. This gospel is not "gospel truth." It must be read, as *Nostra Aetate* teaches, with an understanding of its context, the prevailing patterns of thought and speech at the time the text was written.[4] And yet, this is precisely what most Christians, and indeed most churches, have not yet learned in these forty years since the Vatican document was promulgated.

If we don't learn to contextualize this text of Matthew, then we cannot escape its internal logic, which claims that the Jews are not only liars but are also consciously working to keep people from knowing God's truth, God's Messiah, God's plans for the world's salvation. But how can anyone or any group be so diametrically opposed to God? Only by their alliance with Satan. And so the demonization of the Jews intensifies with this text. The visions of Anne Catherine Emmerich, the German nun whose writings had such a profound influence on Mel Gibson, are filled with scenes in which devils surround the Jews at every point in the story of Jeshu's arrest, torture, and death. And this whole ugly history culminates in a well-known Nazi slogan: "Whoever fights against the Jews, wrestles with the Devil."

I'm saddened at the continued popularity of the obscenely anti-Semitic Mel Gibson film, *The Passion of the Christ*. The videotapes are being sold all over in Christian bookstores and provide "an educational film" for Christian Sunday school teachers. No American bishop has decried the errors of this film. And yet, surveys have revealed that people seeing the film are twice as likely to believe that "The Jews Killed Jesus" than those who have not seen the film. At the time of the Holocaust, only 1 percent of Catholic and Protestant clergymen in Europe spoke out. By and large, the churches remained silent, including the Catholic Church and its pope, Pius XII. Today, the churches are again silent in the face of this new affront to Jeshu, his message, and his ministry. As one rabbi friend of mine has stated, this movie alone has pushed Jewish-Christian dialogue back by fifty years.

So where do we go from here? Laura's appeal to her fellow Jews is astonishingly generous and compassionate. What comparable appeal can I make to my fellow Christians? First, we must honestly and profoundly repent of the crimes against the Jews committed by Christians, Christian churches, and Christian texts (including some of the texts in the Christian Testament). Second, repentance must be accompanied by a firm purpose of amendment, the resolve to commit these crimes no more. Third, this repentance and resolve must be joined by a commitment to the work that must be done to grow beyond our wounded history into an era of mutual respect, dialogue, and love.

Nostra Aetate is rooted in *Dei Verbum*. That is to say, the document on non-Christian religions, especially in its reflections on the church's shared history with the Jewish people, presupposes the rejection of biblical literalism and inerrancy found in the document on revelation. The only way to move beyond an anti-Semitic Christianity is by moving beyond the dogma of a literal and inerrant scriptural text. Dismantling this erroneous view of scripture and revelation is a first and preeminently necessary step toward the goals we envision.

My final appeal to my fellow Christians would be not only to read this book, but also to call together small groups of Jews and Christians to discuss this book paragraph by paragraph, using the questions at the end of each chapter. This can be done in adult educational settings, in Sunday school classes for adolescents, or in family rooms with friends. With so little help coming from the leaders of the Christian churches, though there are exceptions such as Bishop John

Shelby Spong, we have to rely on the grass roots. I would challenge each and every Christian reading this book to become the yeast that can cause the heavy dough of human consciousness to rise. And from that dough of a more enlightened consciousness we can bake a truly wonderful and nourishing bread for all of us at God's table to share.

REFLECTIONS

1. What have I learned from this book?
2. How can I share what I have learned with my family, my coworkers, and my coreligionists?
3. How can I implement these ideas in concrete experiences of Jewish-Christian dialogue?

Invitation to the Reader

The completion of this book ends one phase of its growth and begins another. Our long collaboration and lengthy discussion of texts, our flurry of e-mail messages back and forth, our editing and reediting the material—all this activity has come to an end. But the Latin motto reminds us: *Verba volant sed scripta manent*—"Words fly but what is written remains." The work that gave birth to this text is over, and now it moves on with a life of its own.

We trust that this new life is a fertile beginning. Tracing how the anti-Jewish bias develops in the first of the twenty-seven books of the Christian Testament will lead the careful reader to be alert to this development in the other twenty-six. This is a pressing challenge to our readers. Beyond that, it is a moral imperative for all those who preach these texts or teach them in Sunday schools, adult education sessions, high schools, or university settings.

Readers who go on to read *Constantine's Sword* by James Carroll might be led to explore the way these seeds of anti-Semitism spread like toxic weeds over the next two thousand years, contaminating virtually every soil of our small planet. Progress in weeding out this hateful prejudice must include some familiarity with its tragic history of blood libels, pogroms, ghettos, the Inquisition, expulsions, the

Crusades, and persecutions of every type. Vestiges of this history live on in countless ways. Bombings of synagogues, desecration of Jewish cemeteries, and a resurgence of interest in the notorious forgery that inspired Hitler, *Protocols of the Elders of Zion* (depicting Jews as part of an evil conspiracy to take over the world), are among the more heinous contemporary examples. Even the seemingly innocuous custom of Christians eating an Easter ham has its roots in anti-Semitism: during the greater part of our shared history, eating pork on the holiest day in the Christian calendar was a way of differentiating "true believers" from the "cursed Jews."

Deep dialogue between Jews and Christians is, of course, only a beginning. Islam is now part of American mainline religions, and the dialogue must reach out to include this third great faith descended from Abraham. We all need to grow beyond our tribal boundaries. The sign outside the synagogue that reads "We Support Israel" needs to be replaced with a sign that says "We Support Israel and a Palestinian State Living Together in Peace." The appeals in Muslim magazines to help Palestinian children injured by Israeli incursions into the Palestinian territories need to include an appeal to raise money for Israeli children injured by Palestinian suicide bombers.

We cannot survive as a planetary community if we continue to focus only on the enclaves in which we live. Can we Americans see the world through the eyes of Iranians? They are living surrounded by two American-occupied states with a nuclear-armed Israeli state close by. Does it make sense that they might not totally trust U.S. interests and want some nuclear leverage in the tense world of the Middle East? Can citizens in developing nations understand Americans who take their affluent and high energy-consuming lifestyle for granted? Can Americans understand the resentment this lifestyle generates in the 2.4

billion people who are living on less than one thousand dollars a year? Do Muslims understand how painful it is for Jews when the old anti-Semitic canards used so long by Christians are now gaining new life in many Muslim circles? Do Jews and Christians understand how much it hurts Muslims when all adherents of the faith of Islam are lumped together as fanatic terrorists?

Dialogue is demanding and difficult. It is often painful. It entails deep listening, letting others define themselves, and being willing to confront and transform deep-rooted prejudices in ourselves. It requires the courage to re-envision absolutely everything we tend to cherish and protect, and to relinquish our entrenched vainglorious ego attachments, our inflated sense of "I, me, and mine." This challenge to grow beyond tribalism, to approach others in a fair and reasonable way, is an essential step in our human evolution. It is a step away from violence, warfare, greed, and alienation and a step toward the generosity and joy that accompanies harmonious relationships. When we can stretch enough to appreciate and incorporate the encompassing vision of the great mystics who have moved among us—luminaries such as Jeshu and Muhammad, Rumi and Gandhi, Abraham Joshua Heschel and Martin Luther King Jr.—then we will have learned how to love our neighbor *as* ourself. We can survive only if we are willing to be stretched in this direction of love and unity consciousness.

It is our hope that this book will offer what is a relatively small stretch in the grand scheme of things. But each stretch, however small, allows the next to be a bit deeper. Finally, we attain the necessary suppleness: an enlivened heart that longs for a world free from hatred and rivalry, a vast mind that embraces all humanity as one family, and a powerful will that is strong enough and determined enough to do the great work of *tikkun olam*—the healing of all rifts, the transformation of all hearts. Thus will it come to pass that our small collaboration can be a seed of the large collaboration for which we were born, the flowering of a world community of justice, peace, and love.

Notes

CHAPTER 1: WHAT IS A MESSIAH?

1. Byron Sherwin, "Who Do You Say That I Am?" in *Jesus Through Jewish Eyes: Rabbies and Scholars Engage an Ancient Brother in a New Conversation*, ed. Beatrice Bruteau (Maryknoll, N.Y.: Orbis Books, 2001), 40.
2. Ron Miller, *The Hidden Gospel of Matthew: Annotated and Explained* (Woodstock, Vt.: SkyLight Paths Publishing, 2004), xxiv–xxv.
3. Ibid., 6.

CHAPTER 2: A MIRACULOUS BIRTH?

1. Miller, *Hidden Gospel of Matthew,* 6.
2. Ibid., 8.

CHAPTER 3: A HOMICIDAL JEWISH KING

1. Marcus J. Borg, *The God We Never Knew: Beyond Dogmatic Religion to a More Authentic Contemporary Faith* (San Francisco: HarperSanFrancisco, 1997), 101.
2. Joseph Telushkin, *Jewish Literacy: The Most Important Things to Know about the Jewish Religion, Its People, and Its History* (New York: William Morrow and Co., Inc., 1991), 125.
3. Miller, *Hidden Gospel of Matthew,* 10.

CHAPTER 4: A MAVERICK MENTOR

1. Miller, *Hidden Gospel of Matthew,* 14.

CHAPTER 5: THE MESSAGE AND THE MESSENGER

1. Neil Douglas-Klotz, *The Hidden Gospel: Decoding the Spiritual Message of the Aramaic Jesus* (Wheaton, Ill.: Quest Books, 1999), 85.
2. Ibid., 84.
3. Miller, *Hidden Gospel of Matthew,* 26.

CHAPTER 6: A PROGRAM FOR JEWISH RENEWAL

1. Miller, *Hidden Gospel of Matthew,* 30.
2. The Buddha, from the *Sutta Nipata,* "Discourse on Good Will," in Eknath Easwaran, *God Makes the Rivers to Flow: Sacred Literature of the World* (Tomales, Calif.: Nilgiri Press, 2003), 104.
3. See chapter 16, "Spirituality Is Not Skygazing," in Ron Miller, *The Gospel of Thomas: A Guidebook for Spiritual Practice* (Woodstock, Vt.: SkyLight Paths Publishing, 2004). In the four canonical gospels, we find some ambiguity about the present or future reality of God's reign. In the Gospel of Thomas, however, the presence of this mystery of the moment at hand is unambiguous.

CHAPTER 7: A MASTER OF METAPHOR

1. Coleman Barks, trans., *The Illuminated Rumi* (New York: Broadway Books, 1997), 92, 124.

CHAPTER 10: OPPOSING EVIL WITHOUT EMULATING IT

1. Michael Nagler, *The Search for a Nonviolent Future: A Promise of Peace for Ourselves, Our Families, and Our World* (Maui, Hawaii: Inner Ocean Publishing, 2004), 109. See the entire section "Calling Hitler's Bluff" for further examples of nonviolent protest against Nazi rule, 100–111.

CHAPTER 11: THE MOST CHALLENGING PRACTICE

1. Rabbi Yochanan, Babylonian Talmud, *Megillah* 10b, as quoted in Naom Zion and David Dishon, eds., *The Family Participation Haggadah: A Different Night* (Jerusalem: The Shalom Hartman Institute, 1997), 101.
2. Miller, *Hidden Gospel of Matthew*, 46.
3. Babylonian Talmud, *Berachot* 10a, as quoted in Zion and Dishon, *The Family Participation Haggadah*, 101.

CHAPTER 12: THE LORD'S PRAYER

1. Avrohom Davis, trans., *The Complete Metsudah Siddur* (New York: Ziontalis, 1990), 124.
2. Babylonian Talmud, *Rosh Hashana* 17a.

CHAPTER 13: TRUE TREASURE, TRUE VISION, AND TRUE WORTH

1. Miller, *Hidden Gospel of Matthew*, 52.
2. Abraham Joshua Heschel, *Man Is Not Alone: A Philosophy of Religion* (New York: Farrar, Straus and Giroux, 1951), 92.
3. Michael Lerner, *Spirit Matters* (Charlottesville, Va.: Walsch Books, 2000), 173.
4. Beatrice Bruteau, *The Grand Option: Personal Transformation and a New Creation* (Notre Dame, Ind.: University of Notre Dame Press, 2001). 124. See also Bruteau, *The Holy Thursday Revolution* (Maryknoll, N.Y.: Orbis Books, 2005), 108–10.

CHAPTER 14: A GOLDEN RULE AND A NARROW PATH

1. Miller, *Hidden Gospel of Matthew*, 60.
2. Mahatma Gandhi, in Easwaran, *God Makes the Rivers to Flow,* 202.

CHAPTER 16: THOSE WONDERFUL ROMANS!

1. Larry Dossey, *Healing Words: The Power of Prayer and the Practice of Medicine* (San Francisco: HarperSanFrancisco, 1993), 44.

CHAPTER 17: REDEEMER OR REMINDER?

1. Beatrice Bruteau, *The Easter Mysteries* (New York: The Crossroad Publishing Company, 1995), 167–84.
2. William H. Shannon, ed., *The Hidden Ground of Love: The Letters of Thomas Merton on Religious Experience and Social Concerns* (New York: Farrar, Straus and Giroux, 1985), 526.
3. Bruteau, *Easter Mysteries*, 170.

CHAPTER 18: SIN AS PARALYSIS

1. Douglas Goldhamer and Melinda Stengel, *This Is for Everyone: Universal Principles of Healing Prayer and the Jewish Mystics* (Burdett, N.Y.: Larson Publications, 1999), 15–23.
2. Abraham Joshua Heschel, *God in Search of Man: A Philosophy of Judaism* (New York: Farrar, Straus and Giroux, 1955), 74.

CHAPTER 21: GOOD NEWS?

1. John Shelby Spong, *The Sins of Scripture: Exposing the Bible's Texts of Hate to Reveal the God of Love* (San Francisco: HarperSanFrancisco, 2005), chaps. 23–24.

CHAPTER 23: A CHALLENGING KIND OF PEACE

1. Barks, *Illuminated Rumi*, 108–9.

CHAPTER 24: MIXED MESSAGES

1. Miller, *Hidden Gospel of Matthew*, 90.
2. Ibid.

CHAPTER 25: JESHU THE LAWBREAKER?

1. Abraham Joshua Heschel, *The Sabbath: Its Meaning for Modern Man* (New York: Farrar, Straus and Giroux, 1951), 14, 15, 60.

2. Stanley Ned Rosenbaum, "A Letter from Rabbi Gamaliel ben Gamaliel," in *Jesus Through Jewish Eyes*, 87.
3. Miller, *Hidden Gospel of Matthew*, 98.
4. Rosenbaum, "A Letter from Rabbi Gamaliel ben Gamaliel," 87.
5. Heschel, *The Sabbath*, 68.
6. Telushkin, *Jewish Literacy*, 120–22.

CHAPTER 26: THOSE TERRIBLE PHARISEES!

1. Miller, *Hidden Gospel of Matthew*, 98.
2. Michael Lerner, *Jewish Renewal: A Path to Healing and Transformation* (New York: HarperPerennial, 1995), 95.

CHAPTER 28: WHAT MAKES US UNCLEAN?

1. See Rami Shapiro, *Minyan: Ten Principles for Living a Life of Integrity* (New York: Bell Tower, 1997), 145–55.

CHAPTER 32: A DAMNING DIATRIBE

1. Miller, *Hidden Gospel of Matthew*, 180.
2. See James Carroll, *Constantine's Sword: The Church and the Jews: A History* (Boston: Houghton Mifflin Company, 2001). The author provides an extraordinary, detailed examination of the process of demeaning and demonizing the Jews.
3. Miller, *Hidden Gospel of Matthew*, 184.
4. Spong, *Sins of Scripture*, 12.
5. *Vatican Council II: The Conciliar and Post Conciliar Documents*, ed. Austin Flannery (Northport, N.Y.: Costello Publishing Co., 1975), 757.
6. Ibid., 758.

CHAPTER 34: A FINAL MEAL

1. Miller, *Hidden Gospel of Matthew*, 204.
2. See Bruteau, *Grand Option*, 147–73, for a discussion of the communion paradigm.
3. Miller, *Hidden Gospel of Matthew*, 204.
4. Maxwell Staniforth, trans., *Early Christian Writings: The Apostolic Fathers* (New York: Penguin Books, 1968), 194.

CHAPTER 35: THE UNBEARABLE CURSE

1. Miller, *Hidden Gospel of Matthew*, 214.
2. John Dominic Crossan, *Who Killed Jesus?: Exposing the Roots of Anti-Semitism in the Gospel Story of the Death of Jesus* (San Francisco: HarperSanFrancisco, 1995), 112.
3. Miller, *Hidden Gospel of Matthew*, 214.
4. Ibid.
5. All three quotations are from Crossan, *Who Killed Jesus?*, 158.
6. *Vatican Council II*, 738–42.
7. All three quotations are from *Vatican Council II*, 741.

CHAPTER 36: WORSE THAN LIARS

1. Miller, *Hidden Gospel of Matthew*, 222.
2. Lerner, *Jewish Renewal*, xviii.
3. See Bruteau, *The Holy Thursday Revolution*. The entire book concerns Jeshu's revolutionary agenda and its application to our modern world.
4. *Vatican Council II*, 758.

Suggestions for Further Reading

Borg, Marcus J. *The God We Never Knew: Beyond Dogmatic Religion to a More Authentic Contemporary Faith.* San Francisco: HarperSanFrancisco, 1997.

———. *The Heart of Christianity: Rediscovering a Life of Faith.* San Francisco: HarperSanFrancisco, 2003.

———. *Meeting Jesus Again for the First Time: The Historical Jesus and the Heart of Contemporary Faith.* San Francisco: HarperSanFrancisco, 1994.

———. *Reading the Bible Again for the First Time: Taking the Bible Seriously but Not Literally.* San Francisco: HarperSanFrancisco, 2001.

Bruteau, Beatrice. *The Easter Mysteries.* New York: The Crossroad Publishing Company, 1995.

———. *The Grand Option: Personal Transformation and a New Creation.* Notre Dame, Ind.: University of Notre Dame Press, 2001.

———. *The Holy Thursday Revolution.* Maryknoll, N.Y.: Orbis Books, 2005.

———, ed. *Jesus Through Jewish Eyes: Rabbis and Scholars Engage an Ancient Brother in a New Conversation.* Maryknoll, N.Y.: Orbis Books, 2001.

———, ed. *Merton & Judaism: Holiness in Words: Recognition, Repentance, and Renewal.* Lexington, Ky.: Fons Vitae, 2003.

Buber, Martin. *Tales of the Hasidim.* New York: Schocken Books, 1991.

Carroll, James. *Constantine's Sword: The Church and the Jews: A History.* Boston: Houghton Mifflin, 2001.

Crossan, John Dominic. *The Historical Jesus: The Life of a Mediterranean Jewish Peasant.* San Francisco: HarperSanFrancisco, 1991.

———. *Jesus: A Revolutionary Biography.* San Francisco: HarperSanFrancisco, 1994.

———. *Who Killed Jesus? Exposing the Roots of Anti-Semitism in the Gospel Story of the Death of Jesus.* San Francisco: HarperSanFrancisco, 1995.

Crossan, John Dominic, and Jonathan L. Reed. *Excavating Jesus: Beneath the Stones, Behind the Texts.* San Francisco: HarperSanFrancisco, 2001.

Dossey, Larry, MD. *Healing Words: The Power of Prayer and the Practice of Medicine.* San Francisco: HarperSanFrancisco, 1993.

Douglas-Klotz, Neil. *The Hidden Gospel: Decoding the Spiritual Message of the Aramaic Jesus.* Wheaton, Ill.: Quest Books, 1999.

———. *Prayers of the Cosmos: Meditations on the Aramaic Words of Jesus.* San Francisco: HarperSanFrancisco, 1990.

Easwaran, Eknath. *Meditation: A Simple Eight-Point Program for Translating Spiritual Ideals into Daily Life.* Tomales, Calif.: Nilgiri Press, 1991.

———, ed. *God Makes the Rivers to Flow: Sacred Literature of the World.* Tomales, Calif.: Nilgiri Press, 2003.

———. *Words to Live By: Inspiration for Every Day.* Tomales, Calif.: Nilgiri Press, 1996.

Flannery, Austin, OP, ed. *Vatican Council II: The Conciliar and Post Conciliar Documents,* Northport, N.Y.: Costello Publishing Co., 1975.

Flannery, Edward H. *The Anguish of the Jews: Twenty-three Centuries of Anti-Semitism.* New York: Paulist Press, 1985.

Gillman, Neil. *The Jewish Approach to God: A Brief Introduction for Christians.* Woodstock, Vt.: Jewish Lights Publishing, 2003.

Goldhamer, Douglas, and Melinda Stengel. *This Is for Everyone: Universal Principles of Healing Prayer and the Jewish Mystics.* Burdett, N.Y.: Larson Publications, 1999.

Goldstein, Morris. *Jesus in the Jewish Tradition.* New York: Macmillan, 1950.

Heschel, Abraham Joshua. *God in Search of Man: A Philosophy of Judaism.* New York: Farrar, Straus and Giroux, 1955.

———. *Man Is Not Alone: A Philosophy of Religion.* New York: Farrar, Straus and Giroux, 1951.

———. *The Prophets.* New York: Perennial, 2001.

———. *The Sabbath: Its Meaning for Modern Man.* New York: Farrar, Straus and Giroux, 1951.

Lerner, Michael. *Jewish Renewal: A Path to Healing and Transformation.* New York: HarperPerennial, 1995.

———. *Spirit Matters.* Charlottesville, Va.: Walsch Books, 2000.

Kushner, Lawrence. *Jewish Spirituality: A Brief Introduction for Christians.* Woodstock, Vt.: Jewish Lights Publishing, 2001.

Miller, Ron. *The Gospel of Thomas: A Guidebook for Spiritual Practice.* Woodstock, Vt.: SkyLight Paths Publishing, 2004.

————. *The Hidden Gospel of Matthew: Annotated and Explained.* Woodstock, Vt.: SkyLight Paths Publishing, 2004.

————. *Wisdom of the Carpenter: 365 Prayers and Meditations of Jesus from the Gospel of Thomas, Lost Gospel Q, Secret Book of James, and the New Testament.* Berkeley, Calif.: Seastone, 2002.

Mitchell, Stephen. *The Gospel According to Jesus: A New Translation and Guide to His Essential Teachings for Believers and Unbelievers.* New York: HarperCollins, 1991.

Nagler, Michael N. *The Search for a Nonviolent Future: A Promise of Peace for Ourselves, Our Families, and Our World.* Maui, Hawaii: Inner Ocean Publishing, 2004.

Olitzky, Kerry M. and Daniel Judson. *Jewish Ritual: A Brief Introduction for Christians.* Woodstock, Vt.: Jewish Lights Publishing, 2005.

Sandmel, Samuel. *A Jewish Understanding of the New Testament.* Woodstock, Vt.: SkyLight Paths Publishing, 2004.

Shapiro, Rami. *Hasidic Tales: Annotated and Explained.* Woodstock, Vt.: SkyLight Paths Publishing, 2004.

————. *Minyan: Ten Principles for Living a Life of Integrity.* New York: Bell Tower, 1997.

————. *Wisdom of the Jewish Sages: A Modern Reading of Pirke Avot.* New York: Bell Tower, 1993.

Signer, Michael A. *The Way Into the Relationship between Jews and Non-Jews: Searching for Boundaries and Bridges.* Woodstock, Vt.: Jewish Lights Publishing, 2005.

Spong, John Shelby. *The Sins of Scripture: Exposing the Bible's Texts of Hate to Reveal the God of Love.* San Francisco: HarperSanFrancisco, 2005.

Staniforth, Maxwell, trans. *Early Christian Writings: The Apostolic Fathers.* New York: Penguin Books, 1968.

Telushkin, Joseph. *Jewish Literacy: The Most Important Things to Know about the Jewish Religion, Its People, and Its History.* New York: William Morrow and Co., Inc., 1991.

————. *Jewish Wisdom: Ethical, Spiritual, and Historical Lessons from the Great Works and Thinkers.* New York: W. Morrow, 1994.

Zion, Noam, and David Dishon, eds. *The Family Participation Haggadah: A Different Night.* Jerusalem: The Shalom Hartman Institute, 1997.

AVAILABLE FROM BETTER BOOKSTORES.
TRY YOUR BOOKSTORE FIRST.

Global Spiritual Perspectives

Spiritual Perspectives on America's Role as Superpower

by the Editors at SkyLight Paths

Are we the world's good neighbor or a global bully? Explores broader issues surrounding the use of American power around the world, including in Iraq and the Middle East. From a spiritual perspective, what are America's responsibilities as the only remaining superpower? Contributors:

Dr. Beatrice Bruteau • Rev. Dr. Joan Brown Campbell • Tony Campolo • Rev. Forrest Church • Lama Surya Das • Matthew Fox • Kabir Helminski • Thich Nhat Hanh • Eboo Patel • Abbot M. Basil Pennington, ocso • Dennis Prager • Rosemary Radford Ruether • Wayne Teasdale • Rev. William McD. Tully • Rabbi Arthur Waskow • John Wilson

5½ x 8½, 256 pp, Quality PB, ISBN 1-893361-81-0 **$16.95**

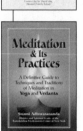

Spiritual Perspectives on Globalization, 2nd Edition

Making Sense of Economic and Cultural Upheaval

by Ira Rifkin; Foreword by Dr. David Little, Harvard Divinity School

What is globalization? What are spiritually minded people saying and doing about it? This lucid introduction surveys the religious landscape, explaining in clear and nonjudgmental language the beliefs that motivate spiritual leaders, activists, theologians, academics, and others involved on all sides of the issue. This edition includes a new Afterword and Discussion Guide designed for group use.

5½ x 8½, 256 pp, Quality PB, ISBN 1-59473-045-8 **$16.99**

Hinduism / Vedanta

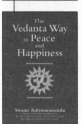

Meditation & Its Practices: A Definitive Guide to Techniques and Traditions of Meditation in Yoga and Vedanta

by Swami Adiswarananda

The complete sourcebook for exploring Hinduism's two most time-honored traditions of meditation. Drawing on both classic and contemporary sources, this comprehensive sourcebook outlines the scientific, psychological, and spiritual elements of Yoga and Vedanta meditation.

6 x 9, 504 pp, HC, ISBN 1-893361-83-7 **$34.95**

Sri Sarada Devi: Her Teachings and Conversations

Translated and with Notes by Swami Nikhilananda

Edited and with an Introduction by Swami Adiswarananda

Brings to life the Holy Mother's teachings on human affliction, self-control, and peace in ways both personal and profound, and illuminates her role as the power, scripture, joy, and guiding spirit of the Ramakrishna Order.

6 x 9, 288 pp, HC, ISBN 1-59473-070-9 **$29.99**

The Vedanta Way to Peace and Happiness

by Swami Adiswarananda

Using language that is accessible to people of all faiths and backgrounds, this book introduces the timeless teachings of Vedanta—divinity of the individual soul, unity of all existence, and oneness with the Divine—ancient wisdom as relevant to human happiness today as it was thousands of years ago.

6 x 9, 240 pp, HC, ISBN 1-59473-034-2 **$29.99**

Or phone, fax, mail or e-mail to: SKYLIGHT PATHS Publishing
Sunset Farm Offices, Route 4 • P.O. Box 237 • Woodstock, Vermont 05091
Tel: (802) 457-4000 • Fax: (802) 457-4004 • www.skylightpaths.com
Credit card orders: (800) 962-4544 (8:30AM–5:30PM ET Monday–Friday)
Generous discounts on quantity orders. SATISFACTION GUARANTEED. Prices subject to change.

Spiritual Biography—SkyLight Lives

SkyLight Lives reintroduces the lives and works of key spiritual figures of our time—people who by their teaching or example have challenged our assumptions about spirituality and have caused us to look at it in new ways.

 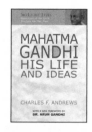  

The Life of Evelyn Underhill
An Intimate Portrait of the Groundbreaking Author of *Mysticism*
by Margaret Cropper; Foreword by Dana Greene
Evelyn Underhill was a passionate writer and teacher who wrote elegantly on mysticism, worship, and devotional life. This is the story of how she made her way toward spiritual maturity, from her early days of agnosticism to the years when her influence was felt throughout the world.
6 x 9, 288 pp, 5 b/w photos, Quality PB, ISBN 1-893361-70-5 **$18.95**

Mahatma Gandhi: His Life and Ideas
by Charles F. Andrews; Foreword by Dr. Arun Gandhi
Examines from a contemporary Christian activist's point of view the religious ideas and political dynamics that influenced the birth of the peaceful resistance movement, the primary tool that Gandhi and the people of his homeland would use to gain India its freedom from British rule.
6 x 9, 336 pp, 5 b/w photos, Quality PB, ISBN 1-893361-89-6 **$18.95**

Simone Weil: A Modern Pilgrimage
by Robert Coles
The extraordinary life of the spiritual philosopher who's been called both saint and madwoman. Robert Coles' intriguing study of Weil is an insightful portrait of the beloved and controversial thinker whose life and writings influenced many (from T. S. Eliot to Adrienne Rich to Albert Camus), and continue to inspire seekers everywhere.
6 x 9, 208 pp, Quality PB, ISBN 1-893361-34-9 **$16.95**

Zen Effects: The Life of Alan Watts
by Monica Furlong
Through his widely popular books and lectures, Alan Watts (1915–1973) did more to introduce Eastern philosophy and religion to Western minds than any figure before or since. Here is the first and only full-length biography of one of the most charismatic spiritual leaders of the twentieth century.
6 x 9, 264 pp, Quality PB, ISBN 1-893361-32-2 **$16.95**

More Spiritual Biography

Bede Griffiths: An Introduction to His Interspiritual Thought
by Wayne Teasdale 6 x 9, 288 pp, Quality PB, ISBN 1-893361-77-2 **$18.95**

Inspired Lives: Exploring the Role of Faith and Spirituality in the Lives of Extraordinary People
by Joanna Laufer and Kenneth S. Lewis 6 x 9, 256 pp, Quality PB, ISBN 1-893361-33-0 **$16.95**

Spiritual Innovators: Seventy-Five Extraordinary People Who Changed the World in the Past Century *Edited by Ira Rifkin and the Editors at SkyLight Paths; Foreword by Robert Coles*
6 x 9, 304 pp, b/w photographs, Quality PB, ISBN 1-893361-50-0 **$16.95**; HC, ISBN 1-893361-43-8 **$24.95**

White Fire: A Portrait of Women Spiritual Leaders in America
by Rabbi Malka Drucker; Photographs by Gay Block
7 x 10, 320 pp, 30+ b/w photos, HC, ISBN 1-893361-64-0 **$24.95**

Children's Spiritual Biography

MULTICULTURAL, NONDENOMINATIONAL, NONSECTARIAN

Ten Amazing People
And How They Changed the World
by Maura D. Shaw; Foreword by Dr. Robert Coles
Full-color illus. by Stephen Marchesi

For ages 7 & up

Black Elk • Dorothy Day • Malcolm X • Mahatma Gandhi • Martin Luther King, Jr. • Mother Teresa • Janusz Korczak • Desmond Tutu • Thich Nhat Hanh • Albert Schweitzer

This vivid, inspirational, and authoritative book will open new possibilities for children by telling the stories of how ten of the past century's greatest leaders changed the world in important ways.

8½ x 11, 48 pp, HC, Full-color illus., ISBN 1-893361-47-0 **$17.95** *For ages 7 & up*

Spiritual Biographies for Young People—For ages 7 and up

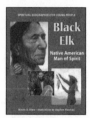
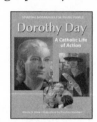
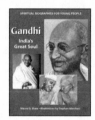
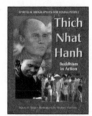

Black Elk: Native American Man of Spirit
by Maura D. Shaw; Full-color illus. by Stephen Marchesi
Through historically accurate illustrations and photos, inspiring age-appropriate activities, and Black Elk's own words, this colorful biography introduces children to a remarkable person who ensured that the traditions and beliefs of his people would not be forgotten.
6¾ x 8¾, 32 pp, HC, Full-color illus., ISBN 1-59473-043-1 **$12.99**

Dorothy Day: A Catholic Life of Action
by Maura D. Shaw; Full-color illus. by Stephen Marchesi
Introduces children to one of the most inspiring women of the twentieth century, a down-to-earth spiritual leader who saw the presence of God in every person she met. Includes practical activities, a timeline, and a list of important words to know.
6¾ x 8¾, 32 pp, HC, Full-color illus., ISBN 1-59473-011-3 **$12.99**

Gandhi: India's Great Soul
by Maura D. Shaw; Full-color illus. by Stephen Marchesi
There are a number of biographies of Gandhi written for young readers, but this is the only one that balances a simple text with illustrations, photographs, and activities that encourage children and adults to talk about how to make changes happen without violence. Introduces children to important concepts of freedom, equality, and justice among people of all backgrounds and religions.
6¾ x 8¾, 32 pp, HC, Full-color illus., ISBN 1-893361-91-8 **$12.95**

Thich Nhat Hanh: Buddhism in Action
by Maura D. Shaw; Full-color illus. by Stephen Marchesi
Warm illustrations, photos, age-appropriate activities, and Thich Nhat Hanh's own poems introduce a great man to children in a way they can understand and enjoy. Includes a list of important Buddhist words to know.
6¾ x 8¾, 32 pp, HC, Full-color illus., ISBN 1-893361-87-X **$12.95**

Children's Spirituality—Board Books

How Did the Animals Help God? (A Board Book)
by Nancy Sohn Swartz, Full-color illus. by Melanie Hall
Abridged from Nancy Sohn Swartz's *In Our Image*, God asks all of nature to offer gifts to humankind—with a promise that they will care for creation in return.
5 x 5, 24 pp, Board Book, Full-color illus., ISBN 1-59473-044-X **$7.99** *For ages 0–4*

Where Is God? (A Board Book)
by Lawrence and Karen Kushner; Full-color illus. by Dawn W. Majewski
A gentle way for young children to explore how God is with us every day, in every way. Abridged from *Because Nothing Looks Like God* by Lawrence and Karen Kushner. 5 x 5, 24 pp, Board, Full-color illus., ISBN 1-893361-17-9 **$7.99** *For ages 0–4*

What Does God Look Like? (A Board Book)
by Lawrence and Karen Kushner; Full-color illus. by Dawn W. Majewski
A simple way for young children to explore the ways that we "see" God. Abridged from *Because Nothing Looks Like God* by Lawrence and Karen Kushner.
5 x 5, 24 pp, Board, Full-color illus., ISBN 1-893361-23-3 **$7.95** *For ages 0–4*

How Does God Make Things Happen? (A Board Book)
by Lawrence and Karen Kushner; Full-color illus. by Dawn W. Majewski
A charming invitation for young children to explore how God makes things happen in our world. Abridged from *Because Nothing Looks Like God* by Lawrence and Karen Kushner. 5 x 5, 24 pp, Board, Full-color illus., ISBN 1-893361-24-1 **$7.95** *For ages 0–4*

What Is God's Name? (A Board Book)
by Sandy Eisenberg Sasso; Full-color illus. by Phoebe Stone
Everyone and everything in the world has a name. What is God's name? Abridged from the award-winning *In God's Name* by Sandy Eisenberg Sasso.
5 x 5, 24 pp, Board, Full-color illus., ISBN 1-893361-10-1 **$7.99** *For ages 0–4*

What You Will See Inside ...

This important new series of books is designed to show children ages 6–10 the Who, What, When, Where, Why and How of traditional houses of worship, liturgical celebrations, and rituals of different world faiths, empowering them to respect and understand their own religious traditions—and those of their friends and neighbors.

What You Will See Inside a Catholic Church
by Reverend Michael Keane; Foreword by Robert J. Keeley, Ed.D.
Full-color photographs by Aaron Pepis
Visually explains the common use of the altar, processional cross, baptismal font, votive candles, and more. 8½ x 10½, 32 pp, HC, ISBN 1-893361-54-3 **$17.95**

Also available in Spanish: **Lo que se puede ver dentro de una iglesia católica**
8½ x 10½, 32 pp, Full-color photos, HC, ISBN 1-893361-66-7 **$16.95**

What You Will See Inside a Hindu Temple
by Dr. Mahendra Jani and Dr. Vandana Jani; Photographs by Neirah Bhargava and Vijay Dave
Colorful, full-page photographs set the scene for concise but informative descriptions of the ways and whys of Hindu worship, faith, and religious life.
8½ x 10½, 32 pp, Full-color photos, HC, ISBN 1-59473-116-0 **$17.99**

What You Will See Inside a Mosque
by Aisha Karen Khan; Photographs by Aaron Pepis
Featuring full-page pictures and concise descriptions, demystifies the celebrations and ceremonies of Islam throughout the year.
8½ x 10½, 32 pp, Full-color photos, HC, ISBN 1-893361-60-8 **$16.95**

What You Will See Inside a Synagogue
by Rabbi Lawrence A. Hoffman and Dr. Ron Wolfson; Full-color photos by Bill Aron
A colorful, fun-to-read introduction that explains the ways and whys of Jewish worship and religious life.
8½ x 10½, 32 pp, Full-color photos, HC, ISBN 1-59473-012-1 **$17.99**

Sacred Texts—SkyLight Illuminations Series
Andrew Harvey, series editor

Offers today's spiritual seeker an enjoyable entry into the great classic texts of the world's spiritual traditions. Each classic is presented in an accessible translation, with facing pages of guided commentary from experts, giving you the keys you need to understand the history, context and meaning of the text. This series enables readers of all backgrounds to experience and understand classic spiritual texts directly, and to make them a part of their lives. Andrew Harvey writes the foreword to each volume, an insightful, personal introduction to each classic.

Bhagavad Gita: Annotated & Explained
Translation by Shri Purohit Swami; Annotation by Kendra Crossen Burroughs
"The very best Gita for first-time readers." —Ken Wilber. Millions of people turn daily to India's most beloved holy book, whose universal appeal has made it popular with non-Hindus and Hindus alike. This edition introduces you to the characters, explains references and philosophical terms, shares the interpretations of famous spiritual leaders and scholars, and more.
5½ x 8½, 192 pp, Quality PB, ISBN 1-893361-28-4 **$16.95**

Dhammapada: Annotated & Explained
Translation by Max Müller and revised by Jack Maguire; Annotation by Jack Maguire
The Dhammapada—believed to have been spoken by the Buddha himself over 2,500 years ago—contain most of Buddhism's central teachings. This timeless text concisely and inspirationally portrays the route a person travels as he or she advances toward enlightenment and describes the fundamental role of mental conditioning in making us who we are.
5½ x 8½, 160 pp, b/w photographs, Quality PB, ISBN 1-893361-42-X **$14.95**

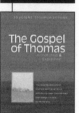

The Divine Feminine in Biblical Wisdom Literature
Selections Annotated & Explained
Translation and annotation by Rabbi Rami Shapiro; Foreword by Rev. Dr. Cynthia Bourgeault
Uses the Hebrew books of Psalms, Proverbs, Song of Songs, Ecclesiastes and Job, and the Wisdom literature books of Sirach and the Wisdom of Solomon to clarify who Wisdom is, what She teaches, and how Her words can help us live justly, wisely, and with compassion.
5½ x 8½, 240 pp, Quality PB, ISBN 1-59473-109-8 **$16.99**

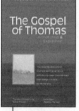

The Gospel of Thomas: Annotated & Explained
Translation and annotation by Stevan Davies
Discovered in 1945, this collection of aphoristic sayings sheds new light on the origins of Christianity and the intriguing figure of Jesus, portraying the Kingdom of God as a present fact about the world, rather than a future promise or future threat.
5½ x 8½, 192 pp, Quality PB, ISBN 1-893361-45-4 **$16.95**

Hasidic Tales: Annotated & Explained
Translation and annotation by Rabbi Rami Shapiro
Introduces the legendary tales of the impassioned Hasidic rabbis, which demonstrate the spiritual power of unabashed joy, offer lessons for leading a holy life, and remind us that the Divine can be found in the everyday.
5½ x 8½, 240 pp, Quality PB, ISBN 1-893361-86-1 **$16.95**

The Hebrew Prophets: Selections Annotated & Explained
Translation and annotation by Rabbi Rami Shapiro
Focuses on the central themes covered by all the Hebrew prophets: moving from ignorance to wisdom, injustice to justice, cruelty to compassion, and despair to joy, and challenges us to engage in justice, kindness and humility in every aspect of our lives.
5½ x 8½, 224 pp, Quality PB, ISBN 1-59473-037-7 **$16.99**

Sacred Texts—SkyLight Illuminations Series
Andrew Harvey, series editor

The Hidden Gospel of Matthew: Annotated & Explained
Translation and annotation by Ron Miller

Takes you deep into the text cherished around the world to discover the words and events that have the strongest connection to the historical Jesus. Reveals the underlying story of Matthew, a story that transcends the traditional theme of an atoning death and focuses instead on Jesus's radical call for personal transformation and social change.

5½ x 8½, 272 pp, Quality PB, ISBN 1-59473-038-5 **$16.99**

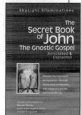

The Secret Book of John
The Gnostic Gospel—Annotated & Explained
Translation and annotation by Stevan Davies

Introduces the most significant and influential text of the ancient Gnostic religion. This central myth of Gnosticism tells the story of how God fell from perfect Oneness to imprisonment in the material world, and how by knowing our divine nature and our divine origins—that we are one with God—we reverse God's descent and find our salvation.

5½ x 8½, 208 pp, Quality PB, ISBN 1-59473-082-2 **$16.99**

Rumi and Islam: Selections from His Stories, Poems, and Discourses—Annotated & Explained
Translation and annotation by Ibrahim Gamard

Offers a new way of thinking about Rumi's poetry. Focuses on Rumi's place within the Sufi tradition of Islam, providing insight into the mystical side of the religion—one that has love of God at its core and sublime wisdom teachings as its pathways.

5½ x 8½, 240 pp, Quality PB, ISBN 1-59473-002-4 **$15.99**

Selections from the Gospel of Sri Ramakrishna
Annotated & Explained
Translation by Swami Nikhilananda; Annotation by Kendra Crossen Burroughs

The words of India's greatest example of God-consciousness and mystical ecstasy in recent history. Introduces the fascinating world of the Indian mystic and the universal appeal of his message that has inspired millions of devotees for more than a century.

5½ x 8½, 240 pp, b/w photographs, Quality PB, ISBN 1-893361-46-2 **$16.95**

Spiritual Writings on Mary: Annotated & Explained
Annotation by Mary Ford-Grabowsky

Selections from influential writers, thinkers, and theologians—ancient and modern, from Western and Eastern backgrounds—examine the role of Mary, the mother of Jesus, as a source of inspiration in history and in life today.

5½ x 8½, 288 pp, Quality PB, ISBN 1-59473-001-6 **$16.99**

The Way of a Pilgrim: Annotated & Explained
Translation and annotation by Gleb Pokrovsky

This classic of Russian spirituality is the delightful account of one man who sets out to learn the prayer of the heart—also known as the "Jesus prayer"—and how the practice transforms his life.

5½ x 8½, 160 pp, Illus., Quality PB, ISBN 1-893361-31-4 **$14.95**

Zohar: Annotated & Explained
Translation and annotation by Daniel C. Matt

The best-selling author of *The Essential Kabbalah* brings together in one place the most important teachings of the Zohar, the canonical text of Jewish mystical tradition. Guides you step by step through the midrash, mystical fantasy, and Hebrew scripture that make up the Zohar, explaining the inner meanings in facing-page commentary.

5½ x 8½, 176 pp, Quality PB, ISBN 1-893361-51-9 **$15.99**

Spiritual Poetry—The Mystic Poets

Experience these mystic poets as you never have before. Each beautiful, compact book includes: A brief introduction to the poet's time and place; a summary of the major themes of the poet's mysticism and religious tradition; essential selections from the poet's most important works; and an appreciative preface by a contemporary spiritual writer.

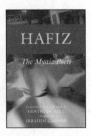   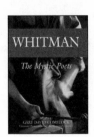

Hafiz: The Mystic Poets
Preface by Ibrahim Gamard
Hafiz is known throughout the world as Persia's greatest poet, with sales of his poems in Iran today only surpassed by those of the Qur'an itself. His probing and joyful verse speaks to people from all backgrounds who long to taste and feel divine love and experience harmony with all living things.
5 x 7¼, 144 pp, HC, ISBN 1-59473-009-1 **$16.99**

Hopkins: The Mystic Poets
Preface by Rev. Thomas Ryan, CSP
Gerard Manley Hopkins, Christian mystical poet, is beloved for his use of fresh language and startling metaphors to describe the world around him. Although his verse is lovely, beneath the surface lies a searching soul, wrestling with and yearning for God.
5 x 7¼, 112 pp, HC, ISBN 1-59473-010-5 **$16.99**

Tagore: The Mystic Poets
Preface by Swami Adiswarananda
Rabindranath Tagore is often considered the "Shakespeare" of modern India. A great mystic, Tagore was the teacher of W. B. Yeats and Robert Frost, the close friend of Albert Einstein and Mahatma Gandhi, and the winner of the Nobel Prize for Literature. This beautiful sampling of Tagore's two most important works, *The Gardener* and *Gitanjali*, offers a glimpse into his spiritual vision that has inspired people around the world.
5 x 7¼, 144 pp, HC, ISBN 1-59473-008-3 **$16.99**

Whitman: The Mystic Poets
Preface by Gary David Comstock
Walt Whitman was the most innovative and influential poet of the nineteenth century. This beautiful sampling of Whitman's most important poetry from *Leaves of Grass,* and selections from his prose writings, offers a glimpse into the spiritual side of his most radical themes— love for country, love for others, and love of Self.
5 x 7¼, 192 pp, HC, ISBN 1-59473-041-5 **$16.99**

Kabbalah from Jewish Lights Publishing

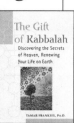

Ehyeh: A Kabbalah for Tomorrow *by Dr. Arthur Green*
6 x 9, 224 pp, Quality PB, ISBN 1-58023-213-2 **$16.99**; HC, ISBN 1-58023-125-X **$21.95**

The Enneagram and Kabbalah: Reading Your Soul *by Rabbi Howard A. Addison*
6 x 9, 176 pp, Quality PB, ISBN 1-58023-001-6 **$15.95**

Finding Joy: A Practical Spiritual Guide to Happiness *by Dannel I. Schwartz with Mark Hass*
6 x 9, 192 pp, Quality PB, ISBN 1-58023-009-1 **$14.95**; HC, ISBN 1-879045-53-2 **$19.95**

The Gift of Kabbalah: Discovering the Secrets of Heaven, Renewing Your Life on Earth
by Tamar Frankiel, Ph.D.
6 x 9, 256 pp, Quality PB, ISBN 1-58023-141-1 **$16.95**; HC, ISBN 1-58023-108-X **$21.95**

Zohar: Annotated & Explained
Translation and annotation by Dr. Daniel C. Matt. Foreword by Andrew Harvey
5½ x 8½, 160 pp, Quality PB, ISBN 1-893361-51-9 **$15.99**

Meditation / Prayer

Prayers to an Evolutionary God
by William Cleary; Afterword by Diarmuid O'Murchu
How is it possible to pray when God is dislocated from heaven, dispersed all around us, and more of a creative force than an all-knowing father? Inspired by the spiritual and scientific teachings of Diarmuid O'Murchu and Teilhard de Chardin, Cleary reveals that religion and science can be combined to create an expanding view of the universe—an evolutionary faith.
6 x 9, 208 pp, HC, ISBN 1-59473-006-7 **$21.99**

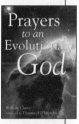

The Song of Songs: A Spiritual Commentary
by M. Basil Pennington, OCSO; Illustrations by Phillip Ratner
Join M. Basil Pennington as he ruminates on the Bible's most challenging mystical text. You will follow a path into the Songs that weaves through his inspired words and the evocative drawings of Jewish artist Phillip Ratner—a path that reveals your own humanity and leads to the deepest delight of your soul.
6 x 9, 160 pp, HC, 14 b/w illus., ISBN 1-59473-004-0 **$19.99**

Women of Color Pray: Voices of Strength, Faith, Healing, Hope, and Courage   *Edited and with Introductions by Christal M. Jackson*
Through these prayers, poetry, lyrics, meditations and affirmations, you will share in the strong and undeniable connection women of color share with God. It will challenge you to explore new ways of prayerful expression.
5 x 7¼, 208 pp, Quality PB, ISBN 1-59473-077-6 **$15.99**

The Art of Public Prayer, 2nd Edition: Not for Clergy Only
by Lawrence A. Hoffman   6 x 9, 288 pp, Quality PB, ISBN 1-893361-06-3 **$18.95**

Finding Grace at the Center: The Beginning of Centering Prayer
by M. Basil Pennington, ocso, Thomas Keating, ocso, and Thomas E. Clarke, SJ
5 x 7¼, 112 pp, HC, ISBN 1-893361-69-1 **$14.95**

A Heart of Stillness: A Complete Guide to Learning the Art of Meditation
by David A. Cooper   5½ x 8½, 272 pp, Quality PB, ISBN 1-893361-03-9 **$16.95**

Meditation without Gurus: A Guide to the Heart of Practice
by Clark Strand   5½ x 8½, 192 pp, Quality PB, ISBN 1-893361-93-4 **$16.95**

Praying with Our Hands: Twenty-One Practices of Embodied Prayer from the World's Spiritual Traditions   *by Jon M. Sweeney; Photographs by Jennifer J. Wilson; Foreword by Mother Tessa Bielecki; Afterword by Taitetsu Unno, PhD*
8 x 8, 96 pp, 22 duotone photographs, Quality PB, ISBN 1-893361-16-0 **$16.95**

Silence, Simplicity & Solitude: A Complete Guide to Spiritual Retreat at Home
by David A. Cooper   5½ x 8½, 336 pp, Quality PB, ISBN 1-893361-04-7 **$16.95**

Three Gates to Meditation Practice: A Personal Journey into Sufism, Buddhism, and Judaism   *by David A. Cooper*   5½ x 8½, 240 pp, Quality PB, ISBN 1-893361-22-5 **$16.95**

Women Pray: Voices through the Ages, from Many Faiths, Cultures, and Traditions
Edited and with introductions by Monica Furlong
5 x 7¼, 256 pp, Quality PB, ISBN 1-59473-071-7 **$15.99**;
Deluxe HC with ribbon marker, ISBN 1-893361-25-X **$19.95**

Spirituality

Prayer for People Who Think Too Much
A Guide to Everyday, Anywhere Prayer from the World's Faith Traditions   *by Mitch Finley*
5½ x 8½, 224 pp, Quality PB, ISBN 1-893361-21-7 **$16.95**; HC, ISBN 1-893361-00-4 **$21.95**

The Shaman's Quest: Journeys in an Ancient Spiritual Practice
by Nevill Drury; with a Basic Introduction to Shamanism by Tom Cowan
5½ x 8½, 208 pp, Quality PB, ISBN 1-893361-68-3 **$16.95**

Show Me Your Way: The Complete Guide to Exploring Interfaith Spiritual Direction
by Howard A. Addison   5½ x 8½, 240 pp, Quality PB, ISBN 1-893361-41-1 **$16.95**;
HC, ISBN 1-893361-12-8 **$21.95**

Spirituality 101: The Indispensable Guide to Keeping—or Finding—Your Spiritual Life
on Campus   *by Harriet L. Schwartz, with contributions from college students at nearly thirty campuses across the United States*   6 x 9, 272 pp, Quality PB, ISBN 1-59473-000-8 **$16.99**

Spiritually Incorrect: Finding God in All the Wrong Places
by Dan Wakefield; Illus. by Marian DelVecchio
5½ x 8½, 192 pp, b/w illus., HC, ISBN 1-893361-88-8 **$21.95**

Spiritual Manifestos: Visions for Renewed Religious Life in America from Young
Spiritual Leaders of Many Faiths   *Edited by Niles Elliot Goldstein; Preface by Martin E. Marty*
6 x 9, 256 pp, HC, ISBN 1-893361-09-8 **$21.95**

A Walk with Four Spiritual Guides: Krishna, Buddha, Jesus, and Ramakrishna
by Andrew Harvey   5½ x 8½, 192 pp, 10 b/w photos & illus., HC, ISBN 1-893361-73-X **$21.95**

What Matters: Spiritual Nourishment for Head and Heart
by Frederick Franck   5 x 7¼, 144 pp, 50+ b/w illus., HC, ISBN 1-59473-013-X **$16.99**

Who Is My God?, 2nd Edition
An Innovative Guide to Finding Your Spiritual Identity
Created by the Editors at SkyLight Paths   6 x 9, 160 pp, Quality PB, ISBN 1-59473-014-8 **$15.99**

Spirituality—A Week Inside

Come and Sit: A Week Inside Meditation Centers
by Marcia Z. Nelson; Foreword by Wayne Teasdale
The insider's guide to meditation in a variety of different spiritual traditions. Traveling through Buddhist, Hindu, Christian, Jewish, and Sufi traditions, this essential guide takes you to different meditation centers to meet the teachers and students and learn about the practices, demystifying the meditation experience.
6 x 9, 224 pp, b/w photographs, Quality PB, ISBN 1-893361-35-7 **$16.95**

Lighting the Lamp of Wisdom: A Week Inside a Yoga Ashram
by John Ittner; Foreword by Dr. David Frawley
This insider's guide to Hindu spiritual life takes you into a typical week of retreat inside a yoga ashram to demystify the experience and show you what to expect from your own visit. Includes a discussion of worship services, meditation and yoga classes, chanting and music, work practice, and more.   6 x 9, 192 pp, b/w photographs, Quality PB, ISBN 1-893361-52-7 **$15.95**; HC, ISBN 1-893361-37-3 **$24.95**

Making a Heart for God: A Week Inside a Catholic Monastery
by Dianne Aprile; Foreword by Brother Patrick Hart, ocso
This essential guide to experiencing life in a Catholic monastery takes you to the Abbey of Gethsemani—the Trappist monastery in Kentucky that was home to author Thomas Merton—to explore the details. "More balanced and informative than the popular *The Cloister Walk* by Kathleen Norris." —*Choice: Current Reviews for Academic Libraries*   6 x 9, 224 pp, b/w photographs, Quality PB, ISBN 1-893361-49-7 **$16.95**; HC, ISBN 1-893361-14-4 **$21.95**

Waking Up: A Week Inside a Zen Monastery
by Jack Maguire; Foreword by John Daido Loori, Roshi
An essential guide to what it's like to spend a week inside a Zen Buddhist monastery.
6 x 9, 224 pp, b/w photographs, Quality PB, ISBN 1-893361-55-1 **$16.95**;
HC, ISBN 1-893361-13-6 **$21.95**

Spirituality

Autumn: A Spiritual Biography of the Season
Edited by Gary Schmidt and Susan M. Felch; Illustrations by Mary Azarian
Autumn is a season of fruition and harvest, of thanksgiving and celebration of abundance and goodness of the earth. But it is also a season that starkly and realistically encourages us to see the limitations of our time. Warm and poignant pieces by Wendell Berry, David James Duncan, Robert Frost, A. Bartlett Giamatti, Kimiko Hahn, P. D. James, Julian of Norwich, Garret Keizer, Tracy Kidder, Anne Lamott, May Sarton, and many others rejoice in autumn as a time of preparation and reflection.
6 x 9, 320 pp, 5 b/w illus., Quality PB, ISBN 1-59473-118-7 **$18.99**; HC, ISBN 1-59473-005-9 **$22.99**

Awakening the Spirit, Inspiring the Soul
30 Stories of Interspiritual Discovery in the Community of Faiths
Edited by Brother Wayne Teasdale and Martha Howard, MD; Foreword by Joan Borysenko, PhD
Thirty original spiritual mini-biographies that showcase the varied ways that people come to faith—and what that means—in today's multi-religious world.
6 x 9, 224 pp, HC, ISBN 1-59473-039-3 **$21.99**

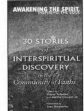

Winter: A Spiritual Biography of the Season
Edited by Gary Schmidt and Susan M. Felch; Illustrations by Barry Moser
Delves into the varied feelings that winter conjures in us, calling up both the barrenness and the beauty of the natural world in wintertime. Includes selections by Will Campbell, Rachel Carson, Annie Dillard, Donald Hall, Ron Hansen, Jane Kenyon, Jamaica Kincaid, Barry Lopez, Kathleen Norris, John Updike, E. B. White, and many others. "This outstanding anthology features top-flight nature and spirituality writers on the fierce, inexorable season of winter.... Remarkably lively and warm, despite the icy subject." —*Publishers Weekly* Starred Review
6 x 9, 288 pp, 6 b/w illus., Deluxe PB w/flaps, ISBN 1-893361-92-6 **$18.95**; HC, ISBN 1-893361-53-5 **$21.95**

The Alphabet of Paradise: An A–Z of Spirituality for Everyday Life
by Howard Cooper 5 x 7¾, 224 pp, Quality PB, ISBN 1-893361-80-2 **$16.95**

Creating a Spiritual Retirement: A Guide to the Unseen Possibilities in Our Lives
by Molly Srode 6 x 9, 208 pp, b/w photos, Quality PB, ISBN 1-59473-050-42 **$14.99**; HC, ISBN 1-893361-75-6 **$19.95**

The Geography of Faith: Underground Conversations on Religious, Political and Social Change *by Daniel Berrigan and Robert Coles; Updated introduction and afterword by the authors* 6 x 9, 224 pp, Quality PB, ISBN 1-893361-40-3 **$16.95**

God Lives in Glass: Reflections of God for Adults through the Eyes of Children
by Robert J. Landy, PhD; Foreword by Sandy Eisenberg Sasso
7 x 6, 64 pp, HC, Full-color illus., ISBN 1-893361-30-6 **$12.95**

God Within: Our Spiritual Future—As Told by Today's New Adults *Edited by Jon M. Sweeney and the Editors at SkyLight Paths* 6 x 9, 176 pp, Quality PB, ISBN 1-893361-15-2 **$14.95**

Jewish Spirituality: A Brief Introduction for Christians *by Lawrence Kushner*
5½ x 8½, 112 pp, Quality PB, ISBN 1-58023-150-0 **$12.95** *(a Jewish Lights book)*

A Jewish Understanding of the New Testament
by Rabbi Samuel Sandmel; New preface by Rabbi David Sandmel
5½ x 8½, 384 pp, Quality PB, ISBN 1-59473-048-2 **$19.99**

Journeys of Simplicity: Traveling Light with Thomas Merton, Basho, Edward Abbey, Annie Dillard & Others *by Philip Harnden* 5 x 7¼, 128 pp, HC, ISBN 1-893361-76-4 **$16.95**

Keeping Spiritual Balance As We Grow Older: More than 65 Creative Ways to Use Purpose, Prayer, and the Power of Spirit to Build a Meaningful Retirement
by Molly and Bernie Srode 8 x 8, 224 pp, Quality PB, ISBN 1-59473-042-3 **$16.99**

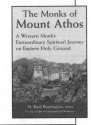

The Monks of Mount Athos: A Western Monk's Extraordinary Spiritual Journey on Eastern Holy Ground *by M. Basil Pennington, ocso; Foreword by Archimandrite Dionysios*
6 x 9, 256 pp, 10+ b/w line drawings, Quality PB, ISBN 1-893361-78-0 **$18.95**

One God Clapping: The Spiritual Path of a Zen Rabbi *by Alan Lew with Sherrill Jaffe*
5½ x 8½, 336 pp, Quality PB, ISBN 1-58023-115-2 **$16.95** *(a Jewish Lights book)*

Spiritual Practice

Divining the Body
Reclaim the Holiness of Your Physical Self *by Jan Phillips*
A practical and inspiring guidebook for connecting the body and soul in spiritual practice. Leads you into a milieu of reverence, mystery and delight, helping you discover a redeemed sense of self.
8 x 8, 256 pp, Quality PB, ISBN 1-59473-080-6 **$16.99**

Finding Time for the Timeless
Spirituality in the Workweek *by John McQuiston II*
Simple, refreshing stories that provide you with examples of how you can refocus and enrich your daily life using prayer or meditation, ritual and other forms of spiritual practice. 5½ x 6½, 208 pp, HC, ISBN 1-59473-035-0 **$17.99**

The Gospel of Thomas: A Guidebook for Spiritual Practice
by Ron Miller; Translations by Stevan Davies
An innovative guide to bring a new spiritual classic into daily life. Offers a way to translate the wisdom of the Gospel of Thomas into daily practice, manifesting in your life the same consciousness revealed in Jesus of Nazareth. Written for readers of all religious backgrounds, this guidebook will help you to apply Jesus's wisdom to your own life and to the world around you.
6 x 9, 160 pp, Quality PB, ISBN 1-59473-047-4 **$14.99**

The Knitting Way: A Guide to Spiritual Self-Discovery
by Linda Skolnik and Janice MacDaniels
Through sharing stories, hands-on explorations and daily cultivation, Skolnik and MacDaniels help you see beyond the surface of a simple craft in order to discover ways in which nuances of knitting can apply to the larger scheme of life and spirituality. Includes original knitting patterns.
7 x 9, 240 pp, Quality PB, ISBN 1-59473-079-2 **$16.99**

Earth, Water, Fire, and Air: Essential Ways of Connecting to Spirit
by Cait Johnson 6 x 9, 224 pp, HC, ISBN 1-893361-65-9 **$19.95**

Forty Days to Begin a Spiritual Life
Today's Most Inspiring Teachers Help You on Your Way
Edited by Maura Shaw and the Editors at SkyLight Paths; Foreword by Dan Wakefield
7 x 9, 144 pp, Quality PB, ISBN 1-893361-48-9 **$16.95**

Labyrinths from the Outside In
Walking to Spiritual Insight—A Beginner's Guide
by Donna Schaper and Carole Ann Camp
6 x 9, 208 pp, b/w illus. and photographs, Quality PB, ISBN 1-893361-18-7 **$16.95**

Practicing the Sacred Art of Listening: A Guide to Enrich Your Relationships
and Kindle Your Spiritual Life—The Listening Center Workshop
by Kay Lindahl 8 x 8, 176 pp, Quality PB, ISBN 1-893361-85-3 **$16.95**

The Sacred Art of Bowing: Preparing to Practice
by Andi Young 5½ x 8½, 128 pp, b/w illus., Quality PB, ISBN 1-893361-82-9 **$14.95**

The Sacred Art of Chant: Preparing to Practice
by Ana Hernandez 5½ x 8½, 192 pp, Quality PB, ISBN 1-59473-036-9 **$15.99**

The Sacred Art of Fasting: Preparing to Practice
by Thomas Ryan, CSP 5½ x 8½, 192 pp, Quality PB, ISBN 1-59473-078-4 **$15.99**

The Sacred Art of Listening: Forty Reflections for Cultivating a Spiritual Practice
by Kay Lindahl; Illustrations by Amy Schnapper
8 x 8, 160 pp, Illus., Quality PB, ISBN 1-893361-44-6 **$16.99**

Sacred Speech: A Practical Guide for Keeping Spirit in Your Speech
by Rev. Donna Schaper 6 x 9, 176 pp, Quality PB, ISBN 1-59473-068-7 **$15.99**;
HC, ISBN 1-893361-74-8 **$21.95**

Midrash Fiction

Daughters of the Desert: Tales of Remarkable Women from Christian, Jewish, and Muslim Traditions   *by Claire Rudolf Murphy, Meghan Nuttall Sayres, Mary Cronk Farrell, Sarah Conover, and Betsy Wharton*

Breathes new life into the old tales of our female ancestors in faith. Uses traditional scriptural passages as starting points, then with vivid detail fills in historical context and place. Chapters reveal the voices of Sarah, Hagar, Huldah, Esther, Salome, Mary Magdalene, Lydia, Khadija, Fatima, and many more. Historical fiction ideal for readers of all ages. Quality paperback includes reader's discussion guide.

5½ x 8½, 208 pp, Quality PB, ISBN 1-59473-106-3 **$14.99**; HC, 192 pp, ISBN 1-893361-72-1 **$19.95**

The Triumph of Eve & Other Subversive Bible Tales
by Matt Biers-Ariel

Many people were taught and remember only a one-dimensional Bible. These engaging retellings are the antidote to this—they're witty, often hilarious, always profound, and invite you to grapple with questions and issues that are often hidden in the original text.

5½ x 8½, 192 pp, HC, ISBN 1-59473-040-7 **$19.99**

Also available:
The Triumph of Eve & Other Subversive Bible Tales Teacher's Guide
8½ x 11, 44 pp, PB, ISBN 1-59473-152-7 **$8.99**

Religious Etiquette / Reference

How to Be a Perfect Stranger, 3rd Edition: The Essential Religious Etiquette Handbook   *Edited by Stuart M. Matlins and Arthur J. Magida*

The indispensable guidebook to help the well-meaning guest when visiting other people's religious ceremonies. A straightforward guide to the rituals and celebrations of the major religions and denominations in the United States and Canada from the perspective of an interested guest of any other faith, based on information obtained from authorities of each religion. Belongs in every living room, library, and office. Covers:

African American Methodist Churches • Assemblies of God • Baha'i • Baptist • Buddhist • Christian Church (Disciples of Christ) • Christian Science (Church of Christ, Scientist) • Churches of Christ • Episcopalian and Anglican • Hindu • Islam • Jehovah's Witnesses • Jewish • Lutheran • Mennonite/Amish • Methodist • Mormon (Church of Jesus Christ of Latter-day Saints) • Native American/First Nations • Orthodox Churches • Pentecostal Church of God • Presbyterian • Quaker (Religious Society of Friends) • Reformed Church in America/Canada • Roman Catholic • Seventh-day Adventist • Sikh • Unitarian Universalist • United Church of Canada • United Church of Christ

6 x 9, 432 pp, Quality PB, ISBN 1-893361-67-5 **$19.95**

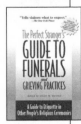

The Perfect Stranger's Guide to Funerals and Grieving Practices: A Guide to Etiquette in Other People's Religious Ceremonies   *Edited by Stuart M. Matlins*
6 x 9, 240 pp, Quality PB, ISBN 1-893361-20-9 **$16.95**

The Perfect Stranger's Guide to Wedding Ceremonies: A Guide to Etiquette in Other People's Religious Ceremonies   *Edited by Stuart M. Matlins*
6 x 9, 208 pp, Quality PB, ISBN 1-893361-19-5 **$16.95**

AVAILABLE FROM BETTER BOOKSTORES.
TRY YOUR BOOKSTORE FIRST.

About SKYLIGHT PATHS Publishing

SkyLight Paths Publishing is creating a place where people of different spiritual traditions come together for challenge and inspiration, a place where we can help each other understand the mystery that lies at the heart of our existence.

Through spirituality, our religious beliefs are increasingly becoming a part of our lives—rather than *apart* from our lives. While many of us may be more interested than ever in spiritual growth, we may be less firmly planted in traditional religion. Yet, we do want to deepen our relationship to the sacred, to learn from our own as well as from other faith traditions, and to practice in new ways.

SkyLight Paths sees both believers and seekers as a community that increasingly transcends traditional boundaries of religion and denomination—people wanting to learn from each other, *walking together, finding the way*.

For your information and convenience, at the back of this book we have provided a list of other SkyLight Paths books you might find interesting and useful. They cover the following subjects:

Buddhism / Zen	Gnosticism	Mysticism
Catholicism	Hinduism /	Poetry
Children's Books	Vedanta	Prayer
Christianity	Inspiration	Religious Etiquette
Comparative	Islam / Sufism	Retirement
Religion	Judaism / Kabbalah /	Spiritual Biography
Current Events	Enneagram	Spiritual Direction
Earth-Based	Meditation	Spirituality
Spirituality	Midrash Fiction	Women's Interest
Global Spiritual	Monasticism	Worship
Perspectives		

Or phone, fax, mail or e-mail to: SKYLIGHT PATHS Publishing
Sunset Farm Offices, Route 4 • P.O. Box 237 • Woodstock, Vermont 05091
Tel: (802) 457-4000 • Fax: (802) 457-4004 • www.skylightpaths.com
Credit card orders: (800) 962-4544 (8:30AM–5:30PM ET Monday–Friday)
Generous discounts on quantity orders. SATISFACTION GUARANTEED. Prices subject to change.

For more information about each book,
visit our website at www.skylightpaths.com